Childhood and the Production of Security

Responding to security scholars' puzzling dearth of attention to children and childhoods, the contributors to this volume reveal the ways in which they not only are already present in security discourses but are actually indispensable to them and to the political projects they make possible. From zones of conflict to everyday life contexts in the (post)industrial Global North, dominant ideas about childhood work to regulate the constitution of political subjects whilst variously enabling and foreclosing a wide range of political possibilities. Whether on the battlefields of Syria, in the halls of the UN, or the conceptual musings of disciplinary Security Studies, claims about or ostensibly on behalf of children are ubiquitous. Recognizing children as engaged political subjects, however, challenges us to bring a sustained critical gaze to the discursive and semiotic deployments of children and childhood in projects not of their making as well as to the ways in which power circulates through and around them.

This book was originally published as a special issue of *Critical Studies on Security*.

J. Marshall Beier is Professor in the Department of Political Science at McMaster University, Canada. His teaching and research centers on issues of political subjecthood with regard to childhood, indigeneity, and the discursive/semiotic production of security more broadly. His recent publications include *The Militarization of Childhood: Thinking Beyond the Global South* (2011), *Canadian Foreign Policy in Critical Perspective* (2010), *Indigenous Diplomacies* (2009), and *International Relations in Uncommon Places: Indigeneity, Cosmology, and the Limits of International Theory* (2005).

Childhood and the Production of Security

Edited by
J. Marshall Beier

Routledge
Taylor & Francis Group

LONDON AND NEW YORK

First published 2017
by Routledge
2 Park Square, Milton Park, Abingdon, Oxfordshire OX14 4RN
711 Third Avenue, New York, NY 10017

Routledge is an imprint of the Taylor & Francis Group, an informa business

First issued in paperback 2018

British Library Cataloguing in Publication Data
A catalogue record for this book is available from the British Library

ISBN 13: 978-1-138-64518-9 (hbk)
ISBN 13: 978-0-367-02626-4 (pbk)

Typeset in Times New Roman
by RefineCatch Limited, Bungay, Suffolk

Publisher's Note
The publisher accepts responsibility for any inconsistencies that may have
arisen during the conversion of this book from journal articles to book chapters,
namely the possible inclusion of journal terminology.

Disclaimer
Every effort has been made to contact copyright holders for their permission to
reprint material in this book. The publishers would be grateful to hear from any
copyright holder who is not here acknowledged and will undertake to rectify
any errors or omissions in future editions of this book.

Contents

Contents

Citation Information

The following chapters were originally published in *Critical Studies on Security*, volume 3, issue 1 (April 2015). When citing this material, please use the original page numbering for each article, as follows:

Chapter 1: Introduction
Children, childhoods, and security studies: an introduction
J. Marshall Beier
Critical Studies on Security, volume 3, issue 1 (April 2015), pp. 1–13

Chapter 2
'Children and armed conflict' and the field of security studies
Cecilia Jacob
Critical Studies on Security, volume 3, issue 1 (April 2015), pp. 14–28

Chapter 3
The state of play: securities of childhood – insecurities of children
Helen Brocklehurst
Critical Studies on Security, volume 3, issue 1 (April 2015), pp. 29–46

Chapter 4
Resilience is its own resistance: the place of children in post-conflict settlement
Alison M. S. Watson
Critical Studies on Security, volume 3, issue 1 (April 2015), pp. 47–61

Chapter 5
Children, civilianhood, and humanitarian securitization
Lorraine Macmillan
Critical Studies on Security, volume 3, issue 1 (April 2015), pp. 62–76

Chapter 6
Telling geopolitical tales: temporality, rationality, and the 'childish' in the ongoing war for the Falklands-Malvinas Islands
Victoria M. Basham
Critical Studies on Security, volume 3, issue 1 (April 2015), pp. 77–89

Chapter 7
Children, violence, and social exclusion: negotiation of everyday insecurity in a Colombian barrio
Helen Berents
Critical Studies on Security, volume 3, issue 1 (April 2015), pp. 90–104

The following chapter was originally published in *Critical Studies on Security*, volume 3, issue 3 (November 2015). When citing this material, please use the original page numbering for the article, as follows:

Chapter 8
Shifting the burden: childhoods, resilience, subjecthood
J. Marshall Beier
Critical Studies on Security, volume 3, issue 3 (November 2015), pp. 237–252

For any permission-related enquiries please visit:
http://www.tandfonline.com/page/help/permissions

Notes on Contributors

Victoria M. Basham is a Senior Lecturer in Politics at the University of Exeter, UK. Her research focuses on issues of gender, race, class, and sexuality in relation to militaries, militarism, and militarization.

J. Marshall Beier is Professor in the Department of Political Science at McMaster University, Canada. His teaching and research centers on issues of political subjecthood with regard to childhood, indigeneity, and the discursive/semiotic production of security more broadly. His recent publications include *The Militarization of Childhood: Thinking Beyond the Global South* (2011), *Canadian Foreign Policy in Critical Perspective* (2010), *Indigenous Diplomacies* (2009), and *International Relations in Uncommon Places: Indigeneity, Cosmology, and the Limits of International Theory* (2005).

Helen Berents is a Lecturer in the School of Justice at the Queensland University of Technology, Australia. Her research explores ways of engaging with conflict-affected young people and strategies for everyday peacebuilding. More broadly, she examines questions of forced migration, theories of childhood, peace and conflict studies, and feminist discourses of marginalization.

Helen Brocklehurst has been a full-time Lecturer at Swansea University, UK, since 2005. She is the author of *Who's Afraid of Children: Children Conflict and International Relations* (2006). She has recently been a consultant for the new International Baccalaureate course on Global Politics and has established a children's book archive on terrorism and war.

Cecilia Jacob is a Research Fellow in the Department of International Relations, The Australian National University, Australia. Her research interests include critical security studies, the politics of civilian protection, and children and armed conflict. She is the author of the book *Child Security in Asia: The Impact of Armed Conflict in Cambodia and Myanmar* (Routledge, 2014).

Lorraine Macmillan is Affiliated Lecturer in the Department of Politics and International Studies, University of Cambridge, UK. Her research interests lie in global North–South relations and their production through news media representations of conflict.

Alison M. S. Watson is Professor in the School of International Relations, University of St. Andrews, UK. Her primary research interest lies in examining grassroots perspectives and marginalized actors within the international system, and, in particular, in considering how their incorporation into the IR discourse may change the questions raised within the discipline itself, as well as in its sub-fields.

Children, childhoods, and security studies: an introduction

J. Marshall Beier

Department of Political Science, McMaster University, Hamilton, ON, Canada

Children and childhoods have not garnered much attention from either mainstream or critical currents of scholarship in International Relations and Security Studies, notwithstanding the significant ways in which they may be inseparable from the fields' subject matters, core concepts, and ideas. Addressing this omission is not a matter of simply 'bringing children in,' however. Rather, it necessitates first coming to terms with how children are already present both as global political actors and as expressed through deeply held ideational commitments that enable and sustain our understandings of and engagements with security. At the same time, this is a presence that has only ever been partial inasmuch as the children and youth of the field's imagining are not imbued with full and unqualified political subjecthood. Recovering robust subjecthood and a more nuanced understanding of lived childhoods promises, among other things, important theoretical correctives and more sophisticated conceptualization of emergent concepts like resilience.

A prize and a puzzle

The 2014 Nobel Peace Prize, presented in Oslo on 10 December 2014 to Malala Yousafzai and Kailash Satyarthi, raises something of a puzzle for and about Security Studies. The joint recipients, recognized for their respective roles in promoting the rights and well-being of children and youth, signal much about the nature and limits of our understanding of the intersections and interplays of childhood/youth and security. At age 17, Ms. Yousafzai is, by half, the youngest-ever recipient of the Prize. She is also likely the better known of the two in many parts of the world, having come to sudden and significant international fame some two years earlier when, then 15 years old, she and two other girls living in Pakistan's troubled Swat Valley – 13-year-old Shazia Ramzan and 16-year-old Kainat Riaz – were shot on their school bus by a member of the Taliban who reportedly asked for Malala by name and sought to make an example of her for her and her family's active advocacy of education for women and girls. Mr. Satyarthi, at age 60, is closer to the average age of Nobel laureates, having spent decades building a global campaign for children's rights, initiated in India in 1980 in the fight against child labor. For a hitherto small number of scholars inquiring into Security Studies' inattention to and somewhat paradoxically deep entanglement with children and childhood, the Nobel Committee's historic elevation of children's security issues in its recognition of Ms. Yusafzai and Mr. Satyarthi is simultaneously an encouraging development and revealing of weightier questions.

'Security,' as bound up in and articulated through the activism of Malala Yousafzai and Kailash Satyarthi, is only very uncomfortably subsumed under the rubric of state security that has long preoccupied mainstream International Relations and Security Studies, together with much in the way of dominant public discourse. At the same time, Security Studies has evinced its own apprehensions, both implicit and explicit, about childhood as an apposite area of disciplinary inquiry. In his famous post-Cold War call to maintain a strict state-centric focus for a Security Studies that seemed amenable to considering other referents, Stephen Walt (1991, 213) specifically listed 'child abuse' among those nontraditional security issues which he feared could dilute the field to the point of threatening its coherence. Walt's point was not that child abuse was somehow a trivial matter or undeserving of urgent attention, but that the enduring problem of interstate war was not likely to fade and, being of such gravity, was one that demanded primacy of place. Exemplary of realist-inspired commitments that continued to cast a long shadow over security scholarship, this position reflected an abiding faith in the state as the arbiter of security and, thus, as appropriately its referent object. Not surprisingly in light of these commitments, mainstream Security Studies, like International Relations writ large, has been relatively inattentive to children and childhoods, operating either on the assumption that the security of the state equates to the security of those within – children included – or that the former is a necessary precondition to the latter.

Rather more peculiar is the dearth of interest by self-consciously critical currents of scholarship on security. Though many of these increasingly manifest (in a disciplinary sense) interventions have been instrumental in creating openings for engagement with children and childhoods, little such dedicated work has emerged. A qualified exception is the vast literature on child soldiers that has arisen together with the idea of human security and increasing interest in so-called 'new wars' (Kaldor 1999). Much of this, however, turns on reductionist renderings of victimhood which have come under challenge (see, for example, Rosen 2005; Hart 2008; Baines 2009; Gilligan 2009) and which mask other circulations of power (Macmillan 2009) in ways that mystify or deny the political subjecthood of children and youth, while doing little to unsettle dominant understandings of either childhood or security (see Tisdall and Punch 2012; Nieuwenhuys 2013). There is much to recommend more in the way of reflexive critical work in this area. Contributions regarding children and youth in connection with, among other things, global political economy, human rights, and militarism (see, for example, Brocklehurst 2006; Watson 2009; Carpenter 2010; Beier 2011) bear important implications with regard to security as well. There is likewise, as Wagnsson, Hellman, and Holmberg (2010) argue, much unrealized promise in taking children's agency seriously in Security Studies, not least in advancing the theorization of 'security' itself.

But, as the various contributions to this special issue also make clear, simply 'adding' children is not enough and attempting to 'find' them is beset by the danger of doing no more than that or, worse, making them what they must be in light of commitments and assumptions that precede them. Feminists and others have alerted us to the analogous perils of 'bringing in,' for example, women (Tickner 1992) or Indigenous peoples (Shaw 2002) in a manner that subjects them both to mainstream frameworks' pronouncements upon ways of knowing and being to which they must then be made to conform if they are to be intelligible. Even if we are properly attentive to the deleterious consequences of forcing children into the conceptual spaces marked out for them in advance by the theoretical mainstream, critical approaches also run the considerable risk of performing similar violences of erasure if they do not bring into relief and interrogate customary and hegemonic renderings of children and childhood. In her contribution herein, Cecilia Jacob points out how this danger might be exacerbated by inadequacies of Critical Security Studies and a privileging of protection over an interest in power, and how it operates to obscure from view alternative imaginings of security and enactments of political subjecthood (Jacob herein, 15). Just as thinking productively about women or Indigenous people in International Relations and Security Studies has meant taking seriously gender and indigeneity in all of their nuance and complexity, so too thinking about children requires theorizing childhood. Failing to do so leaves unchallenged and intact 'common sense' assumptions and commitments as well as the 'subterranean' circulations of power by dint of which we casually reinscribe them.

We can see something of this in some of the framings of the 2014 Nobel Peace Prize and, in particular, of the recipients themselves and the contexts of their activism. Without at all diminishing or in any way calling into question the enormity of the contribution made by either of the 2014 laureates, the politics of political subjecthood at play are nevertheless instructive. It is important to bear in mind that this need not be born of any conscious instrumentality in order to flow together with and reinforce hegemonic narratives and ideas. For instance, while there is certainly much to celebrate about the Prize having been awarded to joint recipients from two South Asian countries – perhaps especially in light of the historically troubled relationship between them – this is something which could also have the unintended effect of reconfirming a widely held sense that issues of child security are at least mostly confined to the global South and thereby to sustain forgetfulness about innumerable forms of insecurity experienced by children the world over, including the global North. That is not to say, of course, that insecurity is not acutely felt by many children and youth in countries of the South. Rather, it is to take note that the problem is not engaged in a political vacuum, as though the gendered and racialized legacies of colonialism somehow play no part or are suspended in the reportage and reception of present events. With this in mind, it is worth considering the extent to which the Nobel laureates might tend to be read as exceptional individuals, not only in connection with their achievements but also in the sense of embodying 'enlightenment' in the midst of forms of 'backwardness' presumed of societies beyond the global North.

On childhood itself, other aspects of framing are no less significant. Among these are matters of critical importance to the relative visibility of children's agency and subjecthood. As much of the world learned (or, elsewhere, was reminded) of Kailash Satyarthi's important work and leading role fighting some of the worst practices of child labor, for instance, the narrative centered him as acting subject. This much is not surprising in the context of the awarding of a Nobel Prize but, as in the case of global origins, it is important to remember also that it is not separable from other entrenched ideas and assumptions – here, those which concern childhood and youth as stages of still-'becoming' or 'incomplete' personhood. Among other things, such framings sustain and reproduce subject/object inscriptions, like protector/protected, and thereby effect erasure of other subject positions. Child laborers' own resistance and broader political subjecthood, though not explicitly denied, are not visible.

Something similar may be at work in the case of Mr. Satyarthi's co-laureate, revealing that underinterrogated knowledges about childhood, though operating on different circuits, are no less relevant to the case of a conspicuous child/youth subject. As noted earlier, Malala Yusafzai was already an activist before the shooting on the school bus – indeed, she was targeted for precisely that reason. But the international fame that arguably led to her being awarded the Nobel Prize arose from the spectacle of the shooting in which the agency and political subjecthood of the shooter, however misguided and repugnant, is conspicuously foregrounded. 'Malala the activist' is thus, in important respects, inseparable from and, at least in part, determined by 'Malala the victim.' This leads us onto a complicated and deeply fraught conceptual terrain for, in fact, Ms. Yusafzai occupies both those subject/object positions – and, in significant ways, they are simultaneously subject *and* object positions – together with others still. What calls out for more careful consideration is how it is that some may register more readily than others.

The real puzzle of the 2014 Nobel Peace Prize for Critical Security Studies is the persistence of unseen (or unacknowledged) circulations of power, expressed through narrations and readings beholden to and reconstitutive of assumptions about childhood that are at work even in our attempts to reveal them. What is apparent here is that the critical faculties honed over the last two decades where a range of other subjects are concerned has achieved precious little purchase when it comes to children. That is not to say that children have been absent from Security Studies. Though seldom imbued with independent agency – and, even where they are, still very much determined by proviso and inscription – they nevertheless populate everyday security discourse in ways that underwrite both mainstream and critical projects and conceptual approaches in the field. Through various points of insertion, the contributors to this special issue bring into relief and disturb assumptions about childhood that work to construct and locate children and youth in security discourse in very particular and circumscribed ways. In so doing, they offer a much-needed corrective to critical scholarship on security that has allowed objectified and essentialized renderings of children and childhood to go largely unchallenged and at times reproduces them.

Constructing childhood

Both textually and semiotically, 'child' is very much a floating signifier – one whose mundane usage is so seemingly ubiquitous that it invites little if any critical introspection and elides the inherent complexity and diversity of childhoods, whether in conceptual formulation or as lived experiences (Mayall 2000). It is also one that marks out in advance much in the way of the essentialized attributes and social locations of the human subjects-cum-objects to whom it is applied. Children, as ontological category, are variously constructed as innocent, dependent, vulnerable, impetuous, dangerous; they are to be cherished, nurtured, protected, regulated, feared. There is, in some senses, a very high degree of consensus about childhood and, in others, little or none at all. Dominant ideas about childhood may be broadly inscribed, bespeaking an aggregate of all persons below some age threshold, for example, or they may be imputed to some more exclusive subset of young people, variously defined along intersecting lines of, among others, race, gender, and class. The definitional struggles map with political ones: whether one is constructed within or without childhood bears critically on issues of agency, rights, protection, and more, in ways that may be enabling or disabling of concrete projects and possibilities. Childhood, like security, is an essentially contested concept.

Defiance of definition

While the idea of children as incomplete adults in the making dates at least to Aristotle, the hegemonic, modern, Western notion of childhood emerged only in the seventeenth century (Cassidy 2012, 57) as exemplified in Rousseau's *Emile* (1979). Despite its long pedigree, it is through Rousseau that the idea of innocent childhood, closer somehow to God or nature and thus unprepared for the vice and avarice of the social world, has perhaps its most enduring expression. What is most clear from *Emile*, and which continues to cast a long shadow by way of the important influence it exerted in the founding of liberal views on education, is Rousseau's commitment to progressive development of the faculties of reason as the *sine qua non* of participation in the social world. That said, he held strong views as to an essential nature of childhood to which reason was fundamentally inimical: 'Childhood,' he wrote, 'has its own way of seeing, thinking, and feeling; nothing is more foolish than to try and substitute our ways. And I should no more expect judgment in a ten-year-old child than I should expect him to be five feet high. Indeed, what use would reason be to him at that age? It is the curb of strength, and the child does not need the curb' (Rousseau 1979, 60). Thus, for Rousseau, childhood was perforce a presocial developmental stage of life and, as such, 'the child' was necessarily to be regarded as *becoming* but not yet *being* a bona fide political subject.

On the one hand, it is dangerous to generalize about historical renditions of children's capacity for reason and understanding. Though the denial of that capacity is a patently persistent motif, coexisting easily with a full spectrum of other ideational commitments across sociopolitical time and space, its congruence with hegemonic sensibilities of the contemporary global North may lead us to gloss over its specificity. Elsewhere and at other times, this has been a rather more complicated and ambiguous terrain than it may seem in our present rendition. The persecution of Anabaptists by Catholics and Protestants alike in Europe through the sixteenth and seventeenth centuries, for example, turned vitally on disputes about children's ability to formulate autonomous choice. Even the most unlikely early modern European philosophers, from Descartes to Locke, betrayed ambivalence about children's faculties of reason (see Krupp 2009). Certainly, along other human historical trajectories and philosophical traditions, and elsewhere in our present moment in time, there is much that unsettles dominant understandings of childhood as merely a stage of 'becoming' and which opens up opportunities to take seriously the heterogeneity of its lived experiences globally and locally.

The indeterminacy of the hegemonic construction of 'the child' comes quickly into relief in the problems that arise from juridical definitional exercises. In her contribution to this special issue, Helen Brocklehurst disturbs the conventional age–linear boundary approach, highlighting the contradictions and intrinsic fuzziness of definitions arrived at in this way (Brocklehurst herein, 29–32). Simply put, asking about the 'when' of childhood misses much in the way of its determinants. In contexts both broad and narrow, childhoods are determined by exigencies of gender, ethnicity, race, class, location, and more. They may be experienced as contingent, changing, and multiple even for the individual, depending on operant relationships or the circumstances of the moment. But the zero plural rendering – *the* child – so unreflexively invoked even in the very name of the 1992 United Nations Convention on the Rights of the Child (UNCRC), for instance, collapses such alterity into a presumed universal conception of childhood that does not withstand critical scrutiny (James 2007, 262; Cordero Arce 2012, 382). Consistent with this universalizing move, the UNCRC defines children as all persons under the age of 18 – though it incorporates numerous qualifications as to capacity at younger ages, these too are universalized. Similarly, the Coalition to Stop the Use of Child Soldiers has settled on the 'straight-18' standard, calling for an international prohibition on recruitment into armed forces before that benchmark age. As David Rosen (2007, 297) points out, this necessitates that 'existing and competing definitions of childhood be abandoned in favor of a single international standard.' As laudable as it may seem on some levels, the encoded assumption of 'straight-18' (that childhood is an innocent stage of life to be protected) is a privileged perspective founded on structural and material privilege that is not and has never been universal, even in the global North (see Cook 2008, 44–45). It cannot accommodate the possibility of child soldiers as autonomous agents with their own motivations, however formulated, and the effect is to flatten complex and varied subject positions, essentializing and separating 'the child' from politics and from independent agency.

The common thread in these and other dominant constructions of childhood is diminution of agency. Where agency is conceded in some way or measure, it is typically an impoverished rendering that does not admit of the possibility of bona fide political subjecthood. Thus, children and youth might be seen to act, but they cannot be read as the autonomous authors of their actions in the same manner as an adult political subject. This amounts to an insistence upon regulation of child and youth agency in ways that contain and reassign the political subjecthood behind it. That is the effect of, for example, casting all child soldiers as victims by dint of their age, notwithstanding that some might actually be pursuing an autonomously reasoned survival strategy. It invalidates the possibility that a child worker's own view of her circumstances might be that she has entered into an employment contract (Scullion 2013) and that the fact of an exploitative relationship of exchange is not, in itself, generally regarded as sufficient basis to question the autonomy of choice of an adult in the same circumstances. Similarly, a moral panic over presumed 'dangerous' young men in the UK may have less to do with any reality of youth violence than with the location of political subjecthood such that its capture and regulation through military service can be promoted (Basham 2011) – here, the state (whose franchise derives from adult citizenry) is recentered as the operant political subject and the inherent contradictions of the 'straight-18' definition of childhood are brought starkly into relief once again.

What calls out for more in the way of critical reflection if we are to productively engage intersections of childhood and security are the everyday ways in which we reproduce subject positions, ascriptions, and inscriptions (Butler 2004) and, thus, the universal child. Childhood as a stage of life to be regulated is central to the Rousseauian commitments that remain integral to prevailing understandings of educa-tion's social purposes and, increasingly, as a technology for the making of neoliberal market participants. Tensions manifest in a multitude of well-known definitional contra-dictions: a young person, by virtue of nothing other than chronological age, may be deemed old enough to be held accountable under criminal law but not old enough to be a juror; she may be free to give military service but not to vote. Such discrepancies between rights and accountability expose social conventions of domination and control. It is noteworthy in this connection that positing an incomplete or deficient capacity for reason has historically been a strategy for resisting empowerment of all manner of marginalized groups. Accordingly, it is important to bear in mind that references to childhood are, in fact, references to adult–child relationships (Johansson 2011, 102) encoding power rela-tions that constitute adults as sociopolitical actors. As such, social reproduction of the universal child of hegemonic imagining is itself an insecurity practice worth unpacking.

These are issues taken up by scholars working in the field of Childhood Studies in ways that better enable us to think about how critical scholarship might best engage intersections between childhood and security. In particular, this growing body of work has opened important avenues of inquiry regarding 'being' and 'becoming' – the crucial distinction mapping with, respectively, 'adult' and 'child' (Jenks 1996; Matthews 1994; Qvortrup 1994). Drawing on Deleuze and Guattari (1984) and Latour (2005), Barbro Bernstein (2011, 104) treats 'being' and 'becoming' not as states defined by objective properties but as outcomes of assemblages 'composed of children's and adults' bodies, discourses of childhood, artefacts, school as an institution, etc.', which work to align being/becoming and adult/child together with, among other binary oppositions, mature/immature, rational/irrational, competent/incompetent, independent/dependent. Approaching the construction of childhood from this perspective opens a space within which to recognize that children and adults alike are in a constant state of simultaneous being and becoming (Bacon and Frankel 2014, 38–39), though hegemonic ideas about childhood function to mystify this. The call to theorize children as beings *and* becomings (Uprichard 2008), if extended to adults also, thus resists the adult world's exclusive claim to political subjecthood.

If children and childhood sometimes seem to defy definition, it might, somewhat paradoxically, be due to the fact that dominant commitments about children as an ontological category of human 'becomings' are so deeply held. The possibility of young people's unqualified legitimate and autonomous political subjecthood so defies prevailing common senses as to be unthinkable, and any such subject transgression is most readily made intelligible as pathology of one sort or another, cast as naïve or misguided or delinquent. The 'human becoming' is thereby re-objectified into something more amenable to sensibilities which insist upon innocent incapacity to formulate a legitimate subject position. The young person is defined by a lack (of maturity, rationality, competence, etc.) and therefore cannot be truly the author of her own actions, whose 'real' determinants must be sought elsewhere (in some guileful interlocutor or other corrupting influence, for example). The inherent indeterminacy of this leads, perhaps inevitably, to clumsy juridical contortions around arbitrary designations like 'straight-18' as the means by which to regulate what is ultimately a critical boundary between political objecthood and subjecthood.

There is much at stake in this when it comes to thinking about childhood in Security Studies. As R.B.J. Walker (1997, 69) argued two decades ago, '[s]ecurity cannot be understood, or reconceptualized, or reconstructed without paying attention to the constitutive account of the political that has made the prevailing accounts of security seem so plausible.' Thinking about childhood in relation to security, then, necessarily entails a challenging of prevailing commitments and common senses concerning the political, in which status quo interests may be deeply invested and by which status quo relations of power are sustained. Fundamentally at issue here are particular renderings and boundaries of political subjecthood which work to objectify children and youth and locate them outside of political life.

Innocent childhood

To say that children are constructed outside of political life is not to say that they are not politicized. More than just an enduring Rousseauian inheritance, the trope of innocent childhood is a powerful political expedient. Indeed, as Robin Bernstein (2011) argues, its always contingent and relatively recent (in historical terms) emergence as an idea is inseparable from its strategic uses in political persuasion. The child as human 'becoming' highlights adult responsibility and seems irresistible as an associative device by which to motivate political action, from the banal references to 'our children's future' that pepper election campaign rhetoric to the often viscerally felt images of suffering children that foreground urgent appeals for response to humanitarian emergencies. In service of politics both benevolent and malign, childhood is metonymically and semiotically employed to great effect as a contiguous referent through which various projects are themselves associated with innocence and virtue. For example, though the archetype of innocent childhood is a racialized one – again, founded on privilege and thus constructing some children outside of innocence and outside of hegemonic understandings of childhood itself – such is its rhetorical sway that, as Bernstein notes, its appropriation became a critical strategy of antiracist resistance politics in early to mid-twentieth-century America. Elsewhere, evocations of the innocence or purity of childhood were, in the same moment, harnessed to overtly racist projects. In these and other ways, innocent childhood functions as an important component of wider discursive economies (Campbell 1992) through which myriad political projects are raised and sustained, from the propagation of Victorian social values (Thiel 2012) to contemporary appeals for intervention (or against intervention) along lines of the Responsibility to Protect doctrine.

As Lorraine Macmillan shows in her contribution to this special issue, innocent childhood and invisibility of children's agency go hand in hand, but the absence this effects also produces things, such as the civilian. Children, at least in the dominant Western construction, are the quintessential innocent civilians. If innocence is a constituent of presumed pre-political life, it entails being held harmless, absolved of political responsibility, and deserving of protection. In short, it is productive of an instrumental boundary between those bodies marked out as legitimate targets of political violence and those which cannot legitimately be understood in that way because they have been constructed outside of political life. Transgressions of the boundary, visiting violence upon those recognized as children (remembering that factors other than age are at play here), may be felt to be especially egregious (Jacob herein, 16) and this, in turn, can be a potent rhetorical resource. Whether in Somalia (Macmillan), Syria (Jacob), or on the streets of Fergusson, Missouri, innocent childhood, predicated on the denial of political subjecthood, functions as metonym for the larger communities of which the (made-) visible child victims of violence are part.

Finding children in Security Studies

The implication for Security Studies is inescapable: children already populate security discourse, most often as innocents to be protected or a social resource for the future, but also as dangerous beings where presumed innocence is subverted by a nefarious force (child soldiers) or is lost for want of regulation (wayward or deviant youth). Children figure prominently as well in security anxieties which cast them as dangerous or potentially dangerous 'becomings.' As Helen Berents notes in her contribution herein, children are apt to be read as dangerous for being 'transgressive' and potentially dangerous when they do not conform to the prevailing normative renderings of childhood (Berents herein, 92). In a particularly extreme formulation, an anti-terror consultation document recently drawn up by the UK Home Office proposed that nursery workers be tasked with identifying very young children considered at risk of radicalization (Tufft 2015). Regardless of whether such a scheme could ever be seen through to practical implementation, its contemplation is nevertheless instructive as to the contingency of innocent childhood and its inseparability from other power circulations. In a similar vein, 'zero tolerance' policies securitize childhood and youth (see Giroux 2001; Saltman, David, and Gabbard 2011; Nguyen 2013) in ways that can all too readily equate autonomous subjecthood with threat. Though less spectacular, the same underlying logics and assumptions are expressed in handwringing about the alleged dire threat or other implications supposed to inhere in demographic 'youth bulges' in other contexts (see, for example, Urdal 2006; Weber 2013).

While agency is conspicuous in all of these examples, it is significant that it is also pathologized. Children/youth are present in their connection to operant security discourses in each case, but that presence is marked out as problematic such that it calls for some sort of remediation or correction. Put another way, though agency might be acknowledged, it is not afforded legitimacy and therefore cannot be abided as robust political subjecthood – the effect is that children are once again reduced to an objectified political problem rather than being recognizable as genuine and autonomous political actors. It might be tempting here to suggest that we ought to explore how such children and childhoods could be more meaningfully engaged in Security Studies but, as noted earlier, that raises the specter of their being rendered as what Security Studies needs them to be. If we are to avoid the inscriptive violences of an 'add children and stir' approach, then, it is imperative that we come to terms with just what it is that extant Security Studies makes of childhood. The first indispensable move in this direction is recognizing that children are already present in Security Studies as much as in security discourses more broadly. This is not limited to those pathologized instances where frighteningly unregulated 'becomings' are understood to pose some danger. The relevance of childhood to Security Studies runs much deeper and in ways that give the lie to any sense that children and childhoods are not always already present.

The importance of finding children in International Relations and Security Studies is not new but, rather, newly recognized (Brocklehurst herein, 34). As Jacob (herein, 15) observes, they are much more present in these disciplinary contexts than we may realize. They pervade constitutive discourses of global politics and security narratives more generally, compellingly invoked as objects of value, of suffering, of hope, and so forth. In this vital sense, they have always been a part of Security Studies, which raises again the puzzle of security scholars' (and especially critical scholars') lack of curiosity about children and childhoods. Their presence, however, is very much as 'furniture of the world,' to borrow Bertrand Russell's (1919, 182) memorable phrase. That is to say, 'the child,' ontologized into a stable referent along lines of dominant constructions, resides beyond the reach of conceptual debates, here rendered not only as presocial but prior to theory as well.

Security discourse relies on well-rehearsed 'knowledge' about childhood whose deferred meaning derives from wider intertextualities but is readily summoned. As we have seen, there is significant indeterminacy and contingency in this so that it functions as a versatile and maneuverable political resource. For instance, the instrumentality of ascriptions of childishness in the Falklands/Malvinas conflict, explored in Victoria Basham's contribution herein, relies on their intelligibility as at least mildly pejorative and demeaning of other subject positions in order for them to function as a discursive technology rationalizing the use and threat of violence. Elsewhere, images and accounts about children themselves, deployed as markers of innocent victimhood, mobilize state violence when they come to stand for aggregate noncombatant groups (Macmillan herein, 64) and, thus, as inherently passive (Watson herein, 52–54) referent objects of humanitarian intervention. Noncombatants do not occupy subject positions with respect to political violence and, as the quintessential innocent civilians, images of children harmed in armed conflict can deal a powerful blow to the perceived legitimacy of the responsible party's own subject position in warfare. As such, they are an increasingly important factor in the management of perception as it pertains to legitimacy in warfare, conferring an advantage on those endowed with the technological wherewithal to sustain a persuasive claim to meaningful discrimination between combatants and non-combatants (Beier 2003).

Children are easily mobilized into 'emotional scenery' underwriting the 'war on terror' or, just as readily, used by aid agencies as the 'hook' by which to gather support for programs whose actual intended beneficiaries may include but are not limited to children

(Brocklehurst herein, 32–33). Together with major children's rights initiatives through the 1990s, the rapid ascendancy of the human security agenda saw the concomitant rise of the use of images of childhood, epitomizing the broadening of security discourse to include new referents in the wake of the Cold War. Civil society groups also made very effective use of these openings. The movement to ban antipersonnel landmines, for example, invested heavily in such imagery, foregrounding the dire consequences suffered by children in mine-affected countries. Child-sized prosthetic limbs were prominently displayed at international meetings, campaign literature centered child landmine victims, and children were pictured on the cover of the International Campaign to Ban Landmines' voluminous annual report, *Landmine Monitor*, in each of its first seven years of publication. Of course, the campaign was undertaken on behalf of all landmine victims, the majority of whom are adults, but the stigmatization of this class of weapons and the startlingly quick completion of an international treaty banning them owed much to the ubiquitous images of child victims who unambiguously register as innocent noncombatants. This, in turn, relied once more upon children's construction outside of political subjecthood and the persistence of popular imaginaries in which theirs is an innocent existence assigned to particular places such as home and school (Macmillan herein, 65), where political violence must not transgress. It is a particular, idealized version of childhood purposefully deployed, and reproduced in the same instant, in furtherance of a political project. And it is contingent on the disappearance from view of actually existing childhoods wherein the implications of such projects are lived experience (Basham herein, 87).

Abstracted and thoroughly objectified, children and childhood are reduced to terrains on which security practices are played out. These can be ideational, as in rhetorical deployments of innocent childhood, or much more literal and corporeal. Starving children's emaciated bodies may impel and come to stand for intervention (Macmillan herein, 68), for example. Differently located but drawing equally on dominant constructions of childhood, Jacob (herein, 16) highlights how children are centerpieces of political contestation on the battlefields of Syria. And, as Alison Watson points out in her contribution, the symbolic meaning of childhood can also cause children to be deliberately selected as targets: another violent context of their reduction to sites of political action by others. They inhabit post-conflict landscapes (Watson herein, 51) as victims: orphaned, abject, and dispossessed, their untimely and inapt autonomy portending further danger in the absence of some benevolent regulation. Children's age can in itself be a significant risk factor for profound insecurity, heightening vulnerability with respect to all manner of dangers and deprivations (Berents herein, 98).

These are just some of the ways in which we find children and childhood already present in Security Studies. We might say that in their incompleteness they are precisely what Security Studies needs them to be, flowing together with and sustaining dominant understandings of sovereignty, authority, order, protection, and much more. The challenge this sets for us, then, is to find what is not fully present, beginning with political subjecthood. This is essential to a progressive rethinking of security as it pertains to children and lived childhoods. Security Studies also stands to benefit from this, both empirically and conceptually. Macmillan (herein, 73) points out that finding children offers, for example, the possibility of a corrective to securitization theory's problematic centering of elites and overemphasis of a very circumscribed range of speech acts. Jacob (herein, 20–22) alerts us to how feminist approaches might inadvertently become implicated in the denial of children's political subjecthood (see also Brocklehurst herein, 41). Mindful of this danger while drawing on feminist scholarship on security as well as theories of agency and everyday life, Berents (herein) finds fieldwork exploration a productive means by which to repopulate not only the structures but the discourse of violence and insecurity in ways that resist children's exclusion. Lived realities of childhood enable alternative political renditions (Berents herein; Basham herein) which, in turn, broach new challenges to accustomed ways of theorizing security, both mainstream and critical.

Taking children and childhoods seriously in Security Studies also raises opportunities to critically engage developing concepts, relatively new to the field, such as resilience. As noted earlier, the conspicuous agency and political subjecthood of Malala Yousafzai's assailant may register more readily than, and is in key respects determinant of, the visibility of Ms. Yousafzai's own political subjecthood. The figure of 'Malala' that has emerged from the act of violence that brought her to global fame is one deeply marked by a trope of resilience, emergent across a range of disciplines and popular discourses in recent years, not least in Childhood Studies and in clinical fields associated with child and youth well-being. In many of its increasingly common articulations, however, it is a concept sorely lacking in positive content. Resilience in many instances does not mean thriving, resilience is too often about surviving. As such, it may tend to summon a rendering of security in decidedly abject terms, much more akin to realist-inspired accounts than to the many reconceptualizations of the last two decades.

Malala Yousafzai's abject resilience is key to understanding her visibility as a political subject. She has refused to be silenced, despite the horrific violence inflicted on her, and that resilience has not only come to define her visible political subjecthood but to bound it too. Again, her prior activism has come to light in consequence of this resilience, itself made visible by way of the agential choices of her assailant. It is worth asking why her resilience continues to be explicitly tied to her survival of the attack and not to her earlier political activism. Surely persistence in taking direct action against the denial of social and political rights under extremely challenging circumstances bespeaks resilience, but the centering instead of the forbearance of the act of violence mystifies this. Here too, then, even in the context of global spectacle, resilience is not disturbed by and does not disturb a very impoverished rendering of the acting political subject. In effect, the subject is made to disappear while in plain view. We begin to get a sense from this of resilience as a necessary but not sufficient condition of genuine and robust political subjecthood, and this suggests new ways of theorizing it.

As the contributions to this special issue reveal, taking children and childhoods seriously in Security Studies suggests new ways of approaching this and other issues of interest to the field more broadly. At the same time, it opens up an area of security discourse whose centrality to so much of what concerns security scholars and practitioners alike is belied by the almost complete lack of attention it has attracted thus far. And, not least, it is revealing of our complicities in the marginalization and silencing of political subjects even at a time when we hope to have become much more attentive to the violences of erasure. Through their various points of entry into this underdeveloped area of inquiry, the contributors herein take on a range of important issues at the intersections of children, childhoods, and security, including but not limited to those sketched in a most preliminary way earlier. In so doing, they complicate our under-standing of security both conceptually and as lived experience and unsettle many of the existing accounts of its subjects, objects, and content.

Funding

Research for this article was supported by an Insight Grant from the Social Sciences and Humanities Research Council of Canada.

References

Bacon, K., and S. Frankel. 2014. "Rethinking Children's Citizenship: Negotiating Structure, Shaping Meanings." *The International Journal of Children's Rights* 22 (1): 21–42. doi:10.1163/15718182-55680003.

Baines, E. K. 2009. "Complex Political Perpetrators: Reflections on Dominic Ongwen." *The Journal of Modern African Studies* 47 (2): 163–191. doi:10.1017/S0022278X09003796.

Basham, V. 2011. "Kids with Guns: Militarization, Masculinities, Moral Panic, and (Dis)Organized Violence." In *The Militarization of Childhood: Thinking Beyond the Global South*, edited by J. M. Beier, 175–193. New York: Palgrave Macmillan.

Beier, J. M. 2003. "Discriminating Tastes: 'Smart' Bombs, Non-Combatants, and Notions of Legitimacy in Warfare." *Security Dialogue* 34 (4): 411–425. doi:10.1177/0967010603344003.

Beier, J. M., ed. 2011. *The Militarization of Childhood: Thinking Beyond the Global South*. New York: Palgrave Macmillan.

Bernstein, R. 2011. *Racial Innocence: Performing American Childhood from Slavery to Civil Rights*. New York: New York University Press.

Brocklehurst, H. 2006. *Who's Afraid of Children? Children, Conflict and International Relations*. Aldershot: Ashgate.

Butler, J. 2004. *Undoing Gender*. London: Routledge.

Campbell, D. 1992. *Writing Security: United States Foreign Policy and the Politics of Identity*. Minneapolis: University of Minnesota Press.

Carpenter, C. R. 2010. *Forgetting Children Born of War: Setting the Human Rights Agenda in Bosnia and Beyond*. New York: Columbia University Press.

Cassidy, C. 2012. "Children's Status, Children's Rights, and 'Dealing With' Children." *The International Journal of Children's Rights* 20 (1): 57–71. doi:10.1163/157181812X608282.

Cook, T. 2008. "'He Was Determined to Go': Underage Soldiers in the Canadian Expeditionary Force." *Histoire Sociale/Social History* 41 (81): 41–74. doi:10.1353/his.0.0009.

Cordero Arce, M. 2012. "Towards an Emancipatory Discourse of Children's Rights." *The International Journal of Children's Rights* 20 (3): 365–421. doi:10.1163/157181812X637127.

Deleuze, G., and F. Guattari. 1984. *Anti-Oedipus: Capitalism and Schizophrenia*. Translated by Robert Hurley, Mark Seem, and Helen R. Lane. London: Athlone Press.

Gilligan, C. 2009. "'Highly Vulnerable?' Political Violence and the Social Construction of Traumatized Children." *Journal of Peace Research* 46 (1): 119–134. doi:10.1177/0022343308098407.

Giroux, H. A. 2001. "Mis/Education and Zero Tolerance: Disposable Youth and the Politics of Domestic Militarization." *Boundary 2* 28 (3): 61–94. doi:10.1215/01903659-28-3-61.

Hart, J. 2008. "Displaced Children's Participation in Political Violence: Towards Greater Understanding of Mobilisation." *Conflict, Security and Development* 8 (3): 277–293. doi:10.1080/14678800802323308.

James, A. 2007. "Giving Voice to Children's Voices: Practices and Problems, Pitfalls and Potentials." *American Anthropologist* 109 (2): 261–272. doi:10.1525/aa.2007.109.2.261.

Jenks, C. 1996. *Childhood*. New York: Routledge.

Johansson, B. 2011. "Doing Adulthood in Childhood Research." *Childhood* 19 (1): 101–114. doi:10.1177/0907568211408362.

Kaldor, M. 1999. *New and Old Wars: Organized Violence in a Global Era*. Stanford: Stanford University Press.

Krupp, A. 2009. *Reason's Children: Childhood in Early Modern Philosophy*. Lewisburg: Bucknell University Press.

Latour, B. 2005. *Reassembling the Social: An Introduction to Actor-Network-Theory*. Oxford: Oxford University Press.

Macmillan, L. 2009. "The Child Soldier in North-South Relations." *International Political Sociology* 3 (1): 36–52. doi:10.1111/j.1749-5687.2008.00062.x.

Matthews, G. B. 1994. *The Philosophy of Childhood.* Cambridge: Harvard University Press.

Mayall, B. 2000. "The Sociology of Childhood in Relation to Children's Rights." *International Journal of Children's Rights* 8 (3): 243–259. doi:10.1163/15718180020494640.

Nguyen, N. 2013. "Scripting 'Safe' Schools: Mapping Urban Education and Zero Tolerance During the Long War." *Review of Education, Pedagogy and Cultural Studies* 35 (4): 277–297. doi:10.1080/10714413.2013.819725.

Nieuwenhuys, O. 2013. "Theorizing Childhood(s): Why We Need Postcolonial Perspectives." *Childhood* 20 (1): 3–8. doi:10.1177/0907568212465534.

Qvortrup, J. 1994. "Childhood Matters: An Introduction." In *Childhood Matters: Social Theory, Practice and Policy,* edited by J. Qvortrup, M. Bardy, G. Sgritta, and H. Wintersberger, 1–24. Aldershot: Avebury.

Rosen, D. M. 2005. *Armies of the Young: Child Soldiers in War and Terrorism.* Piscataway: Rutgers University Press.

Rosen, D. M. 2007. "Child Soldiers, International Humanitarian Law, and the Globalization of Childhood." *American Anthropologist* 109 (2): 296–306. doi:10.1525/AA.2007.109.2.296.

Rousseau, J. J. 1979. *Emile; Or, on Education.* Translated by Allan Bloom. New York: Basic Books.

Russell, B. 1919. *Introduction to Mathematical Philosophy.* London: George Allen & Unwin.

Saltman, K. J., and D. A. Gabbard eds. 2011. *Education as Enforcement: The Militarization and Corporatization of Schools.* New York: Routledge.

Scullion, D. 2013. "Passive Victims or Empowered Actors: Accommodating the Needs of Child Domestic Workers." *The International Journal of Children's Rights* 21 (1): 97–126. doi:10.1163/15718182-55680017.

Shaw, K. 2002. "Indigeneity and the International." *Millennium - Journal of International Studies* 31 (1): 55–81. doi:10.1177/03058298020310010401.

Thiel, L. 2012. "Degenerate 'Innocents': Childhood, Deviance, and Criminality in Nineteenth-Century Texts." In *The Child in British Literature: Literary Constructions of Childhood, Medieval to Contemporary,* edited by A. E. Gavin, 131–145. New York: Palgrave Macmillan.

Tickner, A. N. 1992. *Gender in International Relations: Feminist Perspectives on Achieving Global Security.* New York: Columbia University Press.

Tisdall, E. K. M., and S. Punch. 2012. "Not so 'New'? Looking Critically at Childhood Studies." *Children's Geographies* 10 (3): 249–264. doi:10.1080/14733285.2012.693376.

Tufft, B. 2015. "Nursury Staff to be Forced to Report Toddlers at Risk of Becoming Terrorists." *The Independent* January 4. Accessed January 5. http://www.independent.co.uk/news/uk/politics/nursery-staff-to-be-forced-to-report-toddlers-at-risk-of-becoming-terrorists-9956414.html.

Uprichard, E. 2008. "Children as 'Being and Becomings': Children, Childhood and Temporality." *Children & Society* 22 (4): 303–313. doi:10.1111/j.1099-0860.2007.00110.x.

Urdal, H. 2006. "A Clash of Generations? Youth Bulges and Political Violence." *International Studies Quarterly* 50 (3): 607–629. doi:10.1111/j.1468-2478.2006.00416.x.

Wagnsson, C., M. Hellman, and A. Holmberg. 2010. "The Centrality of Non-traditional Groups for Security in the Globalized Era: The Case of Children." *International Political Sociology* 4 (1): 1–14. doi:10.1111/j.1749-5687.2009.00090.x.

Walker, R. B. J. 1997. "The Subject of Security." In *Critical Security Studies: Concepts and Cases,* edited by K. Krause and. M. C. Williams . 61–80. Minneapolis. University of Minnesota Press.

Walt, S. M. 1991. "The Renaissance of Security Studies." *International Studies Quarterly* 35 (2): 211–239. doi:10.2307/2600471.

Watson, A. M. S. 2009. *The Child in International Political Economy: A Place at the Table.* London: Routledge.

Weber, H. 2013. "Demography and Democracy: The Impact of Youth Cohort Size on Democratic Stability in the World." *Democratization* 20 (2): 335–357. doi:10.1080/13510347.2011.650916.

'Children and armed conflict' and the field of security studies

Cecilia Jacob

Department of International Relations, The Australian National University, Canberra, Australia

Sociological studies in childhood have successfully carved out a research agenda that establishes children as worthy research subjects in their own right. This insight has impacted on international relations (IR) very late compared to similar developments throughout the social sciences given the perceived marginality of children to 'central' IR discussions of power, sovereignty, and security. A number of IR scholars have engaged with critical security studies and pioneered work that has justified the relevance of children to IR. This article goes a step further to build on this emergent body of important literature, advocating a Bourdieu-inspired conceptualization of child security in global politics. This approach to the study of children affected by armed conflict contributes theoretical insights for critical security studies, including the way we see civilians in conflict zones and humanitarian spaces, and pointing to the political implications of locating children in the social-political spaces of conflict and security.

Introduction

Opening analyses in international relations (IR) to include children as significant security actors has much to offer by way of insight into the workings of global politics and security. A number of scholars have argued persuasively why children should be included in the study of IR, in the specific areas of global politics (Brocklehurst 2006), the international political economy (Watson 2009), security studies (Wagnsson, Hellman, and Holmberg 2010), and international humanitarian and human rights law (Carpenter 2010). Topically, scholars in IR and related fields – such as international law and peace studies – interested in children have examined child soldiers (Brett and McCallin 1998; Brett and Specht 2004; Cohn and Goodwin-Gill 1994; Denov 2006, 2010; Happold 2005; Singer 2006; Wessells 2006), the militarization of childhood (Beier 2011; Brocklehurst 2006; Lee-Koo 2011; Mazurana and Carlson 2008), children born of wartime sexual violence (Carpenter 2007, 2010), and children/youth as contributors to post-conflict peace-building (McEvoy-Levy 2006; Wessells and Monteiro 2006). What can we make of this interest in children in conflict, how should we go about theorizing children in IR, and what significance does this bear on the study of security in IR?

Locating children in security studies serves a twofold purpose. Firstly, at a normative level, it concurs with developments in childhood sociology that children are worthy of study in their own right (Corsaro 2010; James and James 2004; James and Prout 1997; Qvortrup et al. 1994) and that childhood – no matter how fluidly defined – is an integral aspect of identity alongside other markers such as gender, ethnicity, class, and religion

(Jenks 1996, 57). Further, explicit theorizing in IR is needed to be specific and articulate about children's security needs and be aware of the practical challenge of tailoring interventions during and after periods of political violence (Jacob 2014). This normative aspect is concerned with recognizing children's rights, agency, claim to human security, and fundamentally, with justice in relation to actors whose voices do not filter into high-level political forums.

Secondly, the approach presented in this article recognizes the importance of the sociological turn in IR and the current inadequacy of ethical and political theorizing of security in critical security studies (Browning and McDonald 2011). Indeed, those of the 'Paris School' in IR – influenced largely by Pierre Bourdieu and Michel Foucault – have argued that an examination of the politics of protection causes us to reorient our frame of reference in thinking about security to asking who should be secured, how they should be secured, and who should do the securing (Huysmans 2006, 2). Engaging with sociological methodology enables us to see power relations, modes of oppression, and alternative practices of securing humanity than those our immediate scholarly categories permit but which may become visible once we open up to cross-disciplinary engagement and rigorous fieldwork (Bigo 2013, 114–127). It is at this juncture, 'seeing' children as constituents of *habitus* and *field* (Bourdieu 1977, 1990) – the same social and political landscape – in which contemporary conflicts are fought, that the linking together of children's security can be theorized. Children are integral to the politics (Brocklehurst 2006), the strategy (Singer 2006), the economics (Watson 2009; Wessells 2007, 3–4), and the casualties of war – including as direct targets of genocide violence. Therefore, seeing the relevance of children as sites of knowledge (Watson 2006) and as significant security actors (Wagnsson, Hellman, and Holmberg 2010) within modes of political competition and social transformation has much to contribute to the study of security in IR.

This article discusses the implications of children and armed conflict (CAAC) for security studies by firstly suggesting ways that children are present in the workings of IR and how their presence could be conceptualized. The second part of the article discusses childhood in relation to feminist IR theory, examining some of the possibilities and problems raised by conceptualizing children in IR through a feminist framework. The final section introduces a Bourdieu-inspired framework for locating and theorizing children in IR. Made possible by the 'practice turn' in IR, this approach shares feminist concerns with power relations and critical modes of theorizing the international. However, this approach also offers new possibilities for, firstly, locating children within the *field* of specific socio-political contexts in global politics such as conflict, or humanitarian spaces; secondly, recognizing the internalized practices of a range of actors within the field in relation to children; and, thirdly, identifying avenues for political intervention through which social transformation can be envisaged.

Children are seen but not heard in IR

To adapt a familiar feminist adage (Enloe 1990), let me ask: where are the children in IR? While far from the 'high' political forums of UN headquarters, embassies, and national parliaments, children in IR are more visible than we realize. For the past three years, the targeting, torture, rape, killing, and mass displacement of children have been cited to illustrate the brutality of the conflict in Syria (Gifkins 2012, 378; Save the Children 2012, 2013). Yet the targeting of children has not just been a side effect of conflict in Syria, but has been constitutive in the development of the conflict: as of 18 December 2013, Save the Children documented on its website that four million children have been seriously affected by the conflict. Children are affected through violence, displacement, disease, and malnutrition, with one-third of all children in Syria being hit, kicked, or shot at due to fighting in the past two years (Save the Children 2013).

Public outrage over the imprisonment and torture of 15 school children by Syrian authorities for spray painting anti-government graffiti in Daraa was the tipping point that catalyzed a series of poplar protests against state-sponsored violence in 2011. The state security forces violently repressed of the wave of public protests that spread across the country, this escalated the crisis that unfolded into the ongoing armed struggle in Syria (Gifkins 2012, 377). Since the outbreak of violence, children have been used as human shields and militants by both the government and opposition forces, have been tortured to gather intelligence on their parents and siblings, and schools have been transformed into 'military staging grounds, temporary bases, detention centres, sniper posts and centres for torture and the interrogation of adults and children' (UN Secretary General 2012, 23). The physical occupation of schools, including the bombardment of schools during military operations in which children have been killed, is one concrete illustration whereby child-hood and war merge within a broader political landscape, the experience and physical presence of children inseparable from the complex levels of violence in the war zones and displacement camps.

In a speech on 21 April 2013, US Secretary of State John Kerry cited the killings of '30 innocent children' by the Syrian government as evidence of the government's target-ing of innocent civilians, justifying the doubling of financial aid to the National Coalition of Syrian Revolutionary and Opposition Forces (Kerry 2013). Innocent children are no doubt an ideal 'civilian' to justify 'humanitarian' interventions (Carpenter 2006, 2013), a discourse central to this conflict. Media reporting has brought the plight of the war-affected children who have been specific targets of state-sponsored atrocities to our television sets and electronic devices. The broadcasting and publication of regular reports, with corresponding footage and photographs, document the horrors of life for children inside Syria and in refugee camps with headlines such as 'Children shot at, tortured and raped in Syria, report says' (*Reuters*, 13 March 2013). Such reporting has spurned civil society demands for states to take action to protect civilians, frustrated at the high-level politics inside the Security Council that prevents the international community from taking decisive action on humanitarian grounds. Children's presence on the battlefield is not just an after-thought but, rather, a centerpiece over which civil society, governments, opposi-tion forces, and humanitarian groups contest political power and security.

The literature on children in international politics concurs that children do play a very symbolic (Brocklehurst 2006) and strategic (Singer 2006; Wessells 2007, 3–4) role in the way that warfare is conducted. Whether the targeting of children themselves is an end in the violence, such as in ethnic cleansing or genocide, or whether children are maimed, raped, tortured, or killed to target family members suspected of being in collusion with the enemy, their presence is indeed instrumental and constitutive to the process of war. Although the quantitative research shows that the human cost of war has declined in sheer numbers since the start of the twentieth century (Melander, Oberg, and Hall 2009), the significant transformation of the *qualitative* nature of conflicts that encompasses a sociological shift through local–global interconnectedness and crimina-lization has a far-reaching impact on civilians that challenges traditional notions of war (Kaldor 2006). These insights raise serious ethical concerns in relation to the multi-plicity of ways that children's rights are violated during conflict and the capacity of IR to address them.

Locating children within security studies requires some conceptual calisthenics as children tend to remain on the margins in discussions of states and wars in both theory and political practice. The idea that women and children are the 'civilians' most vulnerable to conflict and in need of protection features significantly in the popular imagination of children and war, leading to a rather benign presence of children within the broader field of security studies as recipients of humanitarian protection and as victimized child soldiers. There is a tendency in media accounts toward emotive representations of children and war that may indeed sustain a certain 'politics of pity' (Wells 2009, 35–44) in humanitarian discourse and practice.

One of the more positive effects of this stereotyped discourse can be seen in the increased profile of the issue of war-affected children as a priority, for example, on the UN Security Council agenda and in the foreign policies of countries such as Canada where the 'stark images of the situation of war-affected children' convinced 'domestic and international audiences' that protecting war-affected children was morally imperative and proved to be a politically popular position (Sorger and Hoskins 2001, 135–137). A less certain consequence of representing children as non-agents or victims comes into play with domestic debates about the possibility of Western military forces encountering belligerent children in the battlefield. The widespread use of children in nearly every battlefield in the world raises new ethical dilemmas in Western military doctrine (Singer 2006) and international humanitarian law (Kuper 2005). This dynamic has indeed detracted from popular support for humanitarian operations, such as in the debate in Germany about sending troops to the EU peacekeeping mission in the Congo due to the ambiguity of how their soldiers should respond to confrontations with child soldiers in battle (Wagnsson, Hellman, and Holmberg 2010, 5).

The profile of children affected by conflict has increased significantly since the mid-1990s. In the 1990s, coinciding with a number of significant civil conflicts, interest in the humanitarian and ethical aspects of armed conflict led to the popularity of terms such as 'human security' (Commission on Human Security 2003; Human Security Report Project 2005; UNDP 1994), 'New Wars' (Kaldor 2006), and 'Responsibility to Protect' (International Commission on Intervention and State Sovereignty 2001). While these frameworks for thinking about global security have been the subject matter of intense scholarly debates,[1] they have gained significant traction in the international policy arena, particularly in the UN. It is within this overarching context, emphasizing the predominance of intra-state conflict and the revised understanding of the relationship between state sovereignty and human rights (Deng et al. 1996), that a particular emphasis on children affected by armed conflict emerged within the UN.

Following the release of the 1996 'Machel Report' commissioned by the UN on CAAC, the UN created the position of the Special Assistant to the Secretary General on Children and Armed Conflict, with a dedicated office to promote the protection of children in the world's conflict zones. Since the creation of the Office, a total of 10 UN Security Council resolutions on CAAC have been passed to date alongside hundreds of country-specific resolutions passed in the Security Council and General Assembly. Global advocacy networks such as Watchlist on Children and Armed Conflict and Child Soldiers International have contributed to disseminating information about the issue, advocating for governments to take action, and developing guidelines and recommendations for key international actors to better protect children in situations of armed conflict (Watchlist on Children and Armed Conflict 2013). Corresponding developments have taken place in international law, the adoption of the two optional protocols to the UN Convention on the Rights of the Child to protect children from armed conflict and commercial sexual exploitation being significant developments in this area.

In light of these important *institutional* and international *legal* developments that have raised the status of children in global and regional forums (notably the African Union), the location of children within the *political* domain is more challenging, as evidenced by the abstention of China, Russia, Pakistan, and Azerbaijan in 2012 on UNSC Resolution 2068 on CAAC to expand the mandate of this office. Within the international community, discourses of CAAC retain a very paternalistic outlook on childhood that has emphasized a one-dimensional perspective of children's presence in IR. Canada's Department of Foreign Affairs and International Trade (DFAIT), as mentioned above, has prioritized CAAC in its international human rights agenda, stating on its website, 'It is because of the unique vulnerability of children that their rights are of priority concern within Canada's foreign policy' (DFAIT 2013), the emphasis on vulnerability being a central aspect of the discursive construction of the issue in international politics.

The Canadian government has long been a vocal international advocate of CAAC in the international political arena, and alongside the UN and key civil society organizations, such as Watchlist on Children and Armed Conflict, has been instrumental in raising the situation of children and war as a high-profile global security issue.[2] The evocative role that children play is made evident in the framing of humanitarian discourses, justifications for political and military interventions, raising emergency funding, and so on. While laudable that such advocacy has enabled CAAC to gain traction as a global security 'issue', attracting increased resourcing and policy/programming with significant success, there is a danger that the complexity of addressing children in IR be reduced to adding CAAC to a list of human security issues. A token acknowledgement of children risks overlooking the need to unpack further the *implications* of recognizing children's rights, participation, protection, and their agency in conflict and post-conflict settings (Jacob 2014, 54–77). In particular, the emphasis in the discourse on civilian protection as something that is *done to* civilians by exogenous organizations at the point of crisis downplays human resilience and empowerment as vital strategies for promoting the human security of civilians (Chandler 2012; Kaplan 2013).

It is therefore worth paying attention to the insights that can be gained about the workings of conflict by considering the demographic bulk of children and youth in conflict affected societies, many of whom directly participate in hostilities or provide military support roles. Alison Watson (2006) has argued that children's participation as stone-throwers, protestors, and soldiers in contemporary conflict zones is evidence of their agency and represents an important site of knowledge for IR. There are many more empirical studies indicating that children, respecting of course the fluid cognitive and physical capacities of children and youth over time, exercise meaningful agency and political assertiveness during conflict, such as in the case of girls' diverse participations in the Lebanese civil war (Karamé 1995). Such studies also point to important sites for strategic intervention, as illustrated in a study for the United States Institute of Peace by US Colonel John Venhaus. In the study, over 2000 young al-Qaeda recruits who had actively sought to join the organization were interviewed. Venhaus concluded that focusing on providing alternative opportunities and outlets for disenfranchised males during their adolescent years is a vital strategy for the US government that would bring about the 'inevitable' defeat of al-Qaeda and its affiliates (2010, 18). That adolescents are conferred such strategic significance by the US military for combatting terrorism has much to say to the academic discipline of IR that has long failed to pay attention to the 'micro-socio-logical practices' of international politics and security (Adler-Nissen 2013, 5).

A much needed reorientation also includes rethinking who are the relevant stake-holders in post-conflict negotiations and peace-building processes so as not to exclude the experiences, interests, and needs of children in particularly vulnerable circumstances, a prime example being girl soldiers (Denov 2006; Fox 2004; Wessells 2007). Scholars such as Siobhan McEvoy-Levy (2006) and Michael Wessells and Carlinda Monteiro (2006) consider the participation of children and youth in peace negotiations and peace-building processes as crucial to the sustainability of post-conflict peace and inter-community healing and social transformation. This finding is also confirmed in Marc Sommers' (2006) work on former Interahamwe youth in post-genocide Rwanda, which is indeed revealing of the realities that youth with firsthand knowledge and experience of genocide and war have in shaping conflict and post-conflict trajectories. Further, Carolyn Nordstrom's work on war-orphans in Angola points to the resilience, creativity, and capacity of children for community-building that is not taken into account in the adult-centric processes of post-conflict peace-building and reconstruction (2006, 102–107).

In light of the above discussion that contextualized the current status of children in international politics, what direction could be taken to address CAAC in security studies? Solidarist and cosmopolitan accounts of ethics in IR offer a solid normative and legal justification for the imperative of state actors to protect civilians (Bellamy 2011; Dunne and Wheeler 2004), and concur with the humanitarian impulses of the 1990s that propelled CAAC onto the UNSC agenda as a high-priority thematic issue. Yet a more applied understanding of how to reconcile ethical concerns over human rights in IR with the specific and variegated needs of children in practice still remains wanting, despite strong normative justifications within the 'sovereignty as responsibility' rationale. Here I propose that a sociological approach to practice may accommodate some of these practical concerns and account for developments within childhood sociology that offer important theoretical tools for conceptualizing children affected by armed conflict.

A Bourdieu-inspired methodology can assist in transcending the methodological constraints in IR for addressing civilian protection through the concepts of field and habitus. This approach facilitates reorienting the way that the international is conceptua-lized (Adler-Nissen 2013, 7–11; Leander 2011, 296; Mérand and Pouliot 2013, 32–36), breaking down the 'absolute opposition between the collective and the individual' (Bigo 2011, 225), and indeed undermining the prevailing view 'that sociology and international relations work in two different realms with different rules' (Bigo and Walker 2007, 3). In parallel, sociological studies on childhood have been drawing the connections between children as social actors constitutive of their respective societies for over three decades now (Corsaro 2010; James and James 2004; James and Prout 1997). The reorientation within sociology that no longer views children as inhabiting 'different theoretic social worlds' (Jenks 1982, 34) but as constitutive of the broader sociological and political landscape has arrived very late to IR, yet does provide a very important perspective for considering the security of children in conflict zones and post-conflict societies.

A Bourdieu-inspired approach to children in IR raises further important questions about power relations and contestations over definitions and practices of security. As there are overlaps between these concerns and feminist IR theory, the next section will briefly turn to the potentials and limitations of feminist IR theory for theorizing children in IR. Situating children within feminist IR approaches has been an important site of discussions about childhood in IR to date (e.g., Denov 2006; Fox 2004; Lee Koo 2011; Mazurana and Carlson 2008), therefore a few issues will be interrogated in the next section to reflect on this positioning before laying out a Bourdieu-inspired framework in more detail in the final section to provide additional avenues for refining this important work.

Already said and done? IR feminist theory and children

Feminist IR theories have done a great service to IR; they have navigated a path for creative, alternative, and ethically imperative theorizing in a discipline that for a long time experienced the narrowing of its ontological and epistemological scope. A number of IR feminists have engaged feminist methodology to address childhood, for example, Katrina Lee-Koo's (2011) analysis of different images of child soldiers is used to reveal subtle workings of North–South power relations that are reinforced through humanitarian organizations. Likewise, Dyan Mazurana and Khristopher Carlson (2008) employ a feminist framework for analyzing the role of children in armed forces in sustaining armed conflict and war economics, demonstrating the potential of employing feminist and gender analyses of childhood in IR.

There are, however, some tensions and internal contradictions between feminist and childhood scholars that have not been explicitly addressed in IR. In this section, I will break down some of these tensions as they have unconsciously manifested themselves within IR and advocate for a more explicit acknowledgement of these tensions in order to circumvent a possible rift between scholars interested in feminism and childhood, or for scholars promoting children in IR to reject feminism altogether (Burman 2008, 186).

There is a danger that questions of children's rights, agency, participation, and protection could be subsumed within a broader feminist account if the distinction between the agendas of feminist and child rights advocates is not sufficiently qualified. For example, feminists in IR have argued that the repetition of 'womenandchildren' in political speeches (e.g., Bush 2001 cited in Hunt 2010, 117) and media reporting of wars highlight the rendering of women as 'childlike in their innocence about international *realpolitik*' (Enloe 1993, 166). Similarly, in an examination of one of Laura Bush's speeches in 2001, Laura Shepherd argues that:

> The running together of 'womenandchildren' twice in close succession *infantilizes the women* of Afghanistan, denying them both adulthood and agency, affording them only pity and a certain voyeuristic attraction. (Shepherd 2006, 20, emphasis mine)

Yet these phrases may also have as much to tell us about overarching stereotypes and conceptualizations of children in international politics as they do about women. At what point children came to signify a lack of agency and be afforded 'only pity and a certain voyeuristic attraction' in IR does raise a serious need for reflection on a discipline that has become increasingly sensitive to issues of identity, exclusion, and discourse. The absence of deeper interrogation into why children (not women) are valid justifications for war is curious; why are the authors silent about this assumption inherent in the statement? Or why does the juxtaposition of women with *children* not merit any discussion about the positioning of children and children's agency in IR, even if only in passing? Why would a scholar so deeply committed to revealing unjust power relations and identifying those on the margins in IR (Enloe 2004, 19–42) use the phrase 'childlike...innocence about international *realpolitik*' in a way that suggests that children's knowledge, experience, and opinions about world politics are irrelevant? Given that the empirical studies do not concur with this assumption of children's naivety and unproblematic innocence in armed conflict, it is worth interrogating whether this emphasis by the very scholars who claim inclusivity and the need to speak on behalf of the disenfranchised perhaps further crystallizes the irrelevance of children to IR and security studies.

Erica Burman has cautioned against the animosity that feminists (and anti-feminists) have toward the juxtaposition of 'womenandchildren' in discourse, but rather seeks to move the debate forward through a more rigorous examination of children's rights and women's rights in relation to each other. She argues that it is important 'to consider the relations between women's rights and children's rights as neither adversarial, nor equivalent, but as allied – albeit as necessarily structured in tension and contest' (Burman 2008, 177). In her argument we find a nuanced distinction between the conceptualization of these two regimes, but also a refined position that wisely argues against pitting the two regimes against one another. Feminists have long (and understandably) decried the positioning of women alongside children, a labeling that *equates* women with children and suggests women's subordinate and passive status in society. However, child rights activists point out the subordination of children's perspectives that is imposed through a feminist positioning of women *against children* in the rejection of this formulation, rather than acknowledging that their own positioning of children as the subordinate and passive object, is equally problematic (Burman 2008, 180–181). Here Burman seeks to reconcile these animosities by arguing that the source of the tension is not the direct hostility between women and children per se, but rather between women versus women (motherhood is seen as disadvantaging women in relation to 'child-free' mothers), and women versus the institutions of patriarchy including the state.

Burman (2008, 187) argues that childhood studies have come a long way in shifting some of the seeming internal contradictions between children's and women's rights and repositioning their social status in relation to each other. This is yet again evidence of the need for IR scholars to draw more deeply on developments in childhood studies to build on a very nascent conceptualization of children in IR.

Reflecting the other side of the debate, Charli Carpenter has argued that in the case of Bosnia-Herzegovina the issue of children born of wartime sexual violence was subsumed within the women and armed conflict advocacy network. By positioning vulnerable children within the women's advocacy network instead of the child protection network, Carpenter suggests that the rape survivor's needs took precedence over children's protection rights:

> …activists focussing on women were more likely to view the issue (of children born of war) through the lens of the rape survivor's needs than those of her child and to oppose advocacy discourse that might situate rape survivors or their persecuted communities as perpetrators of child abuse. From this perspective, the emphasis tended to be on preventing rape and rape-related pregnancy in the first place rather than responding to the needs of the child as a human rights subject afterward. Although this dynamic is a result in part of the political opportunity structures within and between networks, interpretations of political problems are the result of preexisting narratives about who was wronged during the war. (Carpenter 2010, 186)

What Carpenter shows being played out on the field is a difficulty not just by scholars but also civil society practitioners to reconcile a women's rights agenda with the ambiguous status of children who were also victims in different ways of wartime atrocities. Yet perhaps this contested area of scholarship in IR – the rights of women (many of whom are girls) subjected to rape and the children born of wartime sexual violence – is precisely the intellectual terrain in which IR scholars are able to theorize both the presence of women and children during times of conflict as, in Burman's formulation quoted above, 'neither adversarial, nor equivalent, but as allied – albeit as necessarily structured in tension and contest'.

The literature on children's rights also tends to focus on the individual experience of the child and the child's own capacity to claim/exercise rights (Freeman 1997; Verhellen 1992, 80). When addressing the experience of children in war, and particularly in the 'global South' where family and community relationships are constitutive of the individual child's experience, conceptualizing children's security must take into account their broader socio-political context, modes of survival and protection that are invariably linked to their roles and experiences of war. Indeed, conceptualizing the security of children, particularly very young children, is incomplete without reflecting on children's situations in relation to carers and community that is essential for survival.

Further, women's experiences of war will invariably be differentiated from men's due to their reproductive roles and status in society that structure specific forms of gendered violence against women during war (Cockburn 2004, 24–44; Eisenstein 1996, 43–61). This association of women with reproduction and childhood has been a focus of important feminist work in IR that contributes to the critical analysis of nation-building and justice in post-conflict societies (D'Costa 2011). So here what we find is a need to be more nuanced to prevent positioning feminists in opposition to childhood inadvertently, so that issues of children's rights and agency are not subsumed and subordinated within the broader feminist agenda, and to recognize the need for a purposive and explicit theorization of children in IR that is attuned to the interconnectedness between children and the social relations within which they are embedded – a 'relational autonomy' (Sjoberg and Gentry 2007, 190–196) of children in IR.

This opens up further opportunities for seeing children not only in relation to their mothers (again, many of whom may also be considered children), such as in renderings as children born of wartime sexual violence (Carpenter 2007, 2010), but in relation, for example, to fathers (children being tortured to extract information on alleged affiliation of relatives with rebels in Syria or raped in front of their parents in Libya by militias as a form of terrorism); in relation to militias where their bulk in the fighting population and years of militant activity, including genocide (Sommers 2006), generates rich experiences that are a 'site of knowledge' in IR (Watson 2006; cf. McEvoy-Levy 2006); in relation to the post-conflict community as reproducers of culture (Nordstrom 2006); in relation to processes of post-conflict peace-building (Denov 2006, 2010; Fox 2004); in relation to political and protest movements (McEvoy-Levy 2006; Watson 2006); and so on.

The next section proposes a framework for conceptualizing children not as an isolated category of knowledge but within broader and complex social contexts through a relational ontology that complements feminist IR approaches to studying children and may help in overcoming some of these internal disciplinary tensions.

Childhood as a new frontier for research in security studies

The work of Pierre Bourdieu was referred to above as a way of rethinking the starting point of politics and security (Adler-Nissen 2013, 1). His work was concerned with locating not only the objects of study within their social context but identifying the social relations through which power operates and structures of oppression are established (Bourdieu 1977). As Didier Bigo, drawing on Bourdieu, argues, the categorization of knowledge is an operation of power that is largely 'policed' by epistemic communities – a fact that is of great importance for security studies scholars who should contest the arbitrariness of threat construction and narrowly conceived security practices (Bigo 2013, 125).

From this starting point, an emphasis on practice enables security studies scholars to become aware of the subjective, socially learned and largely unconscious background knowledge that is internalized in actors (*habitus*) inclining them toward certain behaviors in the objective *field* within which actors operate, and the different forms of capital that interact to produce social practice. A *field* is any social space defined by a central struggle, specific arrangements of power, and certain 'rules of the game' (Bourdieu 1977, 40; Mérand and Pouliot 2013, 30). Most closely aligned with a social constructivist position – although with an emphasis on power rather than norms and identity – the practice turn in IR facilitates conceptualizing children by situating them within a given field of power relations and competition where multiple actors interact.

Rather than taking a predetermined bounded subject (such as the state or an organization) as the starting point for theory, various socio-political practices can be scrutinized in a thick sociological setting that could otherwise not be identified (Kopper 2012, 281; Leander 2011, 296). This both overcomes the structure-agency binary in IR and transcends predetermined levels of analysis and constructed binaries such as domestic/international or public/private. Not only is the socio-political space for analysis reconceptualized (Bigo 2011; Huysmans and Nogueira 2012), but it allows for the recognition of multiple actors, in asymmetrical power arrangements, to be present in a given space and to recognize the subjective, material, and ideational processes at work in shaping practice (Leander 2011).

The relational ontology of Bourdieu's work (Mérand and Pouliot 2013, 28–32) creates immense possibilities for conceptualizing children in IR, given the multiple levels and complexity in which children both shape and are shaped by global politics. Situating the Bourdieu-inspired 'practice turn' as part of the broader critical security studies project creates further possibilities for reflecting on the transformative potential of analyses of practice. For example, from a politics of protection approach to the analysis of practice, scholars can interrogate:

> ...how moral and ethical claims can gain political voice; how transformative agency takes form in specific sites in which human beings translate ethical and moral claims into a political encounter characterised by excessive structural constraints...and highly asymmetrical power relations. (Huysmans 2006, 7)

Scholars such as Peter Nyers (2006) and Jef Huysmans (2006) employ a 'politics of protection' framework to build on the recognition of specific arrangements of power to identify sites for political contestation and structural transformation. Although Bourdieu's social theory has a very limited vision of the transformative capacity of political actors, unlike the much more explicit approach of transformative agency advocated by Huysmans and Nyers, his work suggests that raising collective awareness of tacit and unconscious practices can lead to action, a point that is of relevance to critical security studies (Adler-Nissen 2013, 5). Indeed, Bourdieu's work was political in its very nature and purpose. Those interested in engaging with Bourdieu-inspired methodologies in IR have been able to recognize structures of social-political power in ways not possible through rational choice and – until more recently – in social constructivism (Jackson 2009, 112–113). Secondly, this approach moves toward analyzing the political (as opposed to exceptional) nature of security (Bigo 2013, 121). It is in this political space that alternative visions of security can be imagined (Burke 2007, 10) and security practices can be contested and transformed.

To illustrate the practical implications of this perspective, recent research that has mapped the protection regimes for children in conflict and post-conflict zones has identified the presence of a 'protection gap' that emerges from the politicization of the issue of child protection that reinforces the marginal status of children and their agency from the larger discourse of security and the inadequacy of resources dedicated to protecting children (Jacob 2014). This nuanced research illustrates the potential of the conceptual reorientation toward security practice advocated in this article as it assists in identifying practices of security actors that contribute to the production of (in)security of civilians such as children and points to concrete sites of political agency and institutional responsibility that has relevance for policy, advocacy, and institutional transformation that takes us beyond a one-dimensional CAAC thematic approach to child protection.

Conclusion

Children affected by conflict are embedded in specific socio-political contexts and, in the messy 'real world', achieving children's security – particularly in a conflict situation where governance, law, and order are abdicated – is complex. Going back to the current example of Syria, children can be seen as catalyzing the protests that marked the start of the conflict, as fighters, direct targets of violence for interrogation, torture, rape, and killings, caught in the cross-fire, as displaced and thrust into poverty, as tools in political rhetoric, as headline grabbers and media fodder, and as justification for state intervention. Their schools are used as military bases and interrogation centers, and the sectarian violence is tearing apart the cultural, religious, and social fabric that once provided stability to their communities. This is a radical realignment of the entire social space. Children are indeed constituent of the broader socio-political landscape in which the conflict is taking place – not just a category for humanitarian organizations to factor into their operations.

Importantly, for this reason, the impulse toward sociologically oriented and reflexive critical security theory, inspired by Bourdieu's social theory, presents a logical framework for conceptualizing children's security by taking into account the relational nature of social and political practices and the oppressive nature of power structures in armed conflict in which children are situated. For far too long, 'CAAC' has been discussed as a unitary category or a thematic 'issue' in isolation from a broader socio-political context. Furthermore, civilian protection tends to be conceptualized as an external intervention, one that is done by 'humanitarian actors' to 'civilians.' Lacking the capacity to address questions of civilians' own agency and resilience, or indeed to even problematize the category 'civilian' itself, mainstream discourses of children and security need to be unsettled and reinvigorated.

Notes

1. For debates on New Wars, see, *inter alia*, Melander, Oberg, and Hall (2009), Mundy (2011), and Newman (2004). For a range of critical debates on human security, see, *inter alia*, contributions to Chandler and Hynek (2012). A comprehensive literature review of the debates on the concept of Responsibility to Protect is found in Breakey (2011).
2. Such as hosting the first international conference on children affected by conflict in Winnipeg in 2000, co-sponsoring UNSC Resolutions 1882 and 1998 on Children and Armed Conflict among other significant international contributions to establishing CAAC on the international security agenda, see DFAIT Website page 'Children and Armed Conflict': http://www.international.gc.ca/rights-droits/child_soldiers-enfants_soldats.aspx?lang=eng&view=d (accessed 23 November 2013).

References

Adler-Nissen, R. 2013. "Introduction." In *Bourdieu in International Relations: Rethinking Key Concepts in IR*, edited by R. Adler-Nissen, 1–23. London: Routledge.

Beier, J. M., ed. 2011. *The Militarization of Childhood: Thinking Beyond the Global South*. New York: Palgrave Macmillan.

Bellamy, A. 2011. *Global Politics and the Responsibility to Protect: From Words to Deeds*. Oxford: Routledge.

Bigo, D. 2011. "Pierre Bourdieu and International Relations: Power of Practices, Practices of Power." *International Political Sociology* 5 (3): 225–258. doi:10.1111/j.1749-5687.2011.00132.x.

Bigo, D. 2013. "Security." In *Bourdieu in International Relations: Rethinking Key Concepts in IR*, edited by R. Adler-Nissen, 114–130. London: Routledge.

Bigo, D., and R. B. J. Walker. 2007. "Editorial: International, Political, Sociology." *International Political Sociology* 1 (1): 1–5. doi:10.1111/j.1749-5687.2007.00001.x.

Bourdieu, P. 1977. *Outline of a Theory of Practice*. Cambridge: Cambridge University Press.

Bourdieu, P. 1990. *The Logic of Practice*. Cambridge: Polity Press.

Breakey, H. 2011. *The Responsibility to Protect and the Protection of Civilians in Armed Conflicts: Review and Analysis*. Brisbane: Institute for Ethics, Governance and Law, Griffith University.

Brett, R., and M. McCallin. 1998. *Children: The Invisible Soldiers*. Stockholm: Rädda Barnen (Save the Children Sweden).

Brett, R., and I. Specht. 2004. *Young Soldiers: Why They Choose to Fight*. Boulder, CO: Lynne Rienner Publishers.

Brocklehurst, H. 2006. *Who's Afraid of Children: Children, Conflict and International Relations*. Hampshire: Ashgate.

Browning, C. S., and M. McDonald. 2011. "The Future of Critical Security Studies: Ethics and the Politics of Security." *European Journal of International Relations* 19 (2): 1–21. doi:10.1177/1354066111419538.

Burke, A. 2007. *What Security Makes Possible: Some Thoughts on Critical Security Studies*. Canberra: Department of International Relations, RSPAS, Australian National University.

Burman, E. 2008. "Beyond 'Women vs. Children' or 'Womenandchildren': Engendering Childhood and Reformulating Motherhood." *The International Journal of Children's Rights* 16 (2): 177–194. doi:10.1163/157181808X301773.

Carpenter, C. R. 2006. *'Innocent Women and Children': Gender, Norms and the Protection of Civilians*. Hampshire: Ashgate.

Carpenter, C. R., ed. 2007. *Born of War: Protecting Children of Sexual Violence Survivors in Conflict Zones*. Bloomfield, CT: Kumarian Press.

Carpenter, C. R. 2010. *Forgetting Children Born of War: Setting the Human Rights Agenda in Bosnia and Beyond*. New York: Columbia University Press.

Carpenter, C. R. 2013. "The Image before the Weapon: A Critical History of the Distinction between Combatant and Civilian." *Ethics and International Affairs* 27: 107–110. doi:10.1017/S0892679412000809.

Chandler, D. 2012. "Resilience and Human Security: The Post-Interventionist Paradigm." *Security Dialogue* 43 (3): 213–229. doi:10.1177/0967010612444151.

Chandler, D., and N. Hynek, eds. 2012. *Critical Perspectives on Human Security: Rethinking Emancipation and Power in International Relations*. London: Routledge.

Cockburn, C. 2004. "The Continuum of Violence: A Gender Perspective on War and Peace." In *Sites of Violence: Gender and Conflict Zones*, edited by W. Giles and J. Hyndman, 30–44. Berkeley: University of California Press.

Cohn, I., and G. S. Goodwin-Gill. 1994. *Child Soldiers: The Role of Children in Armed Conflict*. Oxford: Clarendon Press.

Commission on Human Security. 2003. *Human Security Now*. New York: United Nations.

Corsaro, W. A. 2010. *The Sociology of Childhood*. Thousand Oaks, CA: Pine Forge Press.

D'Costa, B. 2011. *Nationbuilding, Gender and War Crimes in South Asia*. London: Routledge.

Deng, F. M., S. Kimaro, T. Lyons, D. Rothschild, and I. William Zartman. 1996. *Sovereignty as Responsibility: Conflict Management in Africa*. Washington, DC: Brookings Institution Press.

Denov, M. S. 2006. "Wartime Sexual Violence: Assessing a Human Security Response to War-Affected Girls in Sierra Leone." *Security Dialogue* 37 (3): 319–342. doi:10.1177/0967010606069178.

Denov, M. S. 2010. *Child Soldiers: Sierra Leone's Revolutionary United Front*. Cambridge: Cambridge University Press.

DFAIT (Department of Foreign Affairs and International Trade), Government of Canada. 2013. "Human Rights are an Important Part of Canada's Foreign Policy." Accessed January 17, 2014. http://www.international.gc.ca/rights-droits/index.aspx?lang=eng

Dunne, T., and N. J. Wheeler. 2004. "'We the Peoples': Contending Discourses of Security in Human Rights Theory and Practice." *International Relations* 18 (1): 9–23. doi:10.1177/0047117804041738.

Eisenstein, Z. 1996. *Hatreds: Racialized and Sexualized Conflicts in the 21st Century*. New York: Routledge.

Enloe, C. 1990. *Bananas, Beaches and Bases: Making Feminist Sense of International Politics*. Berkeley: University of California Press.

Enloe, C. 1993. *The Morning After: Sexual Politics at the End of the Cold War*. Berkeley: University of California Press.

Enloe, C. 2004. *The Curious Feminist: Searching for Women in a New Age of Empire*. Berkeley: University of California Press.

Fox, M.-J. 2004. "Girl Soldiers: Human Security and Gendered Insecurity." *Security Dialogue* 35 (4): 465–479. doi:10.1177/0967010604049523.

Freeman, M. 1997. *The Moral Status of Children: Essays on the Rights of the Child*. The Hague: Kluwer Law International.

Gifkins, J. 2012. "Briefing: The UN Security Council Divided: Syria in Crisis." *Global Responsibility to Protect* 4 (3): 377–393. doi:10.1163/1875984X-00403009.

Happold, M. 2005. *Child Soldiers in International Law*. Manchester: Manchester University Press.

Human Security Report Project. 2005. *Human Security Report 2005: War and Peace in the 21st Century*. Vancouver: The University of British Columbia.

Hunt, K. 2010. "The 'War on Terrorism'." In *Gender Matters in Global Politics: A Feminist Introduction to International Relations*, edited by L. J. Shepherd, 116–126. London: Routledge.

Huysmans, J. 2006. "Agency and the Politics of Protection: Implications for Security Studies." In *The Politics of Protection: Sites of Insecurity and Political Agency*, edited by J. Huysmans, A. Dobson, and R. Prokhovnik, 1–18. Oxford: Routledge.

Huysmans, J., and J. P. Nogueira. 2012. "International Political Sociology: Opening Spaces, Stretching Lines." *International Political Sociology* 6 (1): 1–3. doi:10.1111/j.1749-5687.2011.00147.x.

International Commission on Intervention and State Sovereignty. 2001. *Responsibility to Protect*. Ottawa: International Development Research Centre.

Jackson, P. 2009. "Pierre Bourdieu." In *Critical Theorists and International Relations*, edited by J. Edkins and N. Vaughan-Williams, 102–113. London: Routledge.

Jacob, C. 2014. *Child Security in Asia: The Impact of Armed Conflict in Cambodia and Myanmar*. London: Routledge.

James, A., and A. L. James. 2004. *Constructing Childhood: Theory, Policy and Social Practice*. Hampshire: Palgrave Macmillan.

James, A., and A. Prout, eds. 1997. *Constructing and Reconstructing Childhood: Contemporary Issues in the Sociological Study of Childhood*. Hampshire: The Falmer Press.

Jenks, C., ed. 1982. *The Sociology of Childhood: Essential Readings*. London: Batsford Academic and Educational.

Jenks, C. 1996. *Childhood*. London: Routledge.

Kaldor, M. 2006. *New and Old Wars: Organized Violence in a Global Era*. Cambridge, MA: Polity Press.

Kaplan, O. 2013. "Protecting Civilians in Civil War: The Institution of the ATCC in Colombia." *Journal of Peace Research* 50 (3): 351–367. doi:10.1177/0022343313477884.

Karamé, K. H. 1995. "Girls' Participation in Combat: A Case Study from Lebanon." In *Children in the Muslim Middle East*, edited by E. W. Fernea, 378–391. Austin, TX: University of Austin Press.

Kerry, J. 2013. "Remarks with Turkish Foreign Minister Ahmet Davutoglu and Syrian Opposition coalition President Moaz al-Khatib." Adile Sultan Palace, Istanbul, Turkey, April 21.

Kopper, Á. 2012. "The Imaginary of Borders: From a Coloring Book to Cézanne's Paintings." *International Political Sociology* 6 (3): 277–293. doi:10.1111/j.1749-5687.2012.00164.x.

Kuper, J. 2005. *Military Training and Children in Armed Conflict, Law, Policy and Practice*. Leiden: Martinus Nijhoff.

Leander, A. 2011. "The Promises, Problems, and Potentials of a Bourdieu-Inspired Staging of International Relations." *International Political Sociology* 5 (3): 294–313. doi:10.1111/j.1749-5687.2011.00135.x.

Lee-Koo, K. 2011. "Horror and Hope: (Re)presenting Militarised Children in Global North-South Relations." *Third World Quarterly* 32 (4): 725–742. doi:10.1080/01436597.2011.567005.

Mazurana, D., and K. Carlson. 2008. "War Slavery: The Role of Children and Youth in Fighting Forces in Sustaining Armed Conflicts and War Economies in Africa." In *Gender, Violent Conflict, and Development*, edited by D. Zarkov, 205–235. New Delhi: Zubaan Press.

McEvoy-Levy, S., ed. 2006. *Troublemakers or Peacemakers? Youth and Post-Accord Peace Building*. Notre Dame, IN: University of Notre Dame Press.

Melander, E., M. Oberg, and J. Hall. 2009. "Are 'New Wars' More Atrocious? Battle Severity, Civilians Killed and Forced Migration Before and After the End of the Cold War." *European Journal of International Relations* 15 (3): 505–536. doi:10.1177/1354066109338243.

Mérand, F., and V. Pouliot. 2013. "Bourdieu's Concepts." In *Bourdieu in International Relations: Rethinking Key Concepts in IR*, edited by R. Adler-Nissen, 24–44. London: Routledge.

Mundy, J. 2011. "Deconstructing Civil Wars: Beyond the New Wars Debate." *Security Dialogue* 42 (3): 279–295. doi:10.1177/0967010611405378.

Newman, E. 2004. "The 'New Wars' Debate: A Historical Perspective Is Needed." *Security Dialogue* 35 (2): 173–189. doi:10.1177/0967010604044975.

Nordstrom, C. 2006. "The Jagged Edge of Peace." In *Troublemakers or Peacemakers? Youth and Post-Accord Peace Building*, edited by S. McEvoy-Levy, 99–116. Notre Dame, IN: Notre Dame University Press.

Nyers, P. 2006. "Taking Rights, Mediating Wrongs: Disagreements over the Political Agency on Non-Status Refugees." In *The Politics of Protection: Sites of Insecurity and Political Agency*, edited by J. Huysmans, A. Dobson, and R. Prokhovnik, 48–67. Abingdon: Routledge.

Qvortrup, J., M. Bardy, G. Sgritta, and H. Wintersberger, eds. 1994. *Childhood Matters: Social Theory, Practice and Policy*. Aldershot: Avebury.

Save the Children. 2012. *Untold Atrocities: The Stories of Syria's Children*. London: Save the Children.

Save the Children. 2013. *Childhood Under Fire: The Impact of Two Years of Conflict in Syria*. London: Save the Children.

Shepherd, L. J. 2006. "Veiled References: Constructions of Gender in the Bush Administration Discourse on the Attacks on Afghanistan Post-9/11." *International Feminist Journal of Politics* 8 (1): 19–41. doi:10.1080/14616740500415425.

Singer, P. W. 2006. *Children at War*. Berkeley: University of California Press.

Sjoberg, L., and C. E. Gentry. 2007. *Mothers, Monsters, Whores*. London: Zed Books.

Sommers, M. 2006. "In the Shadow of Genocide: Rwanda's Youth Challenge." In *Troublemakers or Peacemakers? Youth and Post-Accord Peace Building*, edited by S. McEvoy-Levy, 81–98. Notre Dame, IN: Notre Dame University Press.

Sorger, C., and E. Hoskins. 2001. "Protecting the Most Vulnerable: War-Affected Children." In *Human Security and the New Diplomacy: Protecting People, Promoting Peace*, edited by R. McRae and D. Hubert, 134–152. Montreal: McGill-Queens University Press.

UNDP (United Nations Development Program). 1994. *Human Development Report 1994: New Dimensions of Human Security*. New York: Oxford University Press.

United Nations Secretary General. 2012. *Report of the Secretary-General to the Security Council (A/66/782-S/2012/261) issued on 26 April 2012*. New York: United Nations.

Venhaus, J. M. 2010. *Why Youth Join Al-Qaeda*. Washington, DC: United States Institute of Peace.

Verhellen, E. 1992. "Changes in the Images of the Child." In *The Ideologies of Children's Rights*, edited by M. Freeman, 79–94. Dordrecht: Kluwer Academic Press.

Wagnsson, C., M. Hellman, and A. Holmberg. 2010. "The Centrality of Non-Traditional Groups for Security in the Globalized Era." *International Political Sociology* 4 (1): 1–14. doi:10.1111/j.1749-5687.2009.00090.x.

Watchlist on Children and Armed Conflict. 2013. *A Checklist for Mainstreaming: Children and Armed Conflict-Friendly Security Council Resolutions*. London: Watchlist on Children and Armed Conflict.

Watson, A. M. S. 2006. "Children and International Relations: A New Site of Knowledge?" *Review of International Studies* 32 (2): 237–250. doi:10.1017/S0260210506007005.

Watson, A. M. S. 2009. *The Child in International Political Economy: A Place at the Table*. London: Routledge.

Wells, K. 2009. *Childhood in a Global Perspective*. Malden: Polity Press.

Wessells, M. 2006. *Child Soldiers: From Violence to Protection*. Cambridge, MA: Harvard University Press.

Wessells, M. 2007. *The Recruitment and Use of Girls in Armed Forces and Groups in Angola: Implications for Ethical Research and Reintegration*. Pittsburgh, PA: Ford Institute for Human Security Working Papers, Ford Institute for Human Security, University of Pittsburgh.

Wessells, M., and C. Monteiro. 2006. "Psychosocial Assistance for Youth: Toward Reconstruction for Peace in Angola." *Journal of Social Issues* 62 (1): 121–139. doi:10.1111/j.1540-4560.2006.00442.x.

The state of play: securities of childhood – insecurities of children

Helen Brocklehurst

Department of Political and Cultural Studies, Swansea University, Swansea, UK

This article is broadly concerned with the positioning of children, both within and outside the subject area of International Relations. It considers the costs of an adult-centric standpoint in security studies and contrasts this with investments made seemingly on behalf of children and their security. It begins by looking at how children and childhoods are constructed and contained – yet also defy categorization – at some cost to their protection. The many competing children and childhoods that are invoked in security discourses and partially sustain their victimcy are then illustrated. It is argued that at their entry point into academia they are essentialized and sentimentalized. Power relations which subvert, yet also rely on children and childhoods can only be disrupted through a reconfiguration of politics and agency which includes an engagement with political literacy on a societal level and acknowledgement of the ubiquitous presence of war in all our lives.

Introduction

At the heart of this article is an attempt to understand why children are undertheorized in International Relations (IRs) and especially in security studies. It will explore why children are a challenging 'category' to think about, but also argue that this only partly explains why so little progress has been made in accommodating them within security studies or challenging security studies to make sense of them. One might argue that political stakeholders and commentators have always recognized children and appealed on their behalf, but vitally the children that are most valued are largely seen and not heard – positioned and increasingly politicized, but not engaged with. Despite their actual integration within political and international webs of power, children as state investments, instruments, symbols, or citizens, are not afforded attention. Although we are surrounded by children and 'completed' children, the majority of these survivors may have been failed. Underestimated, undervalued, and consequently underdeveloped, it is argued here that children protected 'from politics' in this way are also potentially disabled of their – and our – security. The article illustrates two cases in which children are 'hidden in plain sight'. It concludes by asking IR and security studies to engage more fully with the socio-political and gendered dimensions of children and childhood.

The child in the net

There is no doubt that children are contested and 'messy' referents (Beazley et al. 2009, 366). 'Child' is less a lived reality than an assigned concept. There is no agreed definition of a child that is in use worldwide for any purpose. Nor is there agreement on the question of how long childhood is or what its duration should encompass.

> Age is not sufficient in itself as an indicator of childhood, nor does it illustrate why such persons are potentially receiving or deserving of different treatment throughout this time....A unique and transient period of intense physical, mental, emotional and spiritual development; a time span delineated differently across and within communities and cultures; a managed societal or economic initiation; a portal to romanticised and marketable evocations, images and memories – the consideration of childhood presents a unique empirical and theoretical challenge. (Brocklehurst 2006, 1)

The generally accepted definition in development studies and enshrined in international law is that a child is a person under the age of 18 – unless the age of majority is attained earlier. Although UN lobbying is taking place to bring the age of majority closer to 18, such an age span is not typical of most experiences of childhood. As James (2010, 490) notes, '...the category of childhood is fractured not just by the different social constructions of childhood in different political, cultural and economic contexts, but also by the significance of different ages within childhood'. The most common threshold of childhood, prior to which children are treated differently from adults may in fact be closer to 12 years, or even earlier, before puberty, marriage or developed labour capacity. 'Early Childhood', from birth to eight years old, might in fact be the most commonly experienced period of 'childhood' worldwide. Beyond that period, 'older children', 'youth', or younger adults may be indistinguishable. They may work, labour, or hold apprenticeships, hold rights and responsibilities, and be entrusted with the care of other children.

It is also difficult to find even biological/psychological qualities of childhood which might be definitive of it were they not also actually shared by at least some of those who are conventionally treated as adults. Dependency, weakness, disability, immobility, 'child-like'-ness, 'childishness', and irrationality can all characterize adults – including politically active adults. Lifespan and absent or underdeveloped vital organs (especially under five) offer the most straightforward delineators of early childhood, also making the youngest children first in the queue for some forms of protection. Pauses in armed conflict for mass infant immunizations offer one such reminder of this. The less developed children are, the less they cope with, comprehend, and assimilate terror and risk. In addition, very young children's *physical* survival may also be encoded in the psychologically reassuring *proximity* of older, primary caregivers – and potentially vice versa. When a mother dies it doubles the death rate of her surviving sons and quadruples that of her daughters (Hammad and Bindari 2009, 39).

At the other end of the age spectrum, childhood's termination is equally fuzzy. Physical growth is not itself a sole characteristic of childhood in international law. A person's physical or biological maturation will often continue into adolescence and beyond 18, finally stopping near the age of 25. Conversely, in terms of moral and cognitive development, children may reach comparable adult levels between the ages of 12 and 14. Adversity and poverty may make the status of childhood redundant – if not the realities of ongoing development. An early adulthood, designated primarily by gun competency in a Brazilian favela, or by life expectancy of 35 in Afghanistan, does much to explain the capacity and decisions of the individuals trapped within these structures and taking, sustaining, or shaping lives accordingly. The categorization of 'youth' is equally relevant here, straddling the boundary of childhood and yet not indicating full admittance to adulthood. The United Nations Population Fund (UNFPA) defines 'youth' as the age group from 15 to 24 years and 'young people' as those in the range of 10–24 years. Like the status of child, meaning and significance vary greatly across cultures. In Rwanda, the insecurity of a generation has been achieved through the enforcing of a new criterion for adulthood which is beyond the reach of most males – consequently delaying marriages and weakening entire communities (Sommers 2012). The status of 'youth', often assigned beyond the period of 18 and even up to the age of 35, here marks out permanent social impotence.

The ever-lengthening period of protracted immaturity that characterizes Western pre-adult status provides an additional challenge, wherein young people and adults navigate or sustain a relatively undertheorized terrain of rights and responsibilities in sensitive and arguably political contexts such as sex, unpaid labour, military service, or 'pre'-citizenship. Thus childhood is also increasingly understood to be an adult invention, an accretion of ideals, a matrix of boundaries, and an opportunity for transgression which excites both predator and prey – not least in the digital age of childhood 2.0. For some commentators, late or 'teenage' childhood has been reformulated as 'adolescence' – a century old American invention (Maira and Soep 2004, 245) affirming some particulars of emotional underdevelopment and structural dependency but potentially undermining adequate participation.

Legislation typically refracts, retracts and protracts all these related conceptions of child and adult. Sixteen-year-old children in the UK for example are deemed too young to watch pornography or vote at an age when they can choose to procreate or volunteer for the military service. This is not an unusual situation but it is of consequence that partial or whole cognizance of their actions demonstrated in one sphere is not always directly translated to other spheres. What is at stake here is whether we can concede that in various ways we might *all* develop and mature throughout lifetimes. Tellingly, the term 'emerging adulthood' has been coined to capture the insecurities of the years 18–29, which psychologists, sociologists and neuroscientists, increasingly see as a distinct life stage. These developments are also supported within a new journal of the same name. More recently, scientists have suggested that our brains continue to increase in capability through to middle age and beyond.

However, for over a century, age-ridden, linear, developmental perspectives provided little fertile ground for the effective realization and contestation of children's participation and agency (in politics). One paradigm shift later and multidisciplinary research within the 'new social studies of childhood' now provides some antidote and its own fierce debates are instructive. The child is increasingly, if dominantly, theorized as relational and generational – challenging 'a world more used to dealing with dichotomies than continuums' (Such, Walker, and Walker 2005, 322). To this we can add continuations, fluctuations, transitions, reversals, and even denial of agency. Wyness (2006, 234) describes children as 'structurally marginal and situational competent' – a condition that will be sustained not least because the process of researching *with* children has only just begun. A growing number of authors ask that we attend to these pluralities, tensions, and paradoxes.

Scholars also voice concern over whether the new paradigm and its 'emphasis on agency and competency has led to an undervaluing of the interdependencies and range of relationships (human and material) which are fundamental to all children's lives' (Brownlie and Sheach Leith 2011, 206). Others question if childhood studies is 'yet firmly enough established to abandon the political power of the singularity thesis' (James 2010, 488) and suggest that we cannot yet speak of 'a global childhood or know if childhood can or should replace childhoods' (Nieuwenhuys 2013, 8). James has also drawn attention to the very different issues confronting Western industrialized countries and children in the majority South. Learning from both,

> means that not only will the voices of children be heard but that we will also be able to consider how they experience the structural constraints and commonalities of childhood, and how they use their agency to adapt to or modify these in the context of the diversities of their childhoods. (James 2010, 496–497)

Critically, childhood is temporal and fluid. It is both an empirical reality within and between communities and also a sociological construct which may be operationalized. Children's experiences are thus shaped not only by their underdevelopment as persons, but by conceptions of them which are earned and bestowed, constructed and determined, by the many individuals and groups who set and hold expectations of children, individually, collectively, simultaneously, arbitrarily, and even contradictorily (Brocklehurst 2006, 1). By extension, therefore, our conception of adulthood is also uncertain and messy, although this is rarely noted. Who are the 'we' that absorb, reject, or re-create political processes? The growing sociology of childhood (James and Prout 1990) has amply illustrated and problematized agency within childhood – although arguably partial and still unknown – yet there has been no call for a radical articulation of children as political subjects within political disciplines.

This unpromising start to a conceptualization of children and security is a necessary one. To think about children politically engage with many disciplines and multiple realities which anchor down the *child* we may seek to protect or frame the *childhood* that is useful to deploy. As Burman (2008b, 178) urges, we must 'situate ourselves within our accounts of childhood, including our investments – both economic and fantasized – within particular childhoods'.

Children and security

When I began thinking about the presence and the absence of children and childhoods in the discipline of IRs during the late 1990s, I was constantly reminded by my peers that they 'were' thought about. Here the presence of children in the news – most often as infant victims of humanitarian emergencies – or as gun toting teenage boys elided a critical commitment to interpreting their role. Indeed in the 1990s 'the concept of protecting children emerged as a core obligation' (Moeller 2002, 53) – a profitable humanitarian driver which peaked during the moral navel gazing of the new millennium but is still in ascendance through the development of children's rights discourses (Gadda 2008). Security too was a new 'lead concept in the post-cold war world' (Hansen and Buzan 2009, 2) and children were easily mobilized as a face of this breaking new world order. The emotional scenery of this period has continued seamlessly into the 'war on terror', for as Sylvester (2013, 13) notes 'no group is outside war in our global time'.

The shorthand of child – and its subsequent emotional short-circuiting – served General Petreaus well in his appeals to the American nation during the 'war on terror'. His invocations of child abuse by the Taliban to illustrate desperation and immorality was enabled 'precisely because children are thought to be un-political and without agency' (Lee-Koo 2011, 738). 'Afghan children and their experiences became a powerful moral symbol used by belligerents to advance political, military and strategic agendas' (Lee-Koo 2013, 475). Children have thus become 'a social stereotype' (Watson 2009, 6) – convenient signifiers of statehood or instability, typically leading to the wielding of 'humanitarian childhood' (Rosen 2007) reflecting the needs of 'Northern indoor' children (John 2003, 267). In this way the 'African child soldier' prevalent on the Internet is an essential character 'in a catwalk of children that reminds the global North of the infantilism of the global South' (Lee-Koo 2011, 735). In turn, powerful INGOS and charities 'operate an international policy cartel' which deliberately or unintentionally undermines local realities of early childhood (Penn 2011, 110). Analysis of post conflict reconstruction programmes, for example, (Schwartz 2010) shows that it is 'community'-based approaches that most adequately support children's voices and integration of their needs, contributing to a 'stable peace', itself the holy grail of reconstruction. Yet many aid agencies still advocate publicly on behalf of 'children' despite their programmes being necessarily aimed at or contingent on assisting broader social groupings, not least mothers, families, and local communities.

Childhood can thus be shown to be fluid, contested, socially constructed, and shaped by priorities, particularly political priorities. It is not simply natural. Childhood's duration and requirements can be made and un-made and this flexibility provides power for those who deploy children and childhoods in the service of war. Children are part of the calculation of state security and its economics, most starkly in terms of future labour and future wetware for war. Childhood is thus also a 'site for displacement and maneuvering for militarization' (Agathangelou and Killian 2011, 40) and, in the midst of conflict, 'antagonist parties may seek to secure or deprive children of childhood itself' (Netland 2013, 95). Through military orders imposed by Israel, for example, Palestinians have been exclusively reclassified as adults from the age of 16 (Cook, Hanieh, and Kay 2004, 135). They are thus eligible for 'adult' treatment and incarceration and do not have the same rights as their Israeli counterparts of the same age a few streets away. Conversely, the arrival of the pejorative prefix 'child' to 'soldier' does not indicate the beginnings of the practice of soldiering by children. It marks the point at which a society's conception of childhood became incommensurable when harnessed to its concepts of warfare.

It might be argued that societies' unwillingness to think of children as militarized is constructed upon a prior relationship of children to the political. Almost all definitions and concepts of children are premised on a notion of childhood as an experience which has or should have little in common with the political. As Sharon Stephens (1995, 10) notes, children are 'but one in a long trajectory of non-political subjects, including women and the family that are being reclaimed'. Participating and invoked in intra-state and interstate practices of security as investments, instruments, resources, and symbols, children can bring relationships – or dependencies – between the personal and political into sharp relief. It is telling, then, that younger children as a collectivity are often harnessed to passive roles in society, whilst youth have often been perceived or experienced as a potential risk to power (McEvoy-Levy 2006) with both projections downplaying their capability for participation in politics. I have elsewhere explored a separation of political experiences and childhood, theoretically and conceptually, as being symptomatic of three related ways in which the relationship between children and the political is enacted. Concepts of the political and of the child can be demonstrated to be antithetical or contained – a mutual exclusivity which can also be traced back through their respective (Western) disciplines. In examples of political behaviour and military accomplishment, for example, childlike behaviour or weakness is denigrated and discouraged. Boys become men during war and 'innocence is lost'. In the midst of this, explicit or sensationalized use of children elicits significant reaction, but not attention to children's participation. On the contrary it fosters the illusion that children were exceptionally and temporarily drawn in the political sphere and not, in fact, prior members of it. 'Infant power' (Brocklehurst

2006) or the strategic harnessing of a transhistorical, transcultural infant in pleas to the national conscience, symbolic of life and society under threat, is one such instrumentalization of childhood in the service of security. Child soldiers are seen as a political anomaly because they are holding military power, and child victims attract attention as the ultimate essentialized civilians in need of humanitarian and/or political assistance. Childhood innocence becomes 'a useful symbol with which to obscure questions about... interest[s]...[and] power' (Wells 2007, 60). The poster children of famines, the conceptually and legally inept designation of 'child-soldier', the campaigning baby wrapped in a politician, each reinforces rather than counters the perception of children's unnatural place and agency in politics and masks how emotion informs politics, security, and war-making generally. Significant recognition of children's actual daily and low profile interdependence with the political world is obscured or prevented. That children's politicization is simultaneously underplayed in this way actually guarantees their prolific and undisturbed (ab)use in security practices. Children's nationalization and militarization, particularly in social and domestic spheres, arguably precedes, underpins, and sustains many forms of security – real or imagined. In this sense it is mostly our recognition, not children's presence that is new.

This does not, however, mean that they are not thought about within the discipline. The concept of security at the heart of IRs has traditionally been understood as, ultimately, the pursuit of security provided by states on behalf of their people. Children may be implicitly and explicitly referred to in justifications for security practices – children can make 'realism' more real or provide a moral imperative for liberal caution. Children are thus already present within security studies, as resources and instruments of national security and harbored in the idea of human security. What may be less evident is how the language of security is already contained, as if it is distanced from, and ultimately protecting and not using, children. 'Sentimentalisation of children's voices' further masks how 'the problem of children's insecurities lies with structural inequalities' (Wells 2009, 184). The sphere of the child and, per se, the family and mother has been most silenced in IRs which conceptualizes itself as distanced from these referents and fails to recognize their agency.

To look at political children then, requires an engagement with other spaces, other people, other disciplines, and an understanding of IRs' emergence as an exclusive set of knowledge assumptions about the 'international'. An autonomous theory of International Politics has been the central thrust of the discipline, thus the discipline of IRs is firmly implicated in the question of how children and the private sphere are so invisibly politicized and ineffectively secured (Brocklehurst 2006). However one of the paradoxes of society – and potentially security studies – is that it can become 'child-centered' whilst remaining anti-child.

Returning the gaze

Underpinned by a humanitarian or rights-based narrative, 'child soldiers' have had hegemonic capital for humanitarian organizations (Charli 2000) and offer the most widely researched example of children's presence in security. Such virulent advocacy has helped establish a near international 'norm' against their deployment and changes in rehabilitation practices have been realized. However, although we increasingly recognize that young people can be more than victims or perpetrators in war – they are often depended on and dependent on it for survival – responses to children and war (notably its impact and their rights) have not yet eclipsed the careless fetishization of teenage child soldiers, rebel youth, and young suicide bombers that permeate humanitarian narratives of war. The iconography of childhood is perhaps one obstacle to theorizing about children. In the very areas where we might argue that their presence, agency or protection is neglected, our uncritical gaze situates 'children and war'. Selected, consciously and unconsciously, for their emotional appeal, photographic images of children permeate war – and perhaps our theorizing – like no other referent (Holland 1992; Moeller 2002; Wells 2007). Such 'war children' are easily positioned as vulnerable: through the asymmetry of stone throwing; as 'noncombatants par excellence' in the semiotics of landmine campaigning (Beier 2011, 4–5); and, ubiquitously, through the 'disaster pornography' that warscapes sustain (Burman 1994, 239). 'The media, by the success of its artistry, gets caught up in the very processes it seeks to criticize' (Kleinman and Kleinman 1996, 11).

Andersen and Möller specifically caution against the 'discursive-representational security regime' set by photojournalism and note that 'a critique of security that works within the regime of seeing or representational codes of security – as most photojournalism does – runs the risk of confirming both the practices and the idea of security' (Andersen and Moller 2013, 204). There are now many millions of images of child soldiers: armed, maimed, scared, defiant, but also cropped, pasted, and recirculated out of context and copyright. Although there is little research on how captured subjects interpret their visual legacy, the hegemonic image highway of 'Google' is revealing. Using the search engine 'Google image' the search term 'child soldiers' brings up the following eight alternative refinements, informed by web users' collective interests: 'in Africa', 'in Uganda', 'in Sierra Leone', 'crying', 'facts', 'maps', 'dead', and 'international'. One click further in the pursuit of the generic 'child soldier' reveals that images are then automatically organized into themes of 'black and white' (presumably for humanitarian aesthetics), 'Kony' (reference to *Kony 2012*, and the most viral child soldiers campaign in history), 'girl' (illustrative of their pictorial potency), 'cartoon' (perhaps suggestive of image fatigue/arrival of a satirical sensibility), 'quotes', and 'dead'.

In this vast storehouse of misery it is rare to find a photo which does not seek to recreate their vulnerability. There is very little practical advice on how photographs of children public – not least as combatants, or dying – should be selected, solicited, or made. Very few publishers and humanitarian agencies obscure the faces of children and young people in war so that individual recognition is impossible. Notwithstanding the horrific realities of their lives, desperate children have sought attention or been posed by desperate communities and desperate journalists. Dying to be shot and joining the visual collective of 'child soldier' or even 'war child', does not mean that permission has been sought or granted for subsequent circulation of their portrait. Once these images are freely circulating, privacy is violated and, at worst, lives may be endangered through retribution or shame invested on a future adult, their family, or kin. In principle, does responsibility for these risks and children's long-term welfare lie with the image-catcher? Could not permission from children and/or their guardians be established as good practice? Where permission is impractical, or age and competence cannot be ascertained, a limit can be placed on public circulation of these images. An icon can be embedded in the file or image to indicate this. This 'right' can also be extended to any individuals who may not be in a position to consent to their photograph or the consequences of its digital re-circulation. Various styles of photograph can also be promoted. Current practice by some NGOs and publishers includes long distance and group shots, portrait profiles, silhouettes, lowered eyes, sunglasses, headware, and also the later editing of photographs to pixilate or obscure the eyes. Do children feature in war art? Should they? Without such measures, vulnerability may be unwittingly perpetuated by many well-meaning accomplices across the web. For some children in war zones, the capture of their image may have been empowering by the instant affirmation it yielded from their peers. Young people often equate the exercise of power (especially criminal, violent or military activity) with the threshold into adulthood. The acknowledgement of their role, via the opportunity to pose and record it, can further cement this status. In the cases above we are, in effect, speaking for children.

> ...it may amount to strategic short-term media outreach to portray child soldiers as passive clueless victims, as devastated, and as dehumanized tools of war robotically programmed to kill in purportedly senseless African wars. But these images belie a much more sublime, humanistic and granular reality of resilience, agency, potential, and globality. (Drumbl 2012, 482)

And as Martins (2011, 444) notes, there are few examples of Southern counter-discourse in the representation of children and war in Anglophone and Francophone Africa. In these and many ways children's presence is already constituted in what we think of as 'us' and 'what we perceive as threats to "us"' (Zalewski and Enloe 1995, 281). The current viral campaign to 'bring back the girls', over 200 of whom have been abducted by Nigerian-based terrorist group Boko Haram, may also be indicative of not thinking hard enough about 'them' – about children's security. The public naming of all these girls may ultimately direct further harm to their families (Moore 2014).

What our efforts do seem to portray is an attempt to tell or narrate our fears and stories. To cope – or warn – not to solve. It is ironic, but not surprising, therefore, that we have also written books on security *for* young people before we have written fully about young people engaged in war.

Returning the book

In the local library of the town where this article is written, a child can select simplistic, sensational, fatalistic narratives on the 'war on terror' or terrorism, potentially unaware of an award winning graphic novel illustrating the complexity of 9/11 (Jacobsen and Ernie 2006). The publishing of textbooks on 9/11 and the war on terror has not diminished. Arguably, these texts, in their hundreds, reflect a refreshed militarized sub-culture for children and offer a seductive, often gendered, portrayal of war as 'vocation' wherein terrorism is represented and naturalized as a new certainty about which to become excited, fearful, and ultimately to be responded to as a 'good citizen'. Within such fairy tales of New York, fear and difference are cultivated and evil is mitigated by heroism and war (Brocklehurst 2011). In a typical short example for pre-teens, only one page of text may contain a very brief explanation of 9/11 – evidencing Osama Bin Laden's politics. That the word 'Islam' is emboldened – and not the word 'extreme' in the same sentence – is typical of the careless signposting achieved in these security texts. Other picture books offer a graphic depiction of the attacks on the World Trade Center – an ash-ridden snow globe of reality – where bad men were sent from a far away land to fell the towers. Children can currently access these texts, independently of adults, and particularly teachers, creating an under-researched and anarchic dynamic to learning which may be especially attractive to boys. 'In the real-time of Fox News, and in video games', Deck (2004) argues, 'the simplification of cultures and history is itself a form of violence', To this I would add the largely uninvestigated subculture of children's informational literature (Connolly 2008; Geruluk 2012).

The potential impact of such political and military discourse is itself contingent on its place and conceptualization in the curriculum and on the parameters of the political already established in the values of the education system. Should children learn about themselves in relation to international society earlier? If children are capable of learning about religion or citizenship, then why not include the institution of sovereignty or the role of international institutions? At a minimum should we not build links between professional organizations and educational bodies to help craft and review literature consumed by children? Should we be more aware of how children encounter the parameters and constraints of the international, or invitations to fight for international order? The humble book review, largely absent in the UK, may be one important and brave act of counter-security for children. As American library reviewer Bush (2002) noted of one such narrative '….Adolescents who wade through the verbiage will probably derive as fair an outline of bin Laden's life. … However, outdated material, undersourced allegations and breathless prose do little to aid American readers in understanding why they've come under attack'. In this way, 'political literacy' and 'military literacy' are useful ways of thinking about young people's participation in security. Literacy is indicative of our ability to read *and* to think through texts. As Law (2006, 167) argues, education 'to encourage children to think critically and independently' is the 'best defence against being indoctrinated'. However, the perceived value of education and its attendant critical capacities are also shaped by war.

> Indeed, the social topography of militarized masculinity is also evident in the return of the warrior male whose paranoia is endlessly stoked by the existence of a feminized culture of critical thinking, a gay subculture and a liberal ideology that exhibits a disrespect for top-down order and unquestioned authority and discipline. (Giroux 2008, 61)

If war is posited as oppositional to childhood, then the seduction offered by the warrior is also noteworthy.

> As the term 'combatant' is replaced with 'war fighter' in operational and patriotic rhetoric, so too attention is deflected from the agency that was 'soldier' on 'soldier.' War is a given and the war fighter as 'wetware' is needed, recognized, and valued because there *is* war. Through this simple change of language, 'wars' [are] rendered 'natural' and 'inevitable' but also dehumanized [a dissociation from the corporeal realities of war]. (Brocklehurst 2011, 83–84)

The carefully crafted graphic and rhetoric of the 'Warrior-Care' programme in the USA, and its equivalent in the UK, offers another example of how two previously opposed constructs – 'fighting' and 'caring' – have been harnessed into a new palatable form. What, then, of children's potential in a society where teaching itself is feminized and reading is perceived as feminine by young boys? In Australia, for example, critical literacy is 'working against the opposition of masculinity to literacy and language (the feminized knowledges)' (McLeod 2001, 275). In the UK, masculinity is also deployed to encourage literacy. The *National Literacy* Association notes how attention-grabbing titles such as 'War Machines: The Deadliest Weapons in History' (Dougherty 2010), 'will draw children in – especially boys'. As a zone of autonomy and excitement, 'play' itself may be posited as oppositional to education by its participants. 'Do we undervalue play because it is associated with childhood or do we compromise childhood because we trivialise play?' (Wyness 2006, 13).

Historians and sociologists have illustrated how, at the height of the Cold War, civil defence was incorporated into American public education and children and families were subject to both preparations for nuclear attack and education about their role as citizens (Stephens 1997). Children were taught how to use their school desks to 'protect' themselves from falling debris, but they were also taught to cope by not crying and 'to equate emotional maturity with an attitude of calm acceptance toward nuclear war' (Brown 1988, 90). Arguably, the latter placed them and their society at greater risk and perhaps continues to do so through the transmission of values about international security, fear, and correct responses to it (Crawford 2009). The militarization of play (Stahl 2006) and the militarization of digital childhood (Lesley 2011, 143) offer further evidence of children's ongoing capital as spectators, consumers, and, ultimately, stabilizers of war. In the UK, the High Street 'pound' shops sell plastic replica weapons of war and school attendance dips when new 'adult' military games are released. As Deck (2004) notes, 'war games – also known as "real-time strategy" games – seldom deal with causes of war. The games focus on what happens after war has been declared…[making] the period of peace…unreal time'. Toy shops are strongly bifurcated along the lines of warrior males and beautiful, nurturing souls and the largest retailer of toys in the UK has teamed up with the Ministry of Defence in the promotion of a range of dolls. A similar arrangement exists in the USA. Here, 'the business of play works closely with the military to replicate the tools of state violence; the business of state violence in turn capitalizes on playtime for institutional ends' (Stahl 2006, 123). How can we account for a near complete lack of research on children and the militarization of leisure within security studies? Which children are 'targeted' and about whose security are they learning? The causal relations of consumption are complex longitudinal enquiries. How we think – or do not theorize – about children is how we treat children. Simplistic toys, books, and websites which engage young people in security and the circulation of terror may arguably create a pseudo-adult experience of autonomy and excitement – and undermine appeals made to children as future conflict-resolving citizens. Development of critical thinking, or the resilience and emotional dexterity required to survive in adversity, may also better serve some children than protected periods of apparent protection. Yet it is clear that children, like the discipline of IR, are largely unprepared for each other. And '[i]nsofar as politics merely deconstructs power, it paradoxically marginalizes any group that is less fully equipped for political struggle' (Wall 2012, 94).

Back to the future

[W]e need to turn our critical gazes constantly on ourselves to ask if, at each time and in each place, we are theorizing for those most in need. Doing so acknowledges that other outsiders will be excluded by our choices, but has at least the benefit of doing so in a limited and contingent fashion. (Mutimer 2009, 20)

To return to Stephens (1995) original statement, in 20 years children have not really been reclaimed as political, not least by the discipline of politics. Some children and some childhoods have been recognized, yet the empirical, if not 'emotional', neglect of children in IRs is perplexing to the point of instilling academic paralysis. Despite an emerging and substantial literature on the vital political capital of children – through their bodies, minds, and our vulnerability towards particular constructs of childhood – the discipline of IR has not yet exhibited much interest in them (Watson 2009; Beier 2011). Their security remains unrealized and their relevance too is relatively undertheorized.

It is possible to argue that there has been little advancement in the subject of children, childhoods, and security. Reflecting on the mobilizing trope 'women and children',

Puechguirbal (2004, 7) noted barely a decade ago that 'after years of increased awareness and mobilization of women, the language has not fundamentally changed, thus perpetuating the stereotypes that prevent women from becoming more visible and assertive in the public arena'. One might ask if we simply we do not care enough about children. Opportunities are not yet taken. Questions are not posed. Where are children? At what points were men and women also powerful and empowering as somebody's child or some state's children? Where are up to 40% of societies in our analyses of power? Child labour – much of it unpaid and via a currency of sex – is only just entering into economic models with rich work emerging, not least in the context of war. Rape and control of girls and boys is also being systematically uncovered in many state institutions as well as traditional theatres of war. Predation has an axis of age as well as gender. In the UK, waves of prosecutions for sexual abuse are occupying the national press as damaged girlhoods and boyhoods from a lifetime ago are verified. How long until children's contributions – whether passive or active – are calculated in all our webs of power? That scholars of gender and militarization, IR and security studies, have barely lifted the lid on childhood until the last decade (Sjoberg and Via 2010) is thus still disturbing but not surprising. As Enloe prompted decades ago, and Beier (2011) has shown, investments in boys and girls' leisure time remain central to many processes of militarization.

A wider and deeper security analysis might start with the 'peacetime' relationships and power dynamics in the making of people, including forced procreation, infanticide, gendercide, and the politics of nutrition for mothers and infants (Palmer 2009); the realities of how affection shapes a baby's (person's) brain (Gerhardt 2004); and the near global scarcity of midwives. Very young children die easily. 'When you see children as demanding care, the reality of their vulnerability and the necessity of a caring response seem unshakeable' notes Ruddick (1995, 47), yet 'the presence of a child does not guarantee its care'. How do we *know* that we care? As Watson (2007, 31) notes, international discourse, 'can care less for children, because their mothers care more'. Even in terms of individual or community orientated personal 'security', such as health, are we engaged as caretakers? Where does this wedge begin or end? How far does our commitment to care reach? What is the take-up amongst a general population of first aid generally and of child or baby first aid skills specifically? Should children too be systematically trained in basic medical care? Can we unshackle security from the broader issues of politics? Is this not what security ultimately is: the sharp end of a broader and deeper discussion of how we co-exist? When mothers also perish, despite their experience and resourcefulness and perhaps passion to survive for their dependents, this too is a sign of 'a world that is not working' (Booth 2007, 13) – failing to protect children at their most vulnerable ages and stages. If we perceive security more widely in terms of right to appropriate nutrition and survival, the picture looks very different for infants than it does for older children and adults (Kent 1995) and far worse again for female children.

Perhaps relatedly, and despite enormous critical advancements, the many needs of the children we do notice are not met. For all their attention, child soldier rehabilitation programmes touch only a fraction of combatants and typically exclude older children (Celina and Wisler 2007) or fail to provide a structurally adequate guard against remobilization (Stark, Boothby, and Ager 2009; Özerdem and Podder 2011). As Macmillan (2011, 75) also notes, international statutes have problematized participation *in war* rather than militarization, accommodating an absence of legal protection for 15–17 year olds compounded by the imprecision of the term 'participation', which, like 'indirect' or 'hostilities', has no precise meaning in the fog of law. Hamilton (2006) identified as recently as 2006 that there were major gaps in provision of children in complex emergencies: shortcomings included the oversight of domestic abuse and a failure to evaluate children's placements; in both cases, out of sight was out of mind. Men and boys continue to be targeted for sexual violence, rarely reported, and inappropriately documented and treated or addressed and there exists very little longitudinal or evaluative data on the success of interventions or appropriateness of peacebuilding models for girls (Pruitt 2013).

In peacetime, scholars of citizenship note that children's participation – without the constraints of adults' resistance, hindrance, manipulation, decoration, tokenism, tolerance and indulgence (Reddy and Ratna 2002, 18–21) – is also little realized. Commentators even speak of a participation crisis characterized by 'demands for political correctness that lead to the requirement for children to be present in international meetings without sufficient preparation or protection'. Evaluators note that even the most desirable form of participation – 'children sharing participation with adults' – it is not yet evidenced in practice (Van Beers et al. 2006). Yet, as writers such as Morrow (2006) remind us, connecting with children's voices is but a first step. It does not promise agency. In fact children can simply demand that more responsibility is taken by adults. 'There is overwhelming evidence...that children are responsive, creative and measured in responding to calls for their views. The challenge now is to get adults not only to listen, but also to act upon what they hear' (Morrow 2006, 53). As Hartung (2011, 251) notes in groundbreaking work on children's voices, attempts to interpret children as diverse also privilege homogeneity, simplicity, and rationality within their responses. Following this, by learning from children's experiences 'political representation should ultimately mean empowering lived differences to make a difference to interdependent political structures' (Wall 2012, 94). Further, as Wall (2012, 87) argues, children's real democratic representation calls for a new concept of political representation and an 'exercise in *childism*' – 'not just an extension of adult privileges to children, but a restructuring of fundamental social norms in response to children's experiences'.

Partly informed by these debates and the post positivist turn within IRs, we are at the beginning of a more critical juncture in the studies of children and security. Debate has moved on sufficiently for a sub-field to be marked out within which 'sympathies' are being identified – notably 'free-reiners' with an emphasis on child agency or 'caretakers' with an emphasis on child protection – roughly transposed from the sociology of childhood. In their substantial work, D'Costa, Huynh, and Katrina (forthcoming) ask that a middle ground be realized. They argue that critical theory enables a child-centric lens which brings children's lives into focus in analysis of the causes, strategies, and resolutions of conflict. Importantly, it also centralizes children as the site for emancipatory enquiry and,

> explores the complex interplay between the creative agency of children and their distinct vulnerabilities in the face of violence, promotes an approach to children's rights and security in global politics that is both protective and empowering and establishes a meaningful place for children in the adult-centric study of IR and the practice of global politics. (D'Costa, Huynh, and Katrina forthcoming)

Will a 'child-centric' approach always be required? Can we use 'kindered' in a similar way to gendered (Watson 2008)? What does 'infantilization' do to infants? Should we adopt or adapt 'citizenship' for children? A pioneering analysis of adults' recollection and articulation of 'lost childhood' caused by violence is perhaps instructive, broken down into 'lost child-friendliness' (environment) and 'lost childlikeness' (experience) (Netland 2013, 90). Will we have a working vocabulary that accommodates 'child worker', 'child citizen', or 'child politician' as easily as 'child soldier'? Will the term 'child-soldier' become sufficiently unprofitable that it can be replaced by CAFF (Children Affected by Fighting Forces) and therefore permanently foreclose the lumping together of child soldier attributes (Hart 2008)? Will 'minor politics' rescue children 'from the depoliticized territory of the private sphere of the family, or the technical sphere of service delivery' (Dahlberg and Moss 2005, 154)?

Children add an extra level of complexity in that their part may be unknowable: their agency must be read and interpreted reflexively (Spyrou Spyros 2011) and through underdeveloped and unfixed voices. We may have to accept 'methodological immaturity' (Gallacher and Gallagher 2008). Empirically present, simultaneously transient, and conceptually yielding only 'the tip of the iceberg', the slippery underworld of childhood offers a challenging, vitally important, and complementary experience of exploration. Children and their childhoods perhaps sit most comfortably within constructivist and feminist analysis – we can no more 'add' children to the discipline than we can 'add' women. In turn, children as a category are likely to be feminized and yet also framed and bifurcated along traditional male and female lines. Burman (2008a) urges us to look beyond dichotomies such as work versus play and women versus children, the latter being 'neither equivalent nor separable'. And, as Enloe (2010, 218) argues, we also need to be 'conducting a more energetic analysis – one that does not refer lazily to "families," "children," "parents"...*as if* women and men related identically to each'. To think about children's security therefore it would be better to consider women and children's enabling and disabling of each other. The 'complex – even positively messy – understanding of in/security as a discursive terrain' (Rowley and Weldes 2012, 515) is likely to create the most traction here.

The ubiquitous presence of children and, indeed, the development of all kinds of children into all kinds of security bearers, signals their unique complexity as a referent group. If we ask 'where are the children?' would the necessary corollary be to also define 'adults' as a subject of IRs or security? 'Child' might circumscribe both the ambiguous societal and political capital of vulnerable, demanding, and emotionally priceless infants and youth – our neighbouring and most feared cohort. We also cannot use child and adult as mutually exclusive terms. We are all somebody's child. We can all be childlike. But we are not all somebody's adult and we cannot all be adultlike. The development we share with children is increasingly significant. Age and our contingent expectations of it thus might be useful dimensions to explore further in IR. We seem to have a telling paucity in our conceptual arsenal to theorize children. There are probably more types of childhood than snow – but snow has arguably been more adequately represented within, and beyond societies which depend on it.

The unwillingness of the academy to recognize this area of study is a final challenge. Despite the approaches, theories, issues, and maps that crisscross our indiscipline of inhumanity, children have not even made it into the 'periphery' of the 'alternative' of the mainstream theories presented in introductory textbooks. If I look at the most popular textbook in IR today (Baylis, Smith, and Owens 2014) there are only very light mentions of children – mostly as victims, accompanying women and the elderly. Brief examples of children in the construction of the non-combatant 'civilian' (Charli 2000), as part of the 'protection myth' and as participants in warfare can be found. But in the index there is one record for 'youth' and no record at all for children. Found only as occasional needles in this haystack of politics, it will be a long time before young scholars in IR can become scholars of the young. This use of subjects in this introductory text also closely mirrors the 'thread of victimization' in official humanitarian discourse (Haeri and Puechguirbal 2010, 108) 'that closely associates women with children, who, along with the elderly and the disabled are designated as being de facto "vulnerable"'. Students may encounter gender in two hours of teaching across three years of an IRs degree. There seems little point in adding children to this mix and reinforcing this association. In contrast, a final year *optional* project for politics students, on the realities and representation of child soldiers, is annually oversubscribed and typically generates informed critiques and comparisons, including by serving cadet members and former child soldiers. Creating a *separate* space for thinking about children (or gender and warfare) attracts high numbers of students wishing to centre the humanitarian or critical impulse that might have directed them to IR in the first place.

A recent introductory textbook survey of critical security studies mentions children four times in passing (Peoples and Nick 2010) and with little critical purchase, other than mentioning the co-joining of women and children as problematic – for women. Nothing new to report perhaps, although a significant amount of work has been realized and is forthcoming (Seto 2013; Jacob 2013; D'Costa, Huynh, and Katrina forthcoming). In 2005 I was invited to contribute to OUP's *Contemporary Security Studies* textbook. The first edition chapter on 'children and war' attempted to engage with children, childhood, and security more broadly. Subsequent manuscript reviewers stated that there was not enough about child soldiers, who should be the main, 'humanitarian' 'issue' area. 'Child soldiers' thus became the title and focus in two subsequent editions (2009, 2013) although all three chapters were located within a 'broadening and deepening' framework. Ultimately, the fact that this topic is not sufficiently taught led to its elimination of the fourth edition. I do teach about children as political bodies in my *compulsory* courses on IR theory but am increasingly aware that textbooks now act as a legitimizing device. Students are readily skeptical of the validity of children as a referent in the academy and little authority seems to present itself. Relations between political and military stakeholders, academia, educationalists, and commercial publishers clearly need to be fostered or tendered.

As Jacob argues, 'locating the politics that determine children's insecurity as a site for intervention is as important, if not more so, than the political influence or agency exerted by children' (Jacob 2013, 47). Here I would argue that our non-response to children is also a symptom of the security we create. That they are undertheorized and seemingly beyond security studies is a consequence of maneuvers already made. Their security and insecurity are entwined. It is surprising that the volume of vibrant work on 'political children' especially in contexts of security has not yet crystallized into dedicated working groups, or a single journal or book series. This journal's special focus is thus a welcome enterprise. Children's vulnerabilities, agency, their future presence and absence, in practice and on paper, remain all our security challenges. Children and childhoods, then, are apt starting points for thinking about security in its totality.

References

Agathangelou, A. M., and K. D. Killian. 2011. "(Neo) Zones of Violence: Reconstructing Empire on the Bodies of Militarized Youth." In *The Militarization of Childhood: Thinking Beyond the Global South*, edited by J. M. Beier, 17–41. New York: Palgrave Macmillan.

Andersen, R. S., and F. Moller. 2013. "Engaging the Limits of Visibility: Photography, Security and Surveillance." *Security Dialogue* 44 (3): 203–221. doi:10.1177/0967010613484955.

Baylis, J., S. Smith, and P. Owens. 2014. *The Globalization of World Politics: An Introduction to International Relations*. 6th ed. Oxford: Oxford University Press.

Beazley, H., S. Bessell, J. Ennew, and R. Waterson. 2009. "The Right to be Properly Researched: Research with Children in a Messy, Real World." *Children's Geographies* 7 (4): 365–378. doi:10.1080/14733280903234428.

Beier, J. M. 2011. "Introduction: Everyday Zones of Militarization." In *The Militarization of Childhood: Thinking Beyond the Global South*, edited by J. M. Beier, 1–15. New York: Palgrave Macmillan.

Booth, K. 2007. *Theory of World Security*. Cambridge: Cambridge University Press.

Brocklehurst, H. 2006. *Who's Afraid of Children? Children, Conflict and International Relations*. Aldershot: Ashgate.

Brocklehurst, H. 2007. "Children and War." In *Contemporary Security Studies*, edited by A. Collins, 367–382. Oxford: Oxford University Press.

Brocklehurst, H. 2011. "Education and the War on Terror: The Early Years." In *The Militarization of Childhood: Thinking Beyond the Global South*, edited by J. M. Beier, 77–94. New York: Palgrave Macmillan.

Brown, J. 1988. "A is for Atom, B is for Bomb: Civil Defense in American Public Education, 1948–1963." *The Journal of American History* 75 (1): 68–90. doi:10.2307/1889655.

Brownlie, J., and V. M. Sheach Leith. 2011. "Social Bundles: Thinking Through the Infant Body." *Childhood* 18 (2): 196–210. doi:10.1177/0907568210394879.

Burman, E. 1994. "Innocents Abroad: Western Fantasies of Childhood and the Iconography of Emergencies." *Disasters* 18 (3): 238–253. doi:10.1111/j.1467-7717.1994.tb00310.x.

Burman, E. 2008a. "Beyond 'Women Vs. Children' or 'Women and children': Engendering Childhood and Reformulating Motherhood." *The International Journal of Children's Rights* 16 (2): 177–194. doi:10.1163/157181808X301773.

Burman, E. 2008b. *Developments: Child, Image, Nation*. New York: Routledge.

Bush, E. 2002. *The Bulletin of the Center for Children's Books 56*. Vol. 1. Baltimore, MD: The Johns Hopkins University Press.

Celina, D. F., and A. Wisler. 2007. "The Unexplored Power and Potential of Youth as Peacebuilders." *Journal of Peace Conflict & Development* 11: 1–29.

Charli, C. R. 2000. "Forced Maternity, Children's Rights and the Genocide Convention: A Theoretical Analysis." *Journal of Genocide Research* 2 (2): 224–227. doi:10.1080/713677603.

Connolly, P. T. 2008. "Retelling 9/11: How Picture Books Re-Envision National Crises." *The Lion and the Unicorn* 32 (3): 288–303. doi:10.1353/uni.0.0418.

Cook, C., A. Hanieh, and A. Kay. 2004. *Stolen Youth: The Politics of Israel's Detention of Palestinian Children*. London: Pluto Press.

Crawford, N. C. 2009. "Human Nature and World Politics: Rethinking 'Man'." *International Relations* 23 (2): 271–288. doi:10.1177/0047117809104639.

D'Costa, B., K. Huynh, and L.-K. Katrina. Forthcoming. *Children and Global Conflict*. Cambridge: Cambridge University Press.

Dahlberg, G., and P. Moss. 2005. *Ethics and Politics in Early Childhood Education*. London: Routledge Falmer.

Deck, A. 2014. "No Quarter: Demilitarizing the Playground." Art Context. Accessed August 30. http://artcontext.com/crit/essays/noQuarter/.

Dougherty, M. 2010. *War Machines: The Deadliest Weapons in History*. London: A&C Black.

Drumbl, M. A. 2012. "Child Soldiers and Clicktivism: Justice, Myths, and Prevention." *Journal of Human Rights Practice* 4 (3): 481–485. doi:10.1093/jhuman/hus023.

Enloe, C. 2010. *Nimo's War, Emma's War: Making Feminist Sense of the Iraq War*. Berkeley: University of California Press.

Gadda, A. 2008. "Rights, Foucault and Power: A Critical Analysis of the United Nations Convention on the Rights of the Child." *Edinburgh Working Papers in Sociology, no. 31.*

Gallacher, L.-A., and M. Gallagher. 2008. "Methodological Immaturity in Childhood Research?: Thinking through 'Participatory Methods'." *Childhood* 15 (4): 499–516. doi:10.1177/0907568208091672.

Gerhardt, S. 2004. *Why Love Matters: How Affection Shapes a Baby's Brain*. London: Routledge.

Geruluk, D. 2012. *Education, Extremism and Terrorism: What Should Be Taught in Citizenship Education and Why?* London: Continuum.

Giroux, H. A. 2008. "The Militarization of US Higher Education after 9/11." *Theory Culture Society* 25 (5): 56–82. doi:10.1177/0263276408095216.

Haeri, M., and N. Puechguirbal. 2010. "From Helplessness to Agency: Examining the Plurality of Women's Experiences in Armed Conflict." *International Review of the Red Cross* 92 (877): 103–122. doi:10.1017/S1816383110000044.

Hamilton, C. 2006. "Child Protection in Complex Emergencies." In *Dilemmas in Protection of Children During Armed Political Conflict: A Multidisciplinary Perspective*, edited by C. W. Greenbaum, P. Veerman, and N. Bacon-Schnoor, 311–328. Oxford: Hart Publishing.

Hammad, A., and E. Bindari. 2009. "Health Indicators and the Impact of Insecurities on Children." In *Seen, But Not Heard: Placing Children and Youth on the Security Governance Agenda*, edited by D. Nosworthy, 35–54. New Brunswick: Transaction Publishers.

Hansen, L., and B. Buzan. 2009. *The Evolution of International Security Studies*. Cambridge: Cambridge University Press.

Hart, J. 2008. "Children's Participation and International Development: Attending to the Political." *The International Journal of Children's Rights* 16 (3): 407–418. doi:10.1163/157181808X311231.

Hartung, C. 2011. "Governing the 'Agentic' Child Citizen: A Post Structural Analysis of Children's Participation." Unpublished thesis. Faculty of Education, University of Wollongong.

Holland, P. 1992. *What is a Child? Popular Images of Childhood*. London: Virago Press.

Jacob, C. 2013. *Child Security in Asia: The Impact of Political Conflict in Cambodia and Myanmar*. London: Routledge.

Jacobsen, S., and C. Ernie. 2006. *The 9/11 Report: A Graphic Adaptation*. New York: Hill & Wang.

James, A., and A. Prout. eds. 1990. *Constructing and Reconstructing Childhood: Contemporary Issues in the Sociological Study of Childhood*. London: Falmer Press.

James, A. L. 2010. "Competition or Integration? The Next Step in Childhood Studies?" *Childhood* 17 (4): 485–499. doi:10.1177/0907568209350783.

John, M. 2003. *Children, Rights and Power: Charging up for a New Century*. London: Jessica Kingsley.

Kent, G. 1995. *Children in the International Economy*. London: Macmillan.

Kleinman, A., and J. Kleinman. 1996. "The Appeal of Experience; The Dismay of Images: Cultural Appropriations of Suffering in Our Times." *Daedalus* 125 (1): 1–23.

Law, S. 2006. *The War for Children's Minds*. New York: Routledge.

Lee-Koo, K. 2011. "Horror and Hope: (Re)Presenting Militarised Children in Global North–South Relations." *Third World Quarterly* 32 (4): 725–742. doi:10.1080/01436597.2011.567005.

Lee-Koo, K. 2013. "Not Suitable for Children: The Politicisation of Conflict-Affected Children in Post-2001 Afghanistan." *Australian Journal of International Affairs* 67 (4): 475–490. doi:10.1080/10357718.2013.803031.

Lesley, C. 2011. "Mediated War: Imaginative Disembodiment and the Militarization of Childhood." In *The Militarization of Childhood: Thinking Beyond the Global South*, edited by J. M. Beier, 133–152. New York: Palgrave.

Macmillan, L. 2011. "Militarized Children and Sovereign Power." In *The Militarization of Childhood: Thinking Beyond the Global South*, edited by J. M. Beier, 61–76. New York: Palgrave.

Maira, S., and E. Soep. 2004. "United States of Adolescence?: Reconsidering US Youth Culture Studies." *Young* 12 (3): 245–269. doi:10.1177/1103308804044508.

Martins, C. 2011. "The Dangers of the Single Story: Child Soldiers in Literary Fiction and Film." *Childhood* 18 (4): 434–446. doi:10.1177/0907568211400102.

McEvoy-Levy, S., ed. 2006. *Troublemakers or Peacemakers? Youth and Post-Accord Peace Building*. Notre Dame: University of Notre Dame Press.

McLeod, J. 2001. "When Poststructuralism Meets Gender." In *Governing the Child in the New Millennium*, edited by K. Hultqvist and G. Dahlberg, 259–289. London: RoutledgeFalmer.

Moeller, S. D. 2002. "A Hierarchy of Innocence: The Media's Use of Children in the Telling of International News." *The Harvard International Journal of Press/Politics* 7 (1): 36–56. doi:10.1177/1081180X0200700104.

Moore, J. 2014. "Stop Naming Nigeria's Kidnapped Girls." Accessed August 30. http://www. buzzfeed.com/jinamoore/stop-naming-nigerias-kidnapped-girls.

Morrow, V. 2006. "Social Capital: A Flawed Concept." In *Beyond Article 12: Essential Readings in Children's Participation*, edited by H. Van Beers, A. Invernizzi, and B. Milne. Bangkok: Black on White Publications.

Mutimer, D. 2009. "My Critique is Bigger than Yours: Constituting Exclusions in Critical Security Studies." *Studies in Social Justice* 3 (1): 9–22.

Netland, M. 2013. "Exploring 'Lost Childhood': A Study of the Narratives of Palestinians Who Grew Up during the First Intifada." *Childhood* 20 (1): 82–97. doi:10.1177/ 0907568212461329.

Nieuwenhuys, O. 2013. "Theorizing Childhood(s): Why We Need Postcolonial Perspectives." *Childhoods* 20 (1): 3–8. doi:10.1177/0907568212465534.

Özerdem, A., and S. Podder. 2011. "The Long Road Home: Conceptual Debates on Recruitment Experiences and Reintegration Outcomes." In *Child Soldiers: From Recruitment to Reintegration*, edited by Ö. Alpaslan and S. Podder, 3–29. Houndsmills: Palgrave.

Palmer, G. 2009. *The Politics of Breastfeeding: When Breasts Are Bad for Business*. London: Pinter and Martin.

Penn, H. 2011. "Travelling Policies and Global Buzzwords: How International Non-Governmental Organizations and Charities Spread the Word about Early Childhood in the Global South." *Childhood* 18 (1): 94–113. doi:10.1177/0907568210369846.

Peoples, C., and V.-W. Nick. 2010. *Critical Security Studies: An Introduction*. New York: Routledge.

Pruitt, L. 2013. "Fixing the Girls: Neoliberal Discourse and Girls' Participation in Peacebuilding." *International Feminist Journal of Politics* 15 (1): 58–76. doi:10.1080/14616742.2012.699783.

Puechguirbal, N. 2004. "Women and Children: Deconstructing a Paradigm." *Seton Hall Journal of Diplomacy and International Relations* 5 (1): 5–16.

Reddy, N., and K. Ratna. eds. 2002. *A Journey in Children's Participation*. Bangalore: The Concerned for Working Children.

Rosen, D. M. 2007. "Child Soldiers, International Humanitarian Law, and the Globalization of Childhood." *American Anthropologist* 109 (2): 296–306. doi:10.1525/aa.2007.109.2.296.

Rowley, C., and J. Weldes. 2012. "The Evolution of International Security Studies and the Everyday: Suggestions from the Buffyverse." *Security Dialogue* 43: 513–530.

Ruddick, S. 1995. *Maternal Thinking: Towards a Politics of Peace*. Boston, MA: Beacon Press.

Schwartz, S. 2010. *Youth in Post-Conflict Reconstruction: Agents of Change*. Washington, DC: United States Institute of Peace Press.

Seto, D. 2013. *No Place for a War Baby: The Global Politics of Children Born of Wartime Sexual Violence*. London: Ashgate.

Sjoberg, L., and S. Via, eds. 2010. *Gender, War, and Militarism*. Santa Barbara, CA: Praeger.

Sommers, M. 2012. *Stuck: Rwandan Youth and the Struggle for Adulthood*. Athens: University of Georgia Press.

Spyrou Spyros. 2011. "The Limits of Children's Voices: From Authenticity to Critical, Reflexive Representation." *Childhood* 18 (2): 151–165. doi:10.1177/0907568210387834.

Stahl, R. 2006. "Have You Played the War on Terror?" *Critical Studies in Media Communication* 23 (2): 112–130. doi:10.1080/07393180600714489.

Stark, L., N. Boothby, and A. Ager. 2009. "Children and Fighting Forces: 10 Years on from Cape Town." *Disasters* 33 (4): 522–547. doi:10.1111/j.1467-7717.2008.01086.x.

Stephens, S. 1995. "Children and the Politics of Culture in 'Late Capitalism'." In *Children and the Politics of Culture*, edited by S. Stephens, 3–53. Princeton, NJ: Princeton University Press.

Stephens, S. 1997. "Nationalism, Nuclear Policy, and Children in Cold War America." *Childhood* 4 (1): 103–123. doi:10.1177/0907568297004001006.

Such, E., O. Walker, and R. Walker. 2005. "Anti-War Children: Representation of Youth Protests against the Second Iraq War in the British National Press." *Childhood* 12 (3): 301–326. doi:10.1177/0907568205054924.

Sylvester, C. 2013. *War as Experience: Contributions from International Relations and Feminist Analysis*. New York: Routledge.

Van Beers, H., V. P. Chau, J. Ennew, P. Q. Khan, T. T. Long, B. Milne, T. T. A. Nguyet, and V. T. Son. 2006. *Creating an Enabling Environment: Capacity Building in Children's Participation.* Save the Children Sweden, Viet Nam, 2000–2004. Bangkok: Save the Children Sweden.

Wall, J. 2012. "Can Democracy Represent Children? Toward a Politics of Difference." *Childhood* 19 (1): 86–100. doi:10.1177/0907568211406756.

Watson, A. M. S. 2007. "Children Born of Wartime Rape: Rights and Representations." *International Feminist Journal of Politics* 9 (1): 20–34. doi:10.1080/14616740601066242.

Watson, A. M. S. 2008. "Can There Be a 'Kindered' Peace?" *Ethics and International Affairs* 22 (1): 35–42. doi:10.1111/j.1747-7093.2008.00128.x.

Watson, A. M. S. 2009. *The Child in International Political Economy: A Place at the Table.* Abingdon: Routledge.

Wells, K. 2007. "Narratives of Liberation and Narratives of Innocent Suffering: The Rhetorical Uses of Images of Iraqi Children in the British Press." *Visual Communication* 6 (1): 55–71. doi:10.1177/1470357207071465.

Wells, K. 2009. *Childhood in a Global Perspective.* Cambridge: Polity.

Wyness, M. G. 2006. *Childhood and Society: An Introduction to the Sociology of Childhood.* Houndmills: Palgrave.

Zalewski, M., and C. Enloe. 1995. "Questions about Identity in International Relations." In *International Relations Theory Today*, edited by K. Booth and S. Smith, 279–305. Cambridge: Polity Press.

Resilience is its own resistance: the place of children in post-conflict settlement

Alison M. S. Watson

School of International Relations, University of St. Andrews, St Andrews, Fife, UK

In portrayals of contemporary conflict and post-conflict situations, we most often think of children as victims. This article will consider whether such a widespread portrayal is actually counterproductive, both in terms of the conceptualization of childhood and on the conceptualization of the roles that children might play in the international security system. It argues that an emphasis on rationality constrains the way in which we consider who might have agency in the international system and that there is a place for children as distinct actors in post-conflict settings. It is thus a call too for the greater examination of the emotional processes and resilience present in post-conflict settings, and what such resilience may inspire: love, compassion, community, and a recognized place for children as actors in their own right.

In portrayals of contemporary conflict and post-conflict situations, we most often think of children as victims: physically hurt, emotionally traumatized and grief-stricken, robbed of their childhoods and struggling with the long-term impact of loss, in whatever form that loss may take. This article will consider, however, whether such a widespread portrayal is actually counterproductive both in terms of the conceptualization of childhood, and on the conceptualization of the roles that children might play in the international security system. In particular, rather than seeing children as victims, if we instead considered them to be agents in their own right, would our perception of what they may be able to achieve, and in turn what the post-conflict process is able to achieve, be altered? Of course, this issue is not the only one that affects children in the international system. The mechanisms of the liberal peace have been constructed in such a way that anyone classified as 'victim' – by definition, often a condition of powerlessness and domination – finds it difficult to claim agency as the event that has resulted in their being cast as victims has had an emotional and psychological impact that may be perceived as impacting upon their potential to act rationally and hence claim agency. Charbonneau and Parent have written compellingly of this in their examination of the role of liberal thought in the construction of the 'strategy to build a "more peaceful" Afghan state for guaranteeing security,' noting that the,

> focus on women (and children) produces a discourse of an ideal Afghan victim as the target of peace-building. This abstract construction of Afghan life is needed to fit with the conventional images and understandings of Western governments and societies about Afghan life, and women in particular, [and thus] non-political, non-social, and powerless… susceptible to being helped and saved. (Charbonneau and Parent 2010, 97)

It is this abstract construction that results in a failure to connect with the affective dimension of conflict and post-conflict environments, and thus with those elements that may, in actuality, provide the solution to the 'transformation of violent conflict' that has been one of the elements of the liberal peace that has been so heavily criticized (Darby and Mac Ginty 2000, 5). It is also this abstract construction that has served to often undermine the sustainability of peace, for while human security is often promoted as one of the cornerstones of the liberal peace, and policy-makers' rhetoric frequently cites the importance of 'individuals and people' and their lives 'in their homes, in their jobs, in their streets, [and] in their communities' (Ul Haq 1995, 1), in actuality the mechanisms of the liberal peace have been more concerned – though with limited success – with meeting technocratic targets (such as repatriating refugees or reconstructing housing units) than they have with dealing with the very real human emotions that can bedevil post-war societies. These emotions, such as intergroup antipathy, hatred, rage, grief, and the desire for retribution, play an enormous role in shaping post-peace accord communities and can become existential barriers to peace that are demanding of recognition (Kelman 1999, 581). As Jabri has noted, conflict can be,

> a constitutive element of collective identity, reproduced in collective memory through national narratives of past glories in the face of threats against national sovereignty and survival. A self-image based on notions of heroism, valour and justice draws upon such collective memories and is actively reproduced in times of conflict. (Jabri 1996, 139)

Negative emotions, images, and discourses may be powerful enough for the most evident and constructive of solutions to a conflict to be rejected in favor of further harming the other side, even if that means that both sides continue to be hurt in the process. On the other hand, in all conflicts, there will also be some positive emotions at work – so-called 'islands of civility' (Kaldor 1999, 120) – where the seeds of empathy, of engagement with the 'other,' and of understanding (Helena 2004, 87) may provide the potential for future settlement.

In the case of children, these issues are particularly entrenched. Because children are easily conceptualized as victims, but 'very much marginalized as agents, most approaches to building peace marginalize issues surrounding children: they are little discussed in peace-building policies, seldom asked to participate in peace-building projects, and peace-building strategies are rarely informed by knowledge regarding either their wartime experiences or their post-conflict needs' (Watson 2008). This article examines some of the ways in which 'victimhood' and particularly the portrayal of children as 'victims' can impact upon post-conflict societies, especially in terms of its significance to the manifestation of war, and to the creation of peace. In this regard, the article will focus upon two main arguments. First, that the public, and private, significance of the 'victim' portrayal in conflict and post-conflict situations remains under-recognized and under-examined both by policy-makers and practitioners in the prevailing liberal peace-building mechanisms, as well as by academics – when, in reality, the portrayal of any marginalized group as 'victims' has a direct impact on their ability to become political agents and thus claim political rights. Second, that children are particularly under-recognized – some more than others – and that recognizing these children is not a risky strategy but rather one that can provide a key that might help to unlock some of those elements that can prevent stable settlement in a post-conflict environment.

The victims of conflict

During a conflict and its aftermath, the impact of what has occurred, the 'victims' that have suffered, and the losses that have been inflicted upon them, whatever these may be, should always be recognized. The ever-expanding literature on trauma and transitional justice recognizes this. Even, as Errante (1999, 261) notes, the very nature of peace itself may require those that are seeking reconciliation to surrender aspects of the social, symbolic and material world that has sustained them during conflict, and this in itself can provoke feelings of loss. The result is that a sustainable peace requires opposing groups to discharge these feelings of loss, whilst acknowledging that the identities that they have assumed after loss have symbolic meaning. This is just as true for children as it is for adults. If we examine the 'victim' identity in particular, however – with a 'victim' being identified as a person harmed, injured, or killed as a result of a crime, accident, or other event or action – we can recognize that victimhood is constructed in a particular way. Van Dijk undertakes a compelling analysis of the origins of the term 'victimhood' and its implications, noting that:

> The English term victim is derived from the Latin word for sacrificial animal…. In fact, all Western languages use words referring to sacrificial animals for victims of crime… The choice of the victim label for victims of crime in so many languages is puzzling for several reasons… It seems melodramatic and strangely lacking in respect to call human beings suffering from the after effects of crimes slaughtered animals. The victim label precludes any hope of a rapid recovery, or in fact, any recovery at all. Moreover the use of the label puts the behaviour of the perpetrator in a strangely favourable light… in the venerable position of the sacrificing priest. (Van Dijk 2009, 1–2)

This fundamentally Western conception of victimhood is significant enough for those living in the West. In the context of the academic and societal discourse on rape, for example, 'the proposal by American feminists, to replace the negative concept of "victim" with that of "survivor" in cases of violence against women has met with near universal approval' (Van Dijk 2009, 3). As noted by Spalek,

> if the stereotype of victim as 'passive' and 'helpless' is perpetuated in dominant representations of victimhood, during a time when individual strength is valued in society, then both males and females may increasingly refuse to situate themselves in terms of victimhood. (Spalek 2006, 9)

Within the non-Western context, however, those who have been impacted by significant life events may find the 'victim' label deeply 'othering,' because both the label itself, and their response to the context of the life event that has resulted in the labeling, may serve to stigmatize them and render them without agency in both a personal and an institutional context. Those that are marginalized in terms of their identity – whether because of their age, class, ethnicity, gender, race, religion, or sexuality, may be doubly marginalized by being constructed too as 'victims' who have suffered an event that has had an emotional or psychological impact. Take, for example, the issue of grief. Traditions of grief display – whether in the global North or the global South, in the young or in the old, in the feminine gaze or in the masculine one – have influenced perceptions of 'unknowability' that in turn may influence the capacity of particular stakeholders to be taken into account in peace-building processes. The liberal model, and the distant processes of governance that characterize it, assume an ahistorical, atemporal, abstract individual who rationally acts to maximize utility. As a result, the issue of emotions, and the time and effort that it may take to work through these emotions in the aftermath of a life-changing event, are excluded. Yet, the aftermath of any war, for example, is clearly characterized by loss. Death in wartime is often seen only as a statistic, but the reality of loss is that everyday life may have irrevocably changed: part of a family – and indeed the vision of the future of that family – may have been lost forever, and in aggregate communities may thus have been fundamentally altered. The liberal peace thus commits two errors: it either assumes that the antipathy caused by grief is permanent and cannot be resolved, or it assumes that everyone can easily 'move on' from the losses that they have suffered and hence 'act rationally' rather than emotionally, sometimes with the additional provision of monetary compensation to 'cover' the emotional costs associated with loss. In both cases, the result may be a 'reification' of the conflict and, arguably, in turn, with reference to previous arguments, the reification of the perpetrator either because of the creation of a particular set of institutions that do so, or because monetarizing grief results in the erosion of mutual compensation and exchange mechanisms that, for many traditional societies, may have served as the 'core of peace-making' (Ginty 2008, 149).

Moreover, whilst it is well recognized that grief and mourning responses may differ for cultural, racial, and ethnic reasons that are dependent upon gender, age, and the circumstances of the loss (see, for example, Rosenblatt 1993), this may also mean, of course, that grief displays may serve as one of the elements that 'other' us. Thus, for example, the relatively contained nature of private grief and mourning rituals in the Western model, when contrasted with more elaborate displays in non-Western societies, may feed into Western social constructions of non-Western emotionality (and related to this, rationality) as a confirmation of 'otherness' – viewing grief display as a potential indicator of a threat to the maintenance of the societal order – both domestically and internationally – when in fact the opposite may be true – they are performative in just the same way as Western rituals are. In turn, this impacts upon our grief knowledge and the way in which we recognize and use it. This was an issue recognized by Emile Durkheim in *The Elementary Forms of Religious Life* who, as Robben notes, drew on,

> ethnographic accounts of Australian aborigines to argue that the spontaneity of their wailing is deceptive, because all these expressions are clearly prescribed, controlled, and monitored by the community. Durkheim's explanation of such rites is that the death of an individual diminishes the group numerically and socially... Indifference to a death expresses a lack of moral and cultural unity, and an absence of social cohesion and solidarity... collective mourning helps to draw people closer together and invigorate the weakened social group. (Robben 2004, 7–8)

In the case of the child, this 'othering' of grief and mourning practices can be witnessed in historical and cross-cultural accounts of childhood death. In the case of both historical accounts in the industrialized West and contemporary accounts of childhood mortality in developing countries, there has been a degree of debate regarding whether childhood death was/is so frequent that adults became used to it. Nancy Scheper-Hughes examined these arguments for contemporary Brazil when she recognized that:[1]

> a high expectance of child death is a powerful shaper of maternal thinking and practice as evidenced, in particular, in delayed attachment to infants sometimes thought of as temporary household 'visitors.' (Scheper-Hughes 1993, 340)

However, Scheper-Hughes also suggests that these 'differences' may themselves be culturally constructed in that, for example, American mothers:

> are exposed to so much emotional 'prompting' by LaMaze counsellors, doctors, and pediatric nurses that most American women probably do manage to produce the 'appropriate'

sentiments of euphoria, love, and passionate, jealous attachment to the infant while still in hospital. Those who do not, especially if they are poor, single, 'welfare' mothers, run the risk of early social intervention. (Scheper-Hughes 1993, 412)

Moreover, historical accounts often emphasize too the depth of feeling that adults had over the death of their children, however common their occurrence.[2] Grief, then, is a highly personal – culturally and historically specific – experience. It may also be a political one, creating an impetus for activism and constructive resistance. Within the context of conflict, as Judith Butler (2009) has noted, one key contention is that those who have been bereaved may channel their anger and resentment into political militancy as a way of resisting the loss of their sacrifice. By dealing with bereavement through activism, grief may be channeled into various activities such as political agitation, building new social networks, and shaping new identities that give the bereaved a public and political voice (Maxwell 1995, 437). The construction of those who are grieving simply as 'victims' may thus mask a range of examples of political agency that if recognized would change the way in which the post-conflict context is constructed.

In the conflict and post-conflict contexts, children may be perceived as the ultimate victim. Children are affected by conflict in a number of ways. The most obvious of these is when children themselves are physically harmed – either killed or injured. Sometimes children become victims in this way simply as part of the ongoing process of violence. Sometimes, however, children are deliberately targeted, either because they are symbolic of a particular ethnic or religious group, or because they are symbolic of possible future political change, or simply because it is the loss of a child that, arguably, hurts the most (Zelizer 1994). In addition to such direct physical consequences, the long-term physical impact on children of living in an area that is subject to a prolonged terrorist campaign can be significant. A protracted conflict may have a considerable impact on the socioeconomic status of a region and, in such circumstances, it is often children who are the most vulnerable societal group suffering the consequences of a lack of adequate health care, of opportunities for education, and other forms of social and economic deprivation. Whether or not they can simply be classified as 'victims,' however, with all that this term entails regarding the ability of 'victims' to then be able to claim 'agency,' remains to be seen. Indeed, a significant amount of research demonstrates that the reality is actually somewhat different. Finnström's (2006) research with young rebels in Uganda, for example, demonstrates that children perceive themselves not as the passive persona that victimhood would seem to dictate, but rather as negotiating roles that see them neither as victims nor as perpetrators, but as actors – with agency – that negotiate their own political engagement under difficult and exceptional circumstances. This is in line with the work of Wessells (2006, 3) and others who have noted that children are so often portrayed as innocent and without agency, a characterization that would seem to suggest that their only role in a post-conflict environment is to be thought of in terms of the obligations that adults have to them, something that is often stated as part of the rhetoric in post-conflict settlement. In reality, there is evidence that children instead respond to growing up in a war zone – a place where they may see no positive place for themselves in society (Wessells 2006, 3) by negotiating their agency within the conflict environment. Thus, the resort to violence can be a way for children and young people to resist the existing political order; children may participate in a rebel group because it provides a family or peer structure, or a sense of empowerment that may have been otherwise destroyed as a result of the continuing conflict. Being part of a rebel group may also make sense in terms of better access to food and personal protection. The difficulty with this conceptualization, however, is that, as Van Dijk notes,

> The analysed victim narratives tell a very different story to conventional representations of passive suffering. They also reveal how society's response to crime victims tends to turn from sympathy into antipathy when victims defy the expected victim role. (Van Dijk 2009, 3)

Van Dijk's fascinating analysis goes further, and it is worth bearing in mind the current conceptualization of children when considering the following argument:

> It appears a stroke of linguistic genius that by calling those affected by crimes *victims*, society can acknowledge their deep and innocent suffering and at the same time express its firm expectation that they will sacrifice their right of revenge. By calling crime victims *victims* in the image of Jesus Christ, they are socially constructed both as suffering objects worthy of society's compassion and as the active subjects of a sacrifice. (Van Dijk 2009, 7)

Moreover, the notion of 'suffering' is itself often conceptualized in Western terms, which can again be examined within the context of the Western approach to grief. For example, the latter has arguably altered over the last few decades, such that there is now a distinct movement toward more openness surrounding public – especially mass – grief rituals, and a feeling that grieving in this way is a necessary and desirable thing to do. Seltzer (1997, 3) has conceptualized this in terms of the creation of a 'pathological public sphere,' where individual and collective trauma and loss are increasingly legitimized within the public arena. Under such circumstances, the role of 'victim' is one that has become increasingly problematized. Indeed, Seltzer goes one stage further in arguing that we are living in a 'wound culture' where there is a 'public fascination with torn and opened bodies, and torn and opened persons, a collective gathering around shock, trauma and the wound' (Seltzer 1997, 3). Common examples in the literature include the public grief surrounding the death of Princess Diana, as well as the obviously widespread and public outpouring of grief after 9/11. Recent work has also highlighted the public manifestation of grief in Wootton Bassett for the return of those British soldiers lost in Iraq and Afghanistan (Zehfuss 2009, 419).[3] As Schwarcz (1996, 120) recognizes, '[t]he battle over who can speak about sorrow is invariably a battle about words.' Those who are dominant in society often get to effectively write the narrative of what happened during the conflict, and in turn what should happen in its narrative. As Altvater has noted (in Duncan 2013), 'There is power in having a voice.'

For children, however, this issue of voice is a contested one. Although Article 12 of the UN Convention of the Rights of the Child (UNCRC) appears to give children a place to speak for themselves, in reality it still remains within the gift of adults to ensure that this place is given, and that their voices are listened to, and heard. However, children, whilst crucial to the continuity of a particular society's social order (hence the need for their socialization), often remain essentially powerless within it. Moreover, any perceived challenge to this essential powerlessness is seen, in and of itself, as somehow threatening to the maintenance of society as it currently exists. This is particularly the case, as Sharon Stephens notes, for those children who find themselves living a childhood that does not reflect the idealized (often Western) view of what childhood should entail. Children who have been 'victims' of conflict, of socioeconomic disharmony, of justice, become 'risky children' who need to be shaped and controlled in ways that will not threaten the existing societal order, or indeed will not cause too much upheaval in the rapidly changing one (Stephens 1995). Thus, the victim label is a double-edged sword because,

> It offers compassion on condition of meekness. But those who do not comply with the condition of passivity …run a risk of making themselves the target of the feelings of

aggression. … In these cases victims are not just treated as scapegoats symbolically by denying them the right to seek revenge or restitution but in the very real sense that their perceived deviance triggers an outpouring of hatred against them. (Van Dijk 2008, 18)

In terms of the study of childhood, Jo Boyden has examined 'perceptions of childhood … and theories of human responses to adversity that have arisen within the social and medical sciences and highlights their influence on policy and practice in the context of armed conflict.' In particular, she highlights,

> how the idea of childhood as a decontextualized and universal life phase characterized by dependence and vulnerability …interacts with and is reinforced by a view of war-survivors as …traumatized individuals, victims in need of remedial care. (Boyden 2003, 1)

This resonates with the wider literature on victimhood and, in particular, with the reaction that is expected in the face of adversity, which is assumed often to be one of passivity rather than resilience. As Van Dijk notes,

> The theme of resilience is clearly at odds with conventional representations of victimhood in terms of passive suffering and helplessness…. It seems as if an important aspect of the experience of being a victim is experiencing that the personal experience does not fit the internalised stereotypes of passivity and helplessness…. A good victim is before anything else someone who is negatively defined: not intelligent, not visible, not verbal, not angry. The only permitted mode is: keep sobbing and be silent. (Van Dijk 2009, 12–13)

Of course, one of the major problems here lies in the traditional notions of agency that are used to provide various actors with a place in the international system. For Anthony Giddens, 'agency' relates to the capacity to make the appropriate choices within a particular context, and in a way that will have an impact on that context (see Dahl 2009). As Dahl notes,

> In the literature theorising on 'agency', more narrow definitions are often used than those suggested by Giddens. Some researchers emphasise the imprint made by the action without implying… Others emphasise the action itself …and yet others stress the propensity to undertake conscious choices and goal-directed action… (Dahl 2009, 397)

The question of power is also significant here, in that, as Hay (1995, 191) notes, 'power is a question of agency, of influencing or "having an effect" upon the structures which set contexts and define the range of possibilities of others.' Children are generally perceived as not having any 'power,' as defined in a traditional sense, in the international system. As a result, the traditional discussion of their place in that international system has tended to be in terms of their role as victims and dominated persons – as soldiers, as laborers, as refugees, or as slaves. Under such limited conceptions, children are then perceived not to have agency as described in the traditional sense within the Western discourse of international relations (IR). Admittedly, children are affected by the structures that surround them, but they can also affect those same structures. They are more resilient in conflict and post-conflict environments than they are credited with being. Thus, one way to consider agency *vis-à-vis* children is to 'consider agency and structure as integrally related … as the interplay of subject and object within the social world.' Even in their resilience they are demonstrating a form of agency, and in their actions that follow that they may be demonstrating a form of resistance. As James and Prout note:

> Children might employ a variety of modes of agency within and between different social environments ... the possibility [exists] that children locate themselves flexibly and strategically within particular social contexts and that, through focusing on children as competent, individual social actors, we might learn more about the ways in which 'society' and 'social structure' shape social experiences and are themselves refashioned through the social action of members. (James and Prout 1995, 78)

The consequences of this are important, not only for the role that children potentially play in the international system, and the recognition of that role, but also for how we understand the nature of concepts such as power and agency within the discipline of IR. It 'shift[s] our gaze... to the ... putatively powerless' and, in so doing, may reform our consideration of the potential roles that a variety of actors in the international security system may play to one that not only 'genuinely includes the experience of all individuals regardless of race, culture, class and gender', but all individuals regardless of their age as well. It is to this issue that we now turn in detail.

A place for children in the post-conflict state?

The plight of children is little discussed when it comes to agreeing on the minutiae of post-conflict settlement, despite the fact that children are widely recognized – even from within the institutions of the liberal peace itself – as significant to the sustainability of peace. Yet, rather than concentrating upon this specific group as a potential conduit for long-term conflict resolution, those attempting to secure peace tend to assume that a program of post-conflict recovery requires only the redressing of general systemic wrongs that will eventually 'trickle down' to benefit youth along with the rest of the population.

As a result, most approaches to building peace marginalize issues surrounding children: they are little discussed in peace-building policies, seldom asked to participate in peace-building projects, and peace-building strategies are rarely informed by knowledge regarding either their wartime experiences or their post-conflict needs. Yet, given that they are disproportionately affected by conflict, children should be placed center stage, not only as a motivation for a sustainable settlement, but also as actors for peace themselves. Not doing so undermines the potential for successful settlement over the long term and indeed the liberal peace agenda itself. With this in mind, this essay argues for a 'kindering' of peace such that children are recognized as one of the 'fault-lines of the human condition,' which Johan Galtung (1996) has argued are so critical to debates regarding the nature of peace. In fact, no peace treaty has officially considered specific children's rights issues as they relate to a particular conflict. Partly, this is a result of ignorance: policymakers often do not realize the extent of the conflict's impact upon children. Partly, too, it stems from the fact that the parties to treaties seldom consider the knowledge and advice of those who advocate on behalf of children, such as nongovernmental organizations (NGOs), and certainly do not listen to children and youth themselves. Rather, NGOs are expected to support already agreed to post-conflict strategies, and children remain in the background.

The exclusion of children from the peace agreement process, of course, also relates to the dominant construction of children as victims rather than as agents. Ironically, the Western construction of childhood, and the characterization of children within the human rights documents that are meant to protect them as a homogeneous category, leads rather to more marginalization for those children who need to be taken seriously within a post-conflict context. This is because children everywhere are, of course, different: their experiences are different, and these experiences themselves serve to create certain abilities and attitudes that mean that every child is, of course, unique. A child who has lived in a conflict environment for a significant period of time will have developed a set of attitudes and behaviors, will have learned resilience in the face of conflict, will have possibility attained a different place in the family, may now even be the head of that family. On paper they may be young, but their experiences have potentially matured them such that they need to be able to claim their agency and the rights that follow from a younger age than 18. Indeed, for a significant period of time, analysts have recognized the potential that children might have in peace-building processes (see, for example, Cohn 1999) and, in reality, children and youth have taken an active role in creating peace and in ensuring its sustainability. Take, for example, the case of the Children's Peace Movement in Colombia. By the mid-1990s, a series of peace negotiations had begun, spearheaded by a Conciliation Commission that was made up of prominent civic and religious leaders. Although, as a civil society effort, it was much more successful than anything that the government had managed to achieve, the Colombian peace movement as a whole remained weak and fragmented – until the creation of the Children's Movement for Peace. Beginning with a number of young people working in isolation, the movement evolved, without a formal structure, into a significant social force – led by five teenagers – whose contributions to the peace process were recognized in its nomination for a Nobel Peace Prize.

Children can, of course, also disrupt peace if inadequate attention is given to their needs. Peace agreements represent only the beginning of the post-conflict process. The solutions to some of the most pressing and long-term issues that post-conflict societies face depend crucially on children and young populations, especially because it is often the case that children and youth may form a significant percentage of that population. Those children who have actively taken part in hostilities, for example, must, in the aftermath of war, be reintegrated into their home communities. What, however, is their status? They may be children under international law, but they may be criminals, too. Like any other soldier, they face the societal impact of reintegration; but whereas most post-conflict policies provide demobilized adult soldiers with a package of benefits designed to aid such integration, there is no such clear-cut policy for child soldiers, and particularly not for older children. For example, former combatants in Sierra Leone do not receive adequate funding for their reintegration, something that was recognized by Kofi Annan in his report prior to Resolution 1389 on the UN Mission in Sierra Leone (UNAMSIL). In some instances, youth job creation may simply not be a priority for either donors or the presiding government.

Children are also at a disadvantage in terms of land rights in post-conflict societies – a significant issue for those children returning to their homes who find themselves orphaned and perhaps the heads of households. This has been a particular issue in Rwanda, where orphans have been an important class of land claimant and disputant. In general, national legal systems are not yet able to cope with children making such claims, and the result is even more children without a sustainable economic future, something that itself can threaten an already fragile peace. As one World Bank study noted, there is

> robust support for the hypothesis that youth bulges increase the risk of domestic armed conflict, and especially so under conditions of economic stagnation…. . [This is] bad news for regions that currently exhibit both features, often in coexistence with intermediary and unstable political regimes, such as Sub-Saharan Africa and the Arab World.' (Urdal 2004, 22)

The latter is a particularly pertinent example, given the role played by youth in the Arab Spring, their discontent coupled with their use of social media. For example, in terms of the Egyptian case, Stepanova notes that

> the fact that the crisis occurred sooner rather than later, in direct follow-up to protests in Tunisia, was largely due to the initial mobilizing effects of ICT and social media networks. The protests were kickstarted by a Facebook campaign run by the opposition 'April 6 Youth Movement,' which generated tens of thousands of positive responses to the call to rally against government policies. (Stepanova 2011, 1)

Often, however, such dynamics are under-recognized at all stages of a conflict; the current liberal peace approach putting into place a set of norms, when negotiating settlement and its aftermath, that are very much dependent upon states, NGOs, and international organizations for their realization, rather than upon the actions of individuals. They include the encouragement of a democratic political system and the rule of law alongside a liberal market system as a means of achieving economic development. These are very much 'top-down' approaches; however, they require that the necessary institutions and mechanisms are already in place to ensure that such norms can be achieved. Arguably, a more comprehensive solution would encourage the promotion of human rights and human security by fully taking into account grassroots concerns. Listening to youth who have mobilized during a conflict in the post-conflict phase is important, as is recognizing children as agents in their own right. Both would thus become inherent to a successful strategy of conflict resolution, where the root causes of conflict are addressed, all aspects of human security are taken into consideration, and the process of negotiation becomes an inclusive one. The question remains, however, how this can possibly happen within existing frameworks, and in this regard, there are some fundamental difficulties.

We could, for example, argue for far more representation of the interests of children when concluding the terms of peaceful settlement. This could take place in a couple of obvious ways. NGOs advocating for children could consistently be asked their views at the time of the negotiations toward peaceful settlement, rather than it being assumed that their role is important only as administrators of the welfare programs that are instituted in post-conflict zones. This would require policy-makers to consider the effect of the settlement upon children's lives, rather than treat what happens to them simply as an afterthought. In addition, children themselves could be consulted regarding the nature of the peace, and of their requirements in it. One problem with involving children in decision-making processes, however, is in the framing of the boundary between childhood and adulthood. The question of children's agency has become a significant site of negotiation between those who interpret children as fully competent social actors, able to make legitimate claims for the realization of their rights, and those who interpret children as 'still developing' social actors for whom rights claims can only be realized by adult actors on their behalf. The Western categorization of childhood is prevalent. In the aftermath of conflict, there is much discussion of giving children back the childhoods that they have lost as a result of war, but in reality this cannot happen. Children who have been effectively agents in times of conflict, find it very difficult to relinquish this role in a post-conflict environment (in a very similar way to how women in the aftermath of World War II found it difficult to return to a more domestic role, having played an active role in wartime support, e.g., working in munitions factories or as agricultural workers).

O'Neill (1988) has questioned the use of the language of rights when approaching ethical issues as they relate to the child, arguing that a focus on obligations may be more relevant. She argues that because children are dependent (unlike other 'oppressed social groups' in a plea for rights) and vulnerable, the focus should change from the rights of children to the obligations that adults have to them. This is not an uncommon view, but it is a view very much in keeping with Western philosophical tradition; indeed, it characterizes much of the language of those measures that have been designed to address the 'rights' of the child within the international system, such as the UNCRC. Nevertheless, O'Neill concedes that the boundary between childhood and adulthood is blurry. The variety of experiences that children under the age of 18 may have means that some children, notably those O'Neill (1988, 455) terms 'mature minors,' may find themselves as a group in a position partly analogous to that of other oppressed social groups. Arguably, for children in a post-conflict environment this is particularly the case. Thus, childhood, as much as it is a social construct, presents conceptual and practical challenges for policy-makers attempting to negotiate a sustainable settlement. The experiences of children affected by conflict do not constitute the ideal that appears to be fundamental to the Western liberal model. These are not children who have been under parental behest until the age of 18, who have had the chance to play, to develop a network of friends, to feel safe within a secure local environment, to plan for their education. These are children who may have been heads of their households from the age of 12, who may have had to journey far to achieve their version of safety, who may have been forced to take part in the worst forms of child labor to secure some sort of income, and who may have had to kill as a way to survive. Giving them back an ideal childhood is not an option, and so they cannot be treated as if they will revert to being children once peace has been achieved. Rather, children should be seen in the aftermath of war as actors whose opinions are necessary when deciding upon how the reconstruction of the post-conflict society is going to take place, especially over the long term. Moreover, in many societies, children are charged with significant roles at a local level. They may be homemakers, landowners, breadwinners, and peacemakers. Yet, in similar terms to other marginalized groups, their specific interests are not represented at the international level. Moving away from the bias of the 'powerful' toward a consideration of the 'knowledgeable' may thus lead to a more rounded consideration of standard security discourses. Thus, for example, the UN Department of Peacekeeping Operations noted in a 1999 report that what was required for the success of DDR programs was for children to be consulted at various stages of the process. Arguably, the same applies for children involved in conflict more generally. They too should be consulted as a source of knowledge – whether cultural or generational – that would be of use in a post-conflict setting. Instead, however, the marginalization of children in government policy in post-conflict zones around the world results in inadequate care and, in turn, to an increased likelihood of social breakdown and, possibly, the resumption of conflict. Moreover, ignoring the specific needs of children when attempting to build peace actually flies in the face of the liberal peace-building agenda. The point is not to change the wording of a peace settlement so that 'and children' can be inserted at the relevant points, but rather to understand that ignoring children makes it impossible to address crucial elements of conflict resolution. This article has already mentioned the centrality of the notion of human rights to the liberal peace discourse. It must be seen, too, that children are central to contemporary conceptions of human rights. The UNCRC should place children center stage in the quest for the universal application of human rights, and, as such, at the heart of the liberal peace project itself. Peace negotiations should not be reserved to those who can speak in the language of the 'liberal club.' They should be open to those who can provide an alternative – and potentially more fruitful – narrative.

The question remains, of course, of what this narrative might potentially include – and for this, there are a few immediate answers. First of all, it would have to include an examination of children as complete, as opposed to partial, political actors. Currently, there is a temptation to think of children as only being relevant when policies that appear to directly affect them are discussed. Thus, they are confined to discussions of issues of education, child health, and, when things go wrong, youth crime. What about community involvement?; or how to stop alienation from the democratic project?; or how alternative forms of resistance have aided the process of political change? Yet, creating a stable political regime requires all actors to feel enfranchised by the political environment, and continually allowing children to speak only when they are spoken to – or in the ways that adults speak – does nothing to help in the creation of vibrant democracies. Second, there must be the realization that the liberal call for an active civil society actually requires liberal policy-makers to put their money where their mouths are and give civil society groups real political clout, and too to really think where it is that civil society actually happens. Political commentary may be heard on youth radio, in songs, through sport, theatre, and satire, all of which may be divorced from the processes that the liberal peace promotes. Not paying attention to these alternative forms of political enfranchisement is a recipe for long-term failure in post-conflict settings. Third, the dominant policy discourse appears to favor the dominant academic discourse – policy-makers thus largely use the expertise of those who tell them what they want to hear, and who speak to them in the language that they recognize – policy-oriented, committee-based, and legalistic. This is in many ways understandable, because to do otherwise entails a sometimes radical shift in the political agenda and does not offer the short-term solutions that political expediency so clearly requires. Yet, continuing to plough in the same furrow means that there is no hope of political change, and, within that too, no real hope of a long-term and sustainable peace. As Collardey (2011) notes, peace agreements in Burundi, Liberia, and Sierra Leone recognized the significance of children in peace processes and post-conflict settlement. In the 10 years since Liberia, there has been little progress, however. It also begs the question of whether the current policy regime actually is designed for peace, or whether there is more to gain from the maintenance of uncertainty regarding a return to violence. The ideal for any post-conflict situation should be a return to normality and the withdrawal of peacekeepers and the industry that surrounds them. Yet, arguably in the same way that rebel groups may benefit – economically and otherwise – from the continued threat of violence, the peace industry and those who are connected to it – state and non-state actors, governmental and non-governmental organizations, private firms, and individuals – may too have a vested interest in the maintenance of a peace that is uncertain, that is requiring of their continued service, and therefore marginalizing of those actors and issues that are not directly implicated in its resolution. Only by examining the significance of such vested interests, and exploring how they may be overcome, will there ever really be a notion of a long-term peace. More than this, however, this article is a call too – in keeping with a growing body of literature that demonstrates how 'empathy, compassion and wonder...may facilitate more lasting and ingenious forms of social healing and reconciliation' in post-conflict settings (Hutchison and Bleiker 2008, 385) – for the greater examination of the emotional processes and resilience present in post-conflict settings, and what such resilience may inspire: love, compassion, community, and a recognized place for children as actors in their own right.

Acknowledgments

This article has benefitted from a number of discussions around the issues of childhood, agency, emotions, grief, marginalization peace, reconciliation, and voice. The author would very much like to thank Marshall Beier, Bennett Collins, Anne de Graaf, Oliver Richmond, and Arlie Russell Hochschild for their very thoughtful conversations that have greatly aided in the development of the arguments outlined here. The author would also like to thank the two anonymous referees for their comments, which greatly aided contextualization. All errors remain the author's own.

Notes

1. See http://www.faqs.org/childhood/Gr-Im/Grief-Death-Funerals.html.
2. See, for example, the letter written by Joseph Dalton Hooker to Charles Darwin in response to a note that Darwin had written to him: 'I have just buried my darling little girl and read your kind note. I tried hard to make no difference between her and the other children, but she was my very own, the flower of my flock in every one's eyes, the companion of my walks, the first of my children who has shown any love for music and flowers, and the sweetest tempered, affectionate little thing that ever I knew. It will be long before I cease to hear her voice in my ears, or feel her little hand stealing into mine; by the fireside and in the Garden, wherever I go she is there' (Hooker 1918, 62).
3. This has been contrasted with the lack of public recognition of the loss of Muslim lives in the conflict. In the United Kingdom, this issue came to the fore perhaps most obviously in the planned protest through Wootton Bassett by members of Islam4UK (a group now outlawed under UK terror laws) who planned to carry 'symbolic coffins' in memory of civilians killed by coalition forces.

References

Boyden, J. 2003. "Children Under Fire Challenging Assumptions about Children's Resilience." *Children, Youth and Environments* 13 (1): 1–29.

Butler, J. 2009. *Frames of War: When is Life Grievable?* London: Verso.

Charbonneau, B., and G. Parent. 2010. "Managing Life in Afghanistan: Canadian Tales of Peace, Security, and Development." In *Locating Global Order: American Power and Canadian Security After 9/11*, edited by B. Charbonneau and W. S. Cox, 87–106. Vancouver: UBC Press.

Cohn, I. 1999. "The Protection of Children in Peacemaking and Peacekeeping Processes." *Harvard Humanitarian Rights Journal* 12: 129.

Collardey, E. 2011. "1000 Peace Cranes: Exploring Children's Meanings of Peace." *The Peace and Conflict Review* 6 (1). http://www.review.upeace.org/index.cfm?opcion=0&ejemplar=23&entrada=125.

Dahl, G. 2009. "Sociology and Beyond: Agency, Victimisation and the Ethics of Writing." *Asian Journal of Social Science* 37 (3): 391–407. doi:10.1163/156853109X436784.

Darby, J., and R. Mac Ginty. 2000. "Introduction: Comparing Peace Processes." In *The Management of Peace Processes*, edited by J. Darby and R. M. Ginty, 1–15. Basingstoke: Palgrave Macmillan.

Duncan, L. 2013. "How a Community Heals: A Conversation with Denise Altvater." American Friends Service Committee Website, January 10, 2013. Accessed August 29. http://www.afsc.org/friends/how-community-heals-conversation-denise-altvater

Errante, A. 1999. "Peace Work as Grief Work in Mozambique and South Africa: Postconflict Communities as Context for Child and Youth Socialization." *Peace and Conflict: Journal of Peace Psychology* 5 (3): 261–279. doi:10.1207/s15327949pac0503_7.

Finnström, S. 2006. "Wars of the Past and War in the Present: The Lord's Resistance Movement/ Army in Uganda." *Africa: Journal of the International African Institute* 76 (2): 200–220. doi:10.3366/afr.2006.76.2.200.

Galtung, J. 1996. *Peace by Peaceful Means: Peace and Conflict, Development and Civilization.* London: Sage.

Ginty, R. M. 2008. "Indigenous Peace-making Versus the Liberal Peace." *Cooperation and Conflict* 43 (2): 139–163. doi:10.1177/0010836708089080.

Hay, C. 1995. "Structure and Agency." In *Theory and Methods in Political Science*, edited by D. Marsh and G. Stoker, 189–206, New York: St. Martin's Press.

Helena, L. S. 2004. "The Politics of Fear and the Collapse of the Mideast Peace Process." *International Journal of Peace Studies* 9 (1): 85–106.

Hooker, J. D. 1918. *Life and Letters of Sir Joseph Dalton Hooker.* 2 vols. edited by L. Huxley. Cambridge: Cambridge University Press.

Hutchison, E., and R. Bleiker. 2008. "Emotional Reconciliation: Reconstituting Identity and Community after Trauma." *European Journal of Social Theory* 11 (3): 385–403. doi:10.1177/ 1368431008092569.

Jabri, V. 1996. *Discourses on Violence: Conflict Analysis Reconsidered.* Manchester: Manchester University Press.

James, A., and A. Prout. 1995. "Hierarchy, Boundary and Agency: Toward a Theoretical Perspective on Childhood." *Sociological Studies of Children* 7: 77–95.

Kaldor, M. 1999. *New and Old Wars: Organized Violence in a Global Era.* Stanford: Stanford University Press.

Kelman, H. C. 1999. "The Interdependence of Israeli and Palestinian National Identities: The Role of the Other in Existential Conflicts." *Journal of Social Issues* 55 (3): 581–600. doi:10.1111/ 0022-4537.00134.

Maxwell, C. J. C. 1995. "Coping with Bereavement through Activism: Real Grief Imagined Death, and Pseudo-Mourning among Pro-Life Direct Activists." *Ethos* 23 (4): 437–452. doi:10.1525/ eth.1995.23.4.02a00040.

O'Neill, O. 1988. "Children's Rights and Children's Lives." *Ethics* 98 (3): 445–463. doi:10.1086/ 292964.

Robben, A. C. G. M. 2004. "Death and Anthropology: An Introduction." In *Death, Mourning and Burial: A Cross-Cultural Reader*, edited by A. C. G. M. Robben, 1–16. Malden, MA: Wiley Blackwell.

Rosenblatt, P. C. 1993. "Cross-Cultural Variation in the Experience, Expression, and Understanding of Grief." In *Ethnic Variations in Dying, Death and Grief: Diversity in Universality*, edited by D. P. Irish, K. F. Lundquist, and V. J. Nelson, 13–19. Washington, DC: Taylor and Francis.

Scheper-Hughes, N. 1993. *Death without Weeping: The Violence of Everyday Life in Brazil.* Berkeley: University of California Press.

Schwarcz, V. 1996. "The Pane of Sorrow: Public Uses of Personal Grief in China." *Daedalus* 125 (1): 119–148.

Seltzer, M. 1997. "Wound Culture: Trauma in the Pathological Public Sphere." *October* 80: 3–26. doi:10.2307/778805.

Spalek, B. 2006. *Crime Victims, Theory Policy and Practice.* Basingstoke: Palgrave Macmillan.

Stepanova, E. 2011. "The Role of Information Communication Technologies in the Arab Spring." PONARS Eurasia Policy Memo, No. 159. Accessed September 2. http://www.gwu.edu/~ier-esgwu/assets/docs/ponars/pepm_159.pdf.

Stephens, S. 1995. "Children and the Politics of Culture in 'Late Capitalism'." In *Children and the Politics of Culture*, edited by S. Stephens, 3–53. Princeton, NJ: Princeton University Press.

Ul Haq, M. 1995. *Reflections on Human Development.* New York: Oxford University Press.

United Nations Department of Peacekeeping Operations. 1999. "Disarmament, Demobilization and Reintegration of Ex-Combatants in a Peacekeeping Environment: Principles and Guidelines." Accessed March 17, 2015. http://www.peacekeepingbestpractices.unlb.org/PBPS/Library/DPKO %20DDR%20Manual.pdf

Urdal, H. 2004. "The Devil in the Demographics: The Effect of Youth Bulges on Domestic Armed Conflict, 1950–2000." World Bank Social Development Paper No. 14.

Van Dijk, J. 2008. "In the Shadow of Christ? On the Use of the Word 'Victim' for Those Affected by Crime." *Criminal Justice Ethics* 27 (1): 13–24. doi:10.1080/0731129X.2008.9992224.

Van Dijk, J. 2009. "Free the Victim: A Critique of the Western Conception of Victimhood." *International Review of Victimology* 16 (1): 1–33. doi:10.1177/026975800901600101.

Watson, A. M. S. 2008. "Can There Be a 'Kindered' Peace?" *Ethics and International Affairs* 22 (1): 35–42. doi:10.1111/j.1747-7093.2008.00128.x.

Wessells, M. G. 2006. *Child Soldiers: From Violence to Protection*. Cambridge: Harvard University Press.

Zehfuss, M. 2009. "Hierarchies of Grief and the Possibility of War: Remembering UK Fatalities in Iraq." *Millennium – Journal of International Studies* 38 (2): 419–440. doi:10.1177/0305829809347540.

Zelizer, V. A. 1994. *Pricing the Priceless Child*. Princeton, NJ: Princeton University Press.

Children, civilianhood, and humanitarian securitization

Lorraine Macmillan

Department of Politics and International Studies, University of Cambridge, Cambridge, UK

In this article, the influence of the construction of children as civilians over the processes of securitization in the US intervention in Somalia is examined. This is done through an analysis of the US print news media coverage of that event. The study employs two key theoretical frameworks: the first is the social understanding of civilianhood, and the second is the Copenhagen School's theory of securitization. The work concludes that a failure to unpack the value of referent objects of security diminishes the insights that securitization theory can offer. The grammar of securitizing moves cannot be fully comprehended in instances of militarized humanitarian interventions, in particular, without this kind of analysis. Children as suffering civilians draw considerable attention from the world's media and thus an investigation of their role in securitization can be highly informative.

Introduction

The importance of children to the world of international relations has grown markedly in the last three decades. Their heightened salience is amply demonstrated by the near universal adoption of the Convention of the Rights of the Child and the advocacy work from which it sprang. In the world of practice, an increasing number of development and post-conflict reconstruction programs make children their chief concern. The world's media expose us to countless images of suffering children that remain the leitmotif of emergency relief fund-raising campaigns (Burman 1994). Unconventionally fought civil wars in which civilians are disproportionately affected provide a prodigious amount of such imagery. Early media coverage of the Assad regime's actions in Syria proves that conventional weaponry when targeted at civilians can produce equally shocking representations of children's suffering.

Despite the added attention children have attracted, scholarship on children and security is still scant. A small cohort of scholars engage with the security issues children present, but their collective output is small and often appears on the fringes. Consequently, there is insufficient theorization of children's roles in security. This article, as part of this special issue, seeks to partially address that deficiency. In it, the influence of the construction of children as civilians over the processes of securitization is examined. This is achieved through an analysis of the US print news media coverage of the US humanitarian intervention in Somalia in the early 1990s. The study employs two key theoretical frameworks: the first is the social understanding of civilianhood, and the second is the Copenhagen School's theory of securitization. The work concludes that a failure to unpack the value of referent objects of security diminishes the insights that securitization theory can offer. The grammar of securitizing moves cannot be fully comprehended in instances of militarized humanitarian interventions, in particular, without this kind of analysis. Children as suffering civilians draw considerable attention from the world's media, and thus an investigation of their role in securitization has something to teach us.

The article begins with a brief overview of the US intervention in Somalia, explaining how it constituted an extraordinary measure for the United States at the time and how, in addition, it is atypical of traditional subject matter for securitization theorists. A first reading of the public discourse on Somalia carried in several dozen US newspapers follows. Insights from Kinsella's (2004) genealogy of the social construction of civilianhood provide a useful starting point for a second reading of the newspaper texts. The second reading sketches the role played by constructions of child civilians in the securitization and desecuritization of the Somali war. Concluding comments highlight shortcomings in securitization theory that the analysis reveals.

The Somali civil war

The civil war that erupted in Somalia in 1991 quickly gave rise to a humanitarian disaster on a monumental scale. Exacerbated by drought, famine engulfed large swathes of the country. Internal as well as international displacements of refugees were estimated at two million. 'By 1992, almost 4.5 million people, more than half the total number in the country, were threatened with starvation, severe malnutrition and related diseases', the UN reported (United Nations 1997; see also Schmidt 1992). It was said on Capitol Hill that one-quarter of the population under 5 years of age had perished by mid-year (*Congressional Quarterly Weekly Report* 1992). Intense media coverage and mobilization of global civil society groups such as the International Red Cross and Médecins Sans Frontières were followed by mobilization at the governmental level. With support from over 30 nations, the UN embarked on a humanitarian relief mission (UNOSOM I) succeeded by militarized humanitarian intervention of a decidedly muscular kind (UNITAF, UNOSOM II) intended to create peace and stability and rebuild the Somali state and economy. UNITAF was sanctioned by the UN Security Council under a chapter VII mandate (resolution 794), but the multinational force came under US command as the supplier of 80% of troops, 25,000 in number. UNITAF was charged with the task of facilitating aid delivery using 'all necessary means'.

The humanitarian intervention took on particular significance in US public discourse in part because the country had long been a space in which superpower rivalry had played out. Otherwise, the country was of little strategic importance (*Washington Post* 1992b; Doherty 1992). President Siad Barre had utilized this rivalry to extract aid and thus maintain a 21-year-long period of office in which a large degree of coercion was exercised, garnering a reputation for excessive force for his clan. Their 'terror tactics included the indiscriminate slaughter of civilians, mutilating opponents' faces and burning their genitals with acid', it was reported (Mohamed 1992). On his demise, his followers laid 'a deadly web of more than 100,000 mines' in gardens, refugee camps, and on roadsides (Schanke 1991). His eventual fall from power in the absence of superpower support contributed to political destabilization and the collapse of the Somali state shortly afterward. The power vacuum left behind was colonized by a cohort of 'warlords'. Despite US confidence that the simplicity of Somali materiel and warfighting methods would guarantee their success, Somalia became the setting of an ignominious encounter with a local warlord and his cohort (Perlez 1992b). The loss of life was pivotal to the superpower's effective withdrawal subsequently. Notwithstanding its success in averting continued famine, the failure of the multilateral mission to extract Somalia from the grips of warlordism and conflict undermined the UN's reputation and put into question the feasibility of robust peacekeeping operations (*St. Louis Post-Dispatch* 1992; Doughty 1993). Furthermore, the humiliating defeat of US forces was to have negative repercussions for the likelihood of the superpower participating directly in similar ventures again (*All Things Considered* 1993). The loss of life among Pakistani and US peacekeepers exposed the folly of assumptions prevalent at the time of the pacific nature of the post-Cold War global order (*Washington Post* 1992b; *New York Times* 1992; McGrory 1992).

The US intervention in Somalia constitutes an example of securitization, although an unusual one. For the Copenhagen School, securitization occurs when an issue becomes linked to security and is promoted beyond the realm of normal politics through the 'speech acts' made by significant 'securitizing' actors. In the zone of exceptional politics where the issue is debated, there is a true openness to possibilities, a feature normal politics does not display to the same extent. Securitization theorists are mostly occupied with issues that occur *within or impact on the state*. The referent objects of the security issues they examine involve existential level threats to, for example, the citizenry, military forces, or environment of the state. Militarized humanitarian interventions deviate from this form because the referent object of security is a foreign population beyond the boundaries of the state. Even if existential threat to large numbers of foreigners outside the state can be shown, the issue does not normally give rise to securitization. Existential threat to the state or its constituent parts (citizenry, political structures, way of life, etc.) as a consequence of this must be evident. Although no US strategic interests were threatened by war in Somalia, arguably, President George H.W. Bush's ideas for a 'new world order' and the US place within it were at stake if the country did not act. One could also argue that US self-identity as guardian of the 'new world order' was at risk. Apart from existential threat, there were other respects in which Somalia constituted a securitization for the United States, in the way in which it exceeded normal politics, for example. There was sufficient reluctance in Washington to involvement, which considerable debate between Bush, his National Security Council, the Pentagon, and others was needed to overcome. The death of 241 Marines in Beirut in 1983 and a new military doctrine advocating overwhelming (and therefore expensive) force deployment in such situations were only some of the problems to be resolved if intervention were to go ahead.

Of course, much has been made of the influence of humanitarian organizations and the media on the outcome of that debate, although this remains contested. Reports of overwhelming suffering were said to have helped Bush decide on intervention and were important in drumming up pressure from the American public, from the UN, and abroad. Of all lives to be saved, the United States and its public were entreated to come to the aid of a specific group – children – not simply a monolithic block of civilians. Official and grass roots humanitarian organizations mirrored the media's elevation of children's plight (Labonte 2013, 82). Assistant Administrator for the US Agency for International Development told the House Select Committee on Hunger that 'the real tragedy was that of the starving Somali children' (Lofland 2002, 54). Politicians were alive to the publicity surrounding children's plight and apparently motivated by it. Lawrence Eagleburger, acting US Secretary of State at the time, has said that in addition to substantial pressures from Congress, the US president, George Bush, was driven to act by 'pictures of those starving kids' (Glanville 2005, 4). Assuming that there is at least some truth to this claim, then it is important to understand the prominence of constructions of the suffering of child civilians in the discourse and how these structured the field of meaning. This is the matter to which the article now turns.

US public discourse: a first reading

The American-led intervention guaranteed that the Western media would be particularly heavily involved in covering the crisis and in maintaining Somalia at the top of the media agenda (Gordon 1992; *San Francisco Chronicle* 1992b; Richburg 1992b; Gowing 1994). The result is a large stock of articles in the print news media, numbering several thousand. For the discourse analysis that follows, a random sample of over 400 was scrutinized. From this number, representative quotes were extracted to illustrate patterns of representation. Four sets of securitizing actors figured in this discourse: foreign news journalists who authored it and the humanitarians, politicians, and diplomats (international and domestic) they drew on for information and quotes. As the intention here is to show how child civilians figured in the process of securitization, particular emphasis has been placed on them in this reading.

Kinsella's investigation of the social construction of civilianhood over time stresses gender, innocence, and vulnerability. These will be discussed briefly later. For now it is sufficient to note that the latter two signifiers are strongly associated with children in the Western social imaginary, in addition to age. Children are also linked to particular spaces and activities: home or school, play rather than labor. Oftentimes, they are coupled with the activities of the family unit such as socialization, reproduction, and care, and they are frequently embedded in representations of family structure, as daughters and sons, siblings and grandchildren, etc. Ideologies exist in which children are perceived as inherently good or evil, or as individuals in the process of becoming, that is, developing. In the Western social imaginary, childhood is closely related to nature and to the body. These various aspects of childhood are listed here not to define it but to provide markers that orient a first reading of the news media texts (James, Jenks, and Prout 1998; Jenks 1996; Prout and James 1997). In the following sections, they are highlighted where they have been found to be important signifiers in the discourse as a whole. This first reading of the texts is broken into a number of themes that dominated them. They are vulnerability; women and children; family, culture, and masculinity; trauma; irrationality, backwardness, and passivity; the rescuers and the rescued.

Vulnerability

Although highly impersonalized in form, the use of statistics in the texts conveyed the acute vulnerability of the population as the civil war in Somalia got under way. Much of the early reportage, in particular, focused on the sheer numbers of those suffering war-related injuries, famine, or displacement and the rate at which they were dying, conjuring up a profound sense of urgency. *USA Today*, for example, relayed the UN secretary-general's startling assertion that 100,000 had already died after a year of war, that 2.5 million had been displaced, and a third of the population (1.5–2 million) would 'die within the next six months if emergency food supplies do not reach that country soon' (Schmidt 1992). The overwhelming nature of the problems facing the refugees was apparent in descriptions of, for example, how they 'flooded over the border', creating massive 'tent cities' where they landed and forming throngs at feeding centres (Richburg 1992a).

From the texts, it was clear that the population's vulnerability was thought to stem from sources external to the subject such as the state and armed groups, as well as sources internal to the individual such as human biology. The core functions of the public sphere, like the monopoly on the use of force, were lost as the state collapsed. A multiplicity of state institutions crumbled. The 'national currency [had] become worthless and only food [had] any monetary value', Miller (1992) stated. Similar observations were made by others: 'There is no government. No civil service. No commerce. No food' (Power 1992). Social provision, such as medical care, was negligible in its Western sense. In the absence of the rule of law, guns became the chief form of authority, according to Hill (1992). The greatest peril appeared to come from the warring factions themselves. The brutality of clan warlords and their gangs of supporters prompted Africa Watch to remark that Mogadishu had become 'a special place in the annals of human cruelty' (Lyman 1992).

The physical conditions imposed on populations by the war were further external determinants of vulnerability, exacerbating the everyday challenges of survival in what was presented as an unforgiving climate. Somalia was said to be 'one of the unhealthiest places on Earth, where a scratch can become a festering wound in days' (Sammakia 1993). There was little respite offered by a healthcare system crippled by war. One account of the squalid conditions of one Somali hospital described 'the stench of human decay' that greeted the reporter's arrival (Lyman 1992; O'Mara 1992).

Women and children

The conditions took their toll on women and children more than men, according to most depictions. The shelter that starving women could find in the 'punishing heat' might be no more than makeshift huts made from branches and cardboard (Perlez 1991; Hill 1992). Women's isolation from men worsened their predicament. 'The women were the ones who were suffering', the *Dallas Morning News* insisted, 'The men were off fighting, so only the women were occupied with taking care of the children, the old people, even the injured men' (Samuels 1992). But women were also victims of a patriarchal culture in which stoning of women prostitutes still occurred, a punishment the journalist found 'incongruous for the end of the 20th century' (Samuels 1992). The physical dimensions to their vulnerability were frequently rehearsed. The story of several women who were injured on barbed wire barricades while food rioting erupted offers a prime example (LaBelle 1993).

Young children fared little better by Somali culture. Girls were denied education in the Koranic system of schooling, for example (Timms 1994). Many starving children were reduced to sucking on bones, not for nourishment but for the comfort derived from mimicking eating, a UN worker explained (Campagne 1992). During war, it was clear that children were worst affected. Time and again, newspapers reminded readers of their predicament and linked it to warlord and clan behavior. 'I hate them', one child answered when asked about local combatants, their clan violence being the chief obstacle to his development for the press (Campagne 1992). A quarter of all under-fives had perished before US humanitarian intervention had begun and 200 or more children were dying daily in the capital (*Seattle Times* 1992). Some were even killed by soldiers for bags of grain (*San Francisco Chronicle* 1992a). The state of the war-torn country was closely linked to the plight of its children. A French minister, describing his impressions on a visit there, was reported to say, 'I found death, the death of a country and above all of children lying in the streets' (*San Francisco Chronicle* 1992b).

There was no segment of society more symbolic of vulnerability than the orphan population. Physical weakness due to youth and hunger and a lack of protection by family, clan, or the public sphere rendered them the supreme victims of war.

Robbed of their fathers by war and their mothers by famine and disease, thousands of Somali children have been left orphaned, struggling to survive on their own in the chaos of a country in which their villages have been destroyed, their extended families have disappeared and no government structure exists to care for them. (Moore 1993)

Constructed as targets of attack on account of the food they received from international agencies, many orphans were relocated to a leper colony that warlords were too fearful to approach (Pleming 1993). For reporters, the story illustrated the degeneration of the social order in Somalia such that its weakest members could be the targets of violence. Further discussion about Somalis' resistance to the adoption of orphans by foreigners confirmed the suspicion that Somali society did not hold the best interests of children at heart: 'when outsiders have offered to adopt orphans and provide homes for them in the United States or Europe, Muslim tradition and Somali culture have combined to block their efforts' (Moore 1993).

Family, culture, and masculinity

The family and clan was considered the primary vector of a pastoral tradition in Somalia and the 'bedrock of identity'. Yet, they also promoted the 'continual atomization of the society' and a failure to recognize the public good (*St. Petersburg Times* 1992a). A blindness to the public good allowed Somali clans and sub-clans to continue to fight unmoved by the dire need in their midst and intent to actively add to the tragedy, it was argued, by attacking aid shipments for example (Lyman 1992). The clan thus promoted values antithetical to community spirit or peace. It entrenched an aggressive militarism in an individualistic people, Perlez (1991) maintained. Even in high political office, the same sentiments had traction. Former US ambassador to Kenya, Smith Hempstone, described Somalis in a cable to the president as 'natural-born guerrillas… treacherous. The Somali is a killer. The Somali is as tough as his country, and just as unforgiving' (Scarborough 1993).

In the media narrative of the conflict, it was Somali men and adolescent boys who manifested this aggressive national character. In the capital, there were said to be 'thousands of armed, hungry and ill-disciplined men roaming the streets' (Shields 1992). Their lack of self-control was often exacerbated by drugs. Their aggression was untrammeled and 'untrained, frenzied young men' created such anarchy that one reporter dubbed the conflict a 'Western' (Perlez 1992a; Hill 1992). There was such a ready availability of small arms that a US aid official alleged that a 'very high percentage of males above puberty are carrying automatic weapons'. The levels of violence young Somali males dished out were of great concern as was the psychological toll this took on the perpetrators themselves in addition to their victims. It seemed from accounts that thousands of children used as soldiers in the war had lost their moral code. Trauma was the legacy of war for these boys, some as young as 10 or 12 who thereafter were 'haunted by dreams of death' (Ewing 1993).

Trauma

The media rendered the population deeply and in some cases irrevocably affected by exposure to war and famine. 'People were being killed in front of us… Women were being raped in front of us', one Somali recalled (*St. Petersburg Times* 1992a). Large numbers of the population had watched as their family members, sometimes all of them, died from famine (Richburg 1992a). Such stories cast into doubt the prospect of Somalia's recovery. 'The survivors of great famines are broken for all their lives', the *Seattle Times* claimed, 'their children inherit the frailty of their parents. They are a weight that retards the recovery of the people as a whole' (O'Mara 1992).

The psychological damage done during the war was used by some to account for the behavior of some women and children during and after the infamous 'Battle of Mogadishu' in which several US peacekeepers died. The women and children had joined the gunmen in scuppering a US operation and had participated in the public desecration of the bodies of the peacekeepers and a translator who died during the ensuring combat (*Virginian-Pilot* 1993). The revulsion felt by the American public was clearly reflected in newspapers' language. The more restrained of them described the women and children as 'jubilant' as they flaunted a dead man's teeth in their hands to foreign journalists (Continelli 1994). To make sense of these acts as the public uproar in the US grew, *USA Today* consulted a political psychologist who explained the events as the result of the regular 'demonization and dehumanization of the enemy' in war. Another accounted for the triumphalist display as retribution from a nation who had seen many of their own killed by US weapons (Meddis and Greene 1993). The implication of the texts was clear: Somalia's civilians had been corrupted by their experiences of war and now constituted a threat to US peacekeepers.

Irrationality, backwardness, and passivity

Somalis were regularly depicted as uneducated, backward, and child-like. 'Too many youths [...] can shoot a gun but don't know how to read', a UNICEF worker lamented (Timms 1994). The violence they engaged in was described as feuding, and their warfare and materiel as outdated (Perlez 1992b). World politics was thought to lie beyond their grasp (Thompson 1993; Hill 1992; Cappelli 1992; Peterson 1993). They were frequently pictured high on khat that even adolescent boys chewed (Lyman 1992; *Plain Dealer* 1993; Samuels 1992). Somali behavior was regularly constructed as irrational and self-defeating (Shields 1992). They were, in the words of one commentator, 'incapable of giving themselves stable and competent government, even when left alone to try' (Pfaff 1993). Their response to the humanitarianism shown toward them was baffling. '[I]t must be asked', one Canadian journalist mused, 'why people who have been saved from starvation should now be consumed by such savage hatred of their erstwhile benefactors' (Watson 1993).

However, it was the bodies of the starving that did most to convey irrationality. The majority of Somali civilians were represented as little more than frail bodies, as surfaces on which the narratives of death and suffering could be written. A typical account would highlight the state of emaciation of limbs, the slowness of movement, and the dullness of the responses of the starving (Richburg 1992a). Almost invariably, the agency of starving civilians was omitted from the texts and indeed seemed almost impossible given their physical state. The picture drawn of a 4 year old in soiled clothing, 'blink[ing] dully, giving scant attention to the sore on his arms' while an IRC nurse described his imminent death is one such passivating account (Shields 1992). Readers were not spared descriptions of emaciation and the blood, urine, pus, and diarrhea that accompanied many Somalis' last moments. One American nurse compared the scene of starvation to 'a horror movie in which skeletons emerge from their graves to terrorize the living' (Salome 1992).

The rescuers and the rescued

Media accounts regularly depicted the endeavors of the peacekeepers and humanitarian aid workers. They focused on the enormity of the task they faced and the expertise and capabilities they employed in battling it. The American media placed great value on the contribution of US forces, in particular. For instance, one newspaper reported that 11 US planes could transport twice as much food into Somalia as the combined relief agencies had managed in 8 months (Adelman 1992). With UNITAF, the United States could protect relief convoys and ensure aid reached those who needed it rather than the strongest clans (*San Francisco Chronicle* 1992b). It could dispense with the hiring of local gunmen to guard aid (*Economist* 1992; *Washington Post* 1992a). Its military (being the major contributor of forces) could use its strength to put an end to the starving of over a million people and facilitate recovery. It could act, in effect, like a 'cavalry' (*New York Times* 1992). The much-needed care international teams could give could begin with the security that US peacekeepers brought to the country. Accordingly, '[a]id workers could do their job again and they slowly nursed Somalia back from its deathbed' (Sammakia 1993).

With the success of the mission in its early months, there was reason for Americans to express pride. '[The peacekeepers] were acting in the best spirit of America', President Clinton commented (Schafer 1993). The generosity of the American public was a source of satisfaction: 'The idea that kids are dying because no one can spare a handful of grain is not acceptable to most Americans' (Lacknit 1992). The United States had been able to wield its power to good ends. Aid workers faced daunting challenges. 'We're now feeding two or three times the number of children that our feeding centres were designed for', an SCF field director explained. In another report, an American was described running a hospital of 20 beds as the sole hospital service for two million people (Salome 1992). The physical danger the aid staff worked under was considerable, and mortal at times.

There was also a psychological risk attached to the humanitarian mission. Aid workers recalled the scenes of death they had encountered that continued to haunt them (Brink 1992). The psychological ill effects of exposure to war and famine were even felt by US troops. They too were distressed by the sight of rape and of children starving and were 'confused' by Somalis who were hostile to them, throwing stones, spitting, or even shooting at them (Erfrain 1993). This had been expected, however: 'Officials here say that they are more concerned about the psychological impact of human suffering on their soldiers than they are about the threats of Somali street gangs or illness' (Offley 1992).

The Somali crisis provoked a profound emotional response from the family members of aid workers and peacekeepers 'back home'. Families of US peacekeepers were interviewed in the wake of the Battle of Mogadishu and told journalists of their worry and sleeplessness in the days preceding it as the situation in Somalia steadily worsened. Upon witnessing the 'televised horror' of the battle itself, a soldier's mother recalled, 'I went to pieces... Devastated, I wanted to die myself' (Coakley 1993). Revulsion was reflected across the spectrum of newspapers in the aftermath of the battle. A journalist opined, 'The blood of our courageous troops is too precious to spill into this quagmire' (*Salt Lake Tribune* 1993). The conviction was even more visible in the US press coverage that followed the battle. 'Our brave troops' blood means too much to all of us to squander on a war that rightly isn't ours to wage. Let's bring them home' (*Colorado Springs Gazette Telegraph* 1993). A sense of US community was invoked by the battle as it had been by the intervention's instigation.

Child civilians: a second reading

From the sketch of the discourse presented above, three types of subject emerge: civilians, combatants, and humanitarians (peacekeepers and aid workers). As this article claims that the construction of child civilians helped to shape securitization, it is appropriate to turn now to the concept of civilianhood. Legally, civilianhood equates *prima facie* with non-combatant status and invokes the principle of non-combatant immunity (Primoratz 2007). However, Kinsella's genealogy posits a range of powerful social meanings to the term that may be separated here from its weighty legal connotations for the purposes of this analysis. According to Kinsella, the concept of the civilian is related to, *inter alia,* age, corporeality, and family, but gender above all. Kinsella's reading argues that putatively 'natural' female characteristics have long been the basis for distinguishing the category of civilian from combatant. Innocence and a need for protection are especially critical to civilianhood. Indeed, one could say that these two 'feminine' characteristics are the sources of value for civilianhood, the referent objects of security. Historically, effort has been invested in reforming women into individuals with fittingly feminine subjectivities when they have conducted themselves in ways that apparently flout their gender (Elshtain 1998). In contrast, women civilians who performed the roles of men lost their civilian status and were effectively treated as men (Kinsella 2004, 10). In short, the maintenance of the boundaries to conceptualizations of women and civilians required the disciplining of deviant individuals by rehabilitation or reclassification to retain their gendered logic.

For Kinsella, the primary distinction between the civilian and combatant is gender, all other meanings of civilianhood are epiphenomenal. A corollary of the centrality she awards to gender is that other categories of civilians – children, the elderly, the sick, and other non-combatants – must also display typically gendered attributes to qualify as civilians. It is argued here that gender does not exhaust the meaning of civilian. Gender may provide the main logic as the dominant signifier; nonetheless, other key signifiers and articulations in the discourse are noteworthy and crucial to the discourse under scrutiny here. Children, the elderly, and the sick may arrive at innocence and the need for protection through representations and logics that are different from those of gender. The remainder of this section is a reinterpretation of the discourse summarized above. In this re-reading, particular attention is given to the differences in how children's civilian-hood and others' are constructed, especially women as they make up the second most dominant civilian category in the discourse.

In presenting the enormity of the plight Somali civilians faced, journalists liberally employed mortality statistics, death and starvation rates but applied these to only three groups: Somali civilians in general, children, and the under-fives. No statistics were given for women as a separate category, but there was no lack of figures for children. We learned that measles was the primary killer of all under-fives, for example, and that a quarter of all under-fives had died by mid-1992 (Sammakia 1993; *Congressional Quarterly Weekly Report* 1992). In addition to the accenting of age by the use of these categories, children's physical state of weakness induced by war, starvation, or disease was also continuously foregrounded. It appeared from the discourse that children were inherently more physically vulnerable than women. 'Feeble Somalis, many of them children, are expiring as they stand in line for food. Many end up in the makeshift graveyards that now adjoin food kitchens', the *Buffalo News* (1992) bemoaned.

Children's physical vulnerabilities were different too. Women were susceptible to rape by warring parties, but child abuse, where it happened, was never mentioned. Both women and children could be attacked for food, although attacks on children received more attention. The *San Francisco Chronicle* reported that several children were killed in Mogadishu for the grain they had (*San Francisco Chronicle* 1992a). In contrast to children, women were more frequently portrayed as survivors. Consequently, their vulnerability had emotional connotations that children's lacked; they were more often seen grieving for lost family members, for example. Despite the greater emotional distress imputed to women, the psychological impact of the war and famine was more strongly associated with children, and with teenage boys in particular, many of whom were portrayed as perpetrators of violence.

Women's vulnerability in the texts was more elaborated in the sense that it took on a greater variety of forms. Yet it was children's vulnerability to which journalists dedicated more column inches. Moreover, women's vulnerability was more tightly linked to circumstance than children's: for example, women faced the problems of providing food, shelter, and care for their families and had to endure the constraints of a patriarchal culture. As a result, the prevailing social order appeared to be more at risk by women's reduced ability to fulfill their traditional roles. Children's roles were also altered and the social order affected by the lack of education provision for them (although this was poor to begin with) and by the arming of hundreds of adolescents. Yet the ramifications of this were to be felt directly by a small portion of the child population. Furthermore, the meaning awarded this in the texts was expressed as anxiety about the future shape of Somali society. So, while both women and children were constructed as the victims of circumstance (culture, war, famine, attack) and of biology (physical weakness, susceptibility to rape), children's general vulnerability was more rooted in biology and remote from the ongoing crisis than women's.

In the Western social imaginary, children are commonly understood to be in a process of development that adults have completed. This development is a natural unfolding and can be thwarted by negative socializing forces such as exposure to violence. As mentioned above, there was concern expressed in the texts that hundreds of older boys in Mogadishu were involved in conflict and perpetrated crime. '[T]eenage males idled by peace still drive around in heavily armed "technicals"', Samuels (1992) complained. Warlords would feed khat to their 'young gunslingers to keep nerves on alert even if bellies were empty', newspapers maintained (Plain Dealer 1993; Samuels 1992). The absence of reputable sources of socialization over children, such as education rather than warlords, generated further anxiety among commentators. It appeared that the future social order depended on the full development of its young generation's potential, including psychological development, and this was impeded by the crisis.

Yet, there was the possibility of change if Somalis embraced it, but the newspapers were pessimistic about the prospects. For Western onlookers, Somalis' resistance to the healthcare humanitarian agencies provided showed woeful ignorance. Likewise, there was an ignorance of the benefits to be gained from counseling for those traumatized by war, especially children, a situation one Save the Children worker thought 'almost Dickensian' (Ewing 1993). Somali resistance to the adoption of orphans by foreigners was a further example of backwardness that served to punish children and jeopardize their futures (Moore 1993). Hence, many children were vulnerable to corrupting influences and could not avail of reform measures. Yet, children were constructed as intrinsically good in the Western social imaginary and this precluded most errant Somali children from bearing any blame. Only rarely were they held culpable for their misdemeanors by the press.

The construction of civilians as innocent and vulnerable demanded that most occasions of deviance be silenced. Thus, without any sense of contradiction, violent adolescent boys were regrouped with men while younger or non-combatant boys remained associated with women and other children. 'The [Somali] state is dead and its successors are children with AK rifles, holding women and children to ransom' (*Straits Times* 1992). The reworked boundary was unremarkable because violence was still an activity wedded to masculinity and, consequently, those boys who perpetrated it achieved adultness as a result. The shifts of the boundary operated to preserve the general validity of the civilian–combatant distinction and its gender and age-related meanings.

An important technique used in preserving the civilian–combatant boundary was the construction of a Somali hyper-masculinity. This served as a foil against which Somali women's innocence and vulnerability appeared more amplified. The aggression and militarism of Somali men was directed not only toward other Somali men in rival clans but toward Somali women. Somali masculinity was predatory and acted to deepen the victimhood attached to Somali women and the divide between combatants and civilians. The portrayal of Somali civilians as recipients of protection was an equally significant technique in boundary maintenance. The texts paid attention to the protection offered by humanitarians – peacekeepers creating a safe environment for the delivery of aid and aid workers distributing it and for medical care to civilians. The dichotomy between the active rescuers and the vulnerable, passive rescued was illustrated repeatedly with this trope.

The combatant–civilian boundary broke down subsequent to the Battle of Mogadishu in three ways. Firstly, large numbers of civilians were constructed as a threat to peacekeepers rather than under their protection. Secondly, women and children were described as party to the violence meted out to peacekeepers and the desecration of their bodies. Thirdly, the celebrations of civilians at the defeat and death of peacekeepers tarred all civilians with the aggressiveness usually attributed only to men and older boys. Effectively, their complicity with men and adolescent boys eradicated the usual stark contrast between civilians and combatants. The end result was a set of constructions in the media inconsistent with understandings of civilianhood. The withdrawal of US peacekeepers and the protection they offered followed.

In summary, the term civilian has a number of meanings in the social imaginary, the most important of which are innocence and vulnerability, which bring with them the need for protection. Gender and age are also crucially important meanings. In the discourse on Somalia, the manner in which women and children were constructed as innocent and vulnerable varied. Whereas women's vulnerability was more circumstantial, children's derived more from biology and a need for an uncorrupted physical and psychological development path. Despite the violent acts committed by many children, their inherent goodness exonerated them from culpability and their innocence remained intact. Where this stretched innocence excessively, they were awarded combatant status and adulthood by association with men. Thus, of the two civilian categories garnering greatest coverage in the media, the construction of the child civilian was more profound, more robust, and flexible. It was anchored in supposedly immutable facts of nature. It was perhaps for this reason that children achieved greatest visibility in the texts because they demonstrated civilian need more deeply and reliably than women. Gender was insufficient by itself to maintain the difference of women civilians from male combatants; innocence had to be shown and not assumed as it could be for children. Consequently, women's civilian status was more contingent than children's.

Securitization and the Somali child civilian

Several moves are discernable in the securitization of the crisis in Somali. They are listed here without any intention of implying a sequence. The first was the demonstration of urgent overwhelming need that could not be met by alternative means, by the work of charitable agencies or UN peacekeepers on the ground, for example. Secondly, the intervention provided the United States with an opportunity to gain soft power and demonstrate its position in and hopes for a new world order. Thus, intervention was revealed, over time, to be in the best interests of the United States. Thirdly, the intervention was considered to be feasible as warfighting and materiel in Somalia were rudimentary and the risk manageable. Fourthly, the risk to US peacekeepers was outweighed by the obvious humanitarian need of foreign civilians. Fifthly, need translated into the need for protection rather than merely relief supplies or expertise for large parts of the population. Sixthly, that population qualified as civilians in the American social imaginary because they were both vulnerable and innocent. Lastly, vulnerability was undeniable because it was chiefly anchored in children's nature. It was also related – although less powerfully – to the circumstances of women and the ramifications of their failure to uphold the social order. Innocence stemmed largely from children's natural goodness. The logic running through these securitizing moves was reversed by the demonstration of unacceptable risk to US peacekeepers. That this partly came from civilians themselves diminished the validity of constructions of innocence and showed Somali civilians' complicity with their own plight.

Conclusions

This study utilized securitization theory in its attempts to position children more firmly within the realm of security studies. It showed that the successful securitization of the intervention in Somalia relied on the construction of the Somali population as deserving of protection. Children played a fundamental role in this and acted as an important vector in the ascent of Somalia up the US political agenda.

However, securitization theory has its weaknesses and has been subject to extensive critique. Rather than rehearse that critique here, suffice to point to certain strategies adopted in this article to avoid pitfalls the literature has identified. Perhaps the most notable is the charge that political elites' actions are overemphasized in securitization theory to the detriment of others' (Pram Gad and Lund Petersen 2011) and that too much weight is placed on a small number of speech acts at specific moments in time (McDonald 2008, 576; Stritzel 2011, 349–350). Here, a wider range of actors was considered to play a role in securitization. As the debate on Somalia is often taken as the prime example of the influence of the media, it would have been unwise to exclude this set of actors nor their informants. An attempt to paint in the backdrop to the Somali crisis was made and to broaden the number of speech acts that impacted securitization and the period over which they occurred (Abrahamsen 2005). The intertextuality of the speech act was conveyed in this study by attending to the meaning of children in the Western social imaginary and most obviously by the focus placed on the social meaning of civilianhood there (Salter 2008). The author does not suggest that a discourse analysis sidestepped all problems: it omitted the role of an audience, for example, and had to assume that representational practices that were dominant across the US news media discourse reflected the US social imaginary in general (Balzacq 2005). In this way, dominant representational practices operated as a kind of proxy for the audience, although this was not ideal.

However, the chief problem securitization theory presented this analysis was its indifference to how the value of the referent object of security is created in favor of a discussion of threat (McDonald 2008, 578). To have neglected value creation here would have been to entirely overlook the value of children to the discourse and therefore to have passed over the grammar of securitization in the Somali case. Illustrating the existence of existential threat to a referent object was important but insufficient by itself. Threat and vulnerability are two sides of the same coin, and there was utility in unpacking each separately for the Somali case. How children were vulnerable and how, by virtue of their innocence, they were deserving of protection were points of enormous significance in the public discourse that helped bring about securitization.

The Somali case is an example of militarized humanitarian intervention and is not the usual material for securitization scholarship. For countries with a history of peacekeeping, the procedures for involvement in interventions may be normalized and securitization theory may offer few insights as a result. However, for especially dangerous or contentious interventions or those for which the responsibility to protect may be invoked, securitization theory may bring benefits. As long as children's profile in humanitarian emergencies remains high, there is purpose served in scrutinizing their involvement.

References

Abrahamsen, R. 2005. "Blair's Africa: The Politics of Securitization and Fear." *Alternatives* 30 (1): 55–80. doi:10.1177/030437540503000103.

Adelman, K. 1992. "Beacon in the Dark: The Military is There in Times of Disaster." *Tulsa World*, August 29.

All Things Considered. 1993. "US Re-Evaluates its Role in Somalia (Radio Broadcast)." *All Things Considered*, October 6.

Balzacq, T. 2005. "The Three Faces of Securitization: Political Agency, Audience and Context." *European Journal of International Relations* 11 (2): 171–201. doi:10.1177/1354066105052960.

Brink, B. 1992. "The Face of Famine." *Oregonian*, November 30.

Buffalo News. 1992. "World Must Move Quickly to Stop Tragedy in Somalia." *Buffalo News*, August 7.

Burman, E. 1994. "Innocents Abroad: Western Fantasies of Childhood and the Iconography of Emergencies." *Disasters* 18 (3): 238–253. doi:10.1111/j.1467-7717.1994.tb00310.x.

Campagne, J.-P. 1992. "Food Aid Reaches Remote Areas." *Agence France-Presse*, August 27.

Cappelli, V. 1992. "Who Will Help Somalia?" *Christian Science Monitor*, May 1.

Coakley, T. 1993. "Mothers Fear for Sons in War Zone." *Boston Globe*, October 6.

Colorado Springs Gazette Telegraph. 1993. "Pull Troops Out of Somalia Now." *Colorado Springs Gazette Telegraph*, October 5.

Congressional Quarterly Weekly Report. 1992. "Senate Urges UN Force be Deployed in Somalia." *Congressional Quarterly Weekly Report*, August 8.

Continelli, L. 1994. "A Photographer's Album of Horror from Somalia." *Buffalo News*, June 29.

Doherty, C. J. 1992. "African Nations Lose Their Appeal for US Aid as Cold War Thaws." *Congressional Quarterly Weekly Report*, May 16.

Doughty, N. 1993. "World Community May Act Less after Bosnia, Somalia." *Reuters News*, July 14.

Economist. 1992. "Civil War Means Relief Agencies Need Armed Help." *Economist*, May 9.

Elshtain, J. B. 1998. "*Women and War*: Ten Years On." *Review of International Studies* 24 (4): 447–460. doi:10.1017/S0260210598004471.

Erfrain, H. Jr. 1993. "Only Local Heroes: Somalia Vets' Praises are Sung in a Low Key." *Boston Globe*, March 15.

Ewing, J. 1993. "Somalia's Young Suffer Combat Fatigue." *Reuters News*, May 30.

Glanville, L. 2005. "Somalia Reconsidered: An Examination of the Norm of Humanitarian Intervention." *International Affairs* 77 (1): 113–128.

Gordon, M. R. 1992. "TV Army on the Beach Took US by Surprise." *New York Times*, December 10.

Gowing, N. 1994. "What Really Shapes Policy? TV Goads, but Doesn't Guide, Crisis Response." *Wall Street Journal Europe*, July 5.

Hill, A. 1992. "Marriage of Convenience Brings Somalia Food." *Reuters News*, May 7.

James, A., C. Jenks, and A. Prout. 1998. *Theorizing Childhood*. London: Polity Press.

Jenks, C. 1996. *Childhood*. London: Routledge.

Kinsella, H. M. 2004. "Securing the Civilian: Sex and Gender in the Laws of War." Boston Consortium on Gender, Security and Human Rights. Working Paper No. 201.

LaBelle, G. G. 1993. "US Troops Kill Two Militiamen: Sporadic Fighting Overnight." *Associated Press*, September 20.

Labonte, M. 2013. *Human Rights and Humanitarian Norms, Strategic Framing and Intervention: Lessons for the Responsibility to Protect*. Oxford: Routledge.

Lacknit, C. 1992. "Compassion to Drive Giving despite Recession, Charities Say." *Orange County Register*, August 27.

Lofland, V. J. 2002. "Somalia: US intervention and Operation Restore Hope." In *Case Studies in Policy Making and Implementation*, edited by D. A. Williams, 53–64. Newport: Naval War College.

Lyman, R. 1992. "Somalians Struggle to Survive amid Chaos of Civil War." *Austin American-Statesman*, May 14.

McDonald, M. 2008. "Securitization and the Construction of Security." *European Journal of International Relations* 14 (4): 563–587. doi:10.1177/1354066108097553.

McGrory, B. 1992. "In a Reversal, Liberals Back Bush's Decision on Somalia." *Boston Globe*, December 4.

Meddis, S. V., and M. Greene. 1993. "Flaunting War's Fallen: History Shows Not Exclusive to Somalia." *USA Today*, October 6.

Miller, G. 1992. "Violence, Traditions Delay Food Aid to Starving Somalia." *Associated Press*, May 5.

Mohamed, A. 1992. "Somalia: The Political Geography of Starvation." *Atlanta Journal and Constitution*, August 27.

Moore, M. 1993. "Small Victims, Big Struggle: Orphanage Helps Rescue Somalia's Abandoned Children." *Houston Chronicle*, March 14.

New York Times. 1992. "A Foreign Legion for the World." *New York Times*, September 1.

Offley, E. 1992. "Medic Unit Braces for Somalia Desperation." *Seattle Post-Intelligencer*, December 10.

O'Mara, R. 1992. "As the West Shrugs, Heroes Toil in Somalia." *Seattle Times*, August 26.

Perlez, J. 1991. "Somalia Self Destructs and the World Looks On." *New York Times*, December 29.

Perlez, J. 1992a. "Amid Somalia's Frenzy, Family Fights to Survive." *New York Times*, August 26.

Perlez, J. 1992b. "Barrier to Somali Unity: Clan Rivalry." *New York Times*, August 30.

Peterson, S. 1993. "The Anger of Somali Families." *Christian Science Monitor*, October 6.

Pfaff, W. 1993. "UN Could Provide Much Needed Neo-Colonialism in Somalia." *Patriot-News*, June 17.

Plain Dealer. 1993. "Somalis Still Savor Khat: Folks Relish Plant amid War, Famine." *Plain Dealer*, November 29.

Pleming, S. 1993. "Lepers, Orphans Pitched Together in Somali Strife." *Reuters News*, March 21.

Power, J. 1992. "Somalia's Chaos Begs for International Force." *Oregonian*, August 9.

Pram Gad, U., and K. Lund Petersen. 2011. "Concepts of Politics in Securitization Studies." *Security Dialogue* 42 (4–5): 315–328. doi:10.1177/0967010611418716.

Primoratz, I. 2007. "Civilian Immunity in War: Its Grounds, Scope, and Weight." In *Civilian Immunity in War*, edited by I. Primoratz, 21–41. Oxford: Oxford University Press.

Prout, A., and A. James. 1997. "Introduction." In *Constructing and Reconstructing Childhood: Contemporary Issues in the Sociological Study of Childhood*, 2nd ed., edited by A. James, and A. Prout, 106. London: Routledge-Falmer.

Richburg, K. B. 1992a. "Famine, Disease Place Somalis in Death Grip." *Washington Post*, August 11.

Richburg, K. B. 1992b. "Liberians Ask Why US Avoided Their War." *Washington Post*, December 4.

Salome, L. J. 1992. "Civil War, Starvation Transforming Somalia into the 'Land of the Dead'." *Austin American-Statesman*, August 10.

Salt Lake Tribune. 1993. "A War Unworthy of US Troop Involvement." *Salt Lake Tribune*, September 30.

Salter, M. B. 2008. "Securitization and Desecuritization: A Dramaturgical Analysis of the Canadian Air Transport Security Authority." *Journal of International Relations and Development* 11 (4): 321–349. doi:10.1057/jird.2008.20.

Sammakia, N. 1993. "Famine Ebbs but Chaos Thrives in Somalia." *Rocky Mountain News*, December 8.

Samuels, L. 1992. "Fighting Back Somali Civil War Stirs Effort by Some Women to End Mistreatment, Gain More Political Say." *Dallas Morning News*, March 8.

San Francisco Chronicle. 1992a. "Starvation Perils Somalia." *San Francisco Chronicle*, August 7.

San Francisco Chronicle. 1992b. "UN Team Arrives in Somalia to Plan Major Relief Effort." *San Francisco Chronicle*, August 7.

Scarborough, R. 1993. "Mission of Mercy Starts to Remind Many of Vietnam." *Washington Times*, October 6.

Schafer, S. M. 1993. "US Deaths Rise in Somalia: More Troops to Go." *Associated Press*, October 4.

Schanke, D. 1991. "Mines: A Misstep Could Mean Death or Maiming." *Associated Press*, December 2.

Schmidt, E. 1992. "Somalia is Not Alone in Fighting Famine." *USA Today*, August 31.

Seattle Times. 1992. "'We Must Give Them Hope' – Bush Orders Troops to African Nation in UN-Approved Relief Plan." *Times News Service*, December 4.

Shields, T. 1992. "War Chaos Stifling Somalian Relief." *Times Picayune*, May 10.

St. Louis Post-Dispatch. 1992. "Miscues Worsen Somalia's Plight." *St. Louis Post-Dispatch*, August 28.

St. Petersburg Times. 1992a. "Somalia Situation Critical." *St. Petersburg Times*, August 29.

St. Petersburg Times. 1992b. "Warring Factions at Root of Somali Crisis." *St. Petersburg Times*, December 4.

Straits Times. 1992. "Somalia and Yugoslavia Test Limits of UN Intervention." *Straits Times*, November 30.

Stritzel, H. 2011. "Security, the Translation." *Security Dialogue*, 42 (4–5), 343–355. doi:10.1177/0967010611418998.

Thompson, B. 1993. "Woman Helps Schools Start up Again in Somalia." *Times Picayune*, September 23.

Timms, E. 1994. "Koranic Schools Play Key Role in Somalia: They're Helping Restore Education System." *Dallas Morning News*, June 11.

United Nations. 1997. "United Nations Operation in Somalia I." Department of Peacekeeping. Accessed January 18, 2014. www.un.org/Depts/DPKO/Missions/unosomi.htm.

Virginian-Pilot. 1993. "Stuck (For Now) in the Somalia Quagmire: A Fool's Errand?" *Virginian-Pilot*, September 16

Washington Post. 1992a. "Horn of Misery." *Washington Post*, May 2.

Washington Post. 1992b. "New World Disorder." *Washington Post*, April 23.

Watson, P. 1993. "Dozens Killed in Somalia Bloodbath." *Toronto Star*, October 4.

Telling geopolitical tales: temporality, rationality, and the 'childish' in the ongoing war for the Falklands-Malvinas Islands

Victoria M. Basham

Department of Politics, University of Exeter, Exeter, UK

Anniversaries of war often present opportunities for the telling and retelling of tales about the geopolitical; tales of a nation's sovereignty, its identity, its security, and how these are imagined and reimagined through the notion of specific conflicts, their histories, beginnings, ends, and aftermaths. By examining the case of the ongoing 'war' over the Falklands-Malvinas and a particular set of stories where the 'childish' has come to characterize relations and differences between Britain and Argentina, this article explores how the temporality of 'the anniversary' can enable certain claims, about the rationality of war, as a means of safeguarding sovereignty, identity, and security, to become commonsensical. The article argues that more attention should be paid to geopolitical tales of supposedly 'adult' and 'childish' characters because these constructions have the potential to normalize violence as a commonsensical act of strong, adult nations; as an integral part of their national stories that obscures the aggressive role of the state in normalizing and perpetuating violence.

Introduction: telling geopolitical tales

Anniversaries, particularly those marking the outbreak or cessation of wars, present significant opportunities for the telling of geopolitical tales and the reproduction of geopolitical 'truths'. As markers of an 'event' in which questions and performances of sovereignty, territory, security, and national identity invariably coalesce, anniversaries of war are never just recurrent dates in the calendar where 'the past' is consciously brought into the present; they are always productive of political and social relations. As a calendric feature, all anniversaries 'arise from, and are perpetuated by, social require-ments'; their meaning and marking relies on common, social, and mutually held under-standings of time and its significance to the collective (Sorokin and Merton 1937, 626). As examples of what Sorokin and Merton (1937) call 'social time', war anniversaries can provide 'opportunities for remembrance and recreation that cut across and reinvent time' (Hutchings 2007, 72), while simultaneously producing temporal boundaries and distinc-tions about the nature of the past, present, and future (Lundborg 2012). Anniversaries of war often nurture attempts to 'fix' the meaning of the practices of violence conjured into memory, practices that, though neither temporally nor spatially stable, often constitute the shifting foundations on which claims about national boundaries, roles, and identities are frequently built (Edkins 2003; Till 2003). Anniversaries of war may also foster stories that justify and legitimate the death and violence the events they mark entailed (Dodds 2012) and, more often than not, they are characterized by political discourses that seek to affirm an imagined past or pasts regarded as 'useful for justifying present interests' (Staudinger in Wodak et al. 2009, 70).

In light of the productive and social characteristics of anniversaries, and given that people frequently attach a distinctive significance to any calendric date 'that is in any way outstanding' (Forrest 1993, 445), it is perhaps unsurprising that recent anniversaries of the 1982 Falklands-Malvinas War have marked renewed and reinvigorated rounds of (ongoing) tale-telling by British, Argentinian, and Islander representatives, officials, politicians, media, and publics alike. The discursive reproduction of the War and the contested sovereignty of the Falklands-Malvinas Islands began long ago, is likely to ensue for much time to come, and takes many forms, from the cultural and social to the legal and economic. However, there is one particular configuration of political discourses that has resurfaced in recent years that can reveal much about how ideas of national identity, sovereignty, and security coalesce to animate certain forms of geopolitical practice over others. The discursive tropes that concern me herein are those that draw on the notion of the 'childish'. From claims that Argentina acts like a playground bully to the notion that the United Kingdom cannot accept basic facts that would be apparent to small children, ideas and beliefs about what comes to be understood as 'childish' permeate the politics of the Falkland-Malvinas.

What we come to recognize as childhood (the spatial and temporal limits of what precedes adulthood) and the child or children (the personhood prior to adulthood) is configured and reconfigured within different social spaces and temporalities; childhood and 'the child' is the outcome of social transformations and continuities, not a natural state of being (Ariès 1962; Holmer Nadesan 2010). Indeed, our understandings of childhood are often not much at all about the lived experiences of the young, but about our collective beliefs about what children are, can be, and should be. Equally, what therefore enables us to determine whether something or someone is identifiable as 'childish' in nature or behavior – who and what comes to be understood as resembling or reminiscent of a 'child' – is also historically, socially, and culturally contingent.

One of the most significant functions of the notion of the modern child is its capacity to produce and reproduce modern 'man' as the agent of action, rationality, maturity, and order (Jenks 2005). What has come to characterize the rational adult, capable of expressing their reasoned will, is their transcendence of the partiality that plagues childhood as a space of the 'pre-social, potentially social, [and] in the process of becoming social' (Alanen 1988, 56). Since the nineteenth century, this notion of the unfinished adult has grown especially with the proliferation of psychiatry. Childhood became a potential origin for abnormality in later life in this period, and adults became at risk from the condition of 'arrested development', a term denoting an adult, who had seemingly transcended childhood, acting out 'like a child' rather than an adult according to prevalent social norms of what constituted these subjectivities (Foucault 2003).

As such, the child has come to be 'defined only by what the child is not but is subsequently going to be, and not by what the child presently is' (Alanen 1988, 56). It is in this context of becoming, of being incomplete, that the child becomes at once familiar yet strange to those who have come to be socially recognizable as 'adult'. After all, adults were once children; indeed, the very condition of being reassured that one is an adult is that one is no longer a child. As social beings who are simultaneously 'like us' but 'not like us', children are not merely what adults are not, however, but are more like what Simmel (1971) and Bauman (1991) call 'strangers'. Strangers 'are not perceived as individuals, but as strangers of a certain type' (Simmel 1971, 148), and they require processes of assimilation not only to overcome their strangeness but to be considered as individuals capable of expressing reason. Whereas adults are drivers of agency, children are vehicles for structure.

The heroes of many a geopolitical tale are rational and ordered actors, not children or sufferers of arrested development. They are individual agents in control of their destinies and the destinies of others, but who have often had to confront muddled and irrational others in order to save the nation or the world from invasion, economic collapse, nuclear destruction, and so on. As various feminists have argued, though (*inter alia* Tickner 1992; Petersen 1998; Steans 1998), claims to rationality ought to invite caution. They often entail 'a reinforcement of the superiority of masculine characteristics such as rationality, resolve and strength' and frequently, with them, 'strong' military responses (Basham and Vaughan-Williams 2013, 516). Accusations of 'childish' behavior can thus denigrate some practices while normalizing others. As attempts to define the scope for political agency, they can play a significant role in determining what courses of action are most intelligible and come to be considered 'sensible'.

In what follows, I focus primarily on British claims about the supposed childishness of Argentina in the ongoing 'war' over the Falklands-Malvinas. I examine two mutually reinforcing ways in which Argentina is defined as behaving in ways supposedly more befitting children than adults: that Argentina is a 'sore loser', unable to accept defeat and Britain's legitimate claim to the Falklands, and that Argentina is a 'bully', acting out because it cannot get its way. I focus on these two particular tales in order to suggest that characterizing Argentina as a somewhat puerile and fledgling nation allows Britain to define and consolidate itself on the world stage as a rational adult nation worthy of being listened to. I attempt to demonstrate that this particular formation of identity, sovereignty, and security enables military violence to become an integral part of the British national story, obscuring the aggressive role of the state in perpetuating violence over other practices. I conclude, however, by considering how different tales are possible; tales that might disrupt the notion of the 'rational' adult by questioning how the lived realities of children may serve as an important reminder of the *ir*rationality of war.

Sore losers: 1833 and all that

War is the *raison d'être* of the modern state. The sovereignty of states is 'produced and defined by organised violence'; states proffer citizens security in exchange for their compliance and it is war, therefore, that produces and defines political community (Edkins 2003, 6). As a ubiquitous aspect of the national story, war engenders tales about its history, about specific wars themselves, and about the aftermath of war. The 74 days of military violence in 1982 that has come to be known in Britain as The Falklands War and in Argentina as La Guerra de las Malvinas has been the subject of many stories. One especially salient telling for Argentina is of a breach of national sovereignty. The history of the War is of Las Islas Malvinas being forcibly seized in 1833 by a colonial power and of Argentina trying to regain its stolen territory ever since. The War in this story is a tale of reasserting a sovereign right to the Islands by sending troops there in 1982 to secure them, at the cost of an estimated 650 Argentine lives. Since the end of the War, a villainous Britain has consistently refused to engage in a legitimate dialogue with Argentina over the sovereignty of the Islands, which it continues to illegally colonize and militarize.

For Britain, an alternative but equally salient telling of the Falklands War is that the Islands have been British sovereign territory since 1833. The War of 1982 came about because the security of the Britons who legitimately resided there came under threat from

Argentine aggression. This necessitated sending troops to the Islands at the cost 255 British servicemen and merchant seamen's lives, and the lives of 3 women Islanders.[1] In Britain's tale, the aftermath of the War has been characterized firstly by the suspension of diplomatic relations between Britain and Argentina until 1990 and, since then, by relations with Argentina that have shifted from dialogical to hostile due to Argentina's refusal to accept the reality that the Falklands are British.

While wars are the very condition of the state, they also have the capacity to unsettle the routinized temporality of social and political life (Edkins 2003). As something 'unexpected', war can constitute an affront to an everyday life imagined, performed, and experienced as continuity. For traumas like wars to be socially intelligible, therefore, re-imaginings are often necessary; and these frequently invoke 'a linear narrative of national heroism' (Edkins 2003, xv). This is especially apparent in Britain's tale of the War. As Femenia (2000, 42) argues, when Argentine troops surrendered on 14 June 1982,

> both countries were left with the symbolic treasure over which they fought; Britain was left with a renewed sense of British world greatness and Argentina appropriated the role of victimized, heroic David resisting the prepotency of the superpowers.

Trauma's destabilizing capacity has necessitated the rehabilitation of the War as an integral part of both nations' national stories and one particularly important effect of the reassertion of linearity is that the War appears to have 'tragically confirmed for each national player... that war is a legitimate means to get to know who they are, and what they stand for' (Femenia 2000, 42). In one tale of the Falklands-Malvinas, a victim requires a stubborn aggressor. In another, a victor requires a loser. In both, however, the War is central to the intelligibility of those roles.

Recent anniversaries of the Falklands-Malvinas War suggest these stories of the War remain significant to the production of both nations as sovereign. On the 30th anniversary of the start of military hostilities, an anniversary with a number imbued with an almost 'magic' quality, Argentine President Cristina Fernández De Kirchner (in *BBC News Online* 2012) marked the occasion with a speech in which she reasserted Argentina's claim to the Islands but also its peaceful stance. She told the assembled crowd that with every day that goes by British control of the Islands

> looks more ridiculous, more absurd to the eyes of the world...It is an injustice that in the 21st Century there are still colonial enclaves... 16 colonial enclaves throughout the world – 10 of those belonging to the United Kingdom...We also demand that so they stop usurping our environment, our natural resources, our oil...[but] wars only bring backwardness and hatred.

Similarly, Argentine Foreign Minister Héctor Timerman (2013) has insisted that Las Islas Malvinas are a 'colonized territory' and a 'militarized enclave of an extra-regional power', that they rightfully belong to Argentina, and that the ongoing dispute is a 'matter of sovereignty and territorial integrity' for Argentina. British Prime Minister David Cameron's speech on the 30th anniversary of the War conjures a different telling of sovereignty, however. He stated that

> [t]hirty years ago today the people of the Falkland Islands suffered an act of aggression that sought to rob them of their freedom and their way of life. Today is a day for commemoration and reflection: a day to remember all those who lost their lives in the conflict – the members of our armed forces, as well as the Argentinian personnel who died. (Cameron in *BBC News Online* 2012)

Cameron (in *BBC News Online* 2012) went on to applaud the 'heroism' of British troops and their role in 'righting a profound wrong' and reminded his audience that

> Britain remains staunchly committed to upholding the right of the Falkland Islanders, and of the Falkland Islanders alone, to determine their own future. That was the fundamental principle that was at stake 30 years ago: and that is the principle which we solemnly reaffirm today.

These competing tales of sovereignty are the context for the United Kingdom's repeated refusal to engage in discussions of sovereignty over the Islands with Argentina, on the grounds that it will only do so if and when the Islanders welcome these talks. Though giving due consideration to the wishes of the Islanders is important, Britain's refusal to engage with Argentina also reinforces the notion that Argentina is a sore loser. As David Cameron (2011) put it to the House of Commons in 2011, 'as long as the Falkland Islands want to be sovereign British territory, they should remain sovereign British territory – full stop, end of story'. Argentina appears as like a haranguing child, who despite being told to play fair insists on getting its way, who needs to be told by the rational adult that enough is enough. Though adults are accused of being sore losers, a sense of arrested development – the inability to fully transcend childhood – is often blamed for such behavior. As Goodheart (2011, 527) argues,

> We have been taught from childhood not to be sore losers in the realization that it is only a game. A grandparent playing with his grandson learns how much easier it is to teach him the rules than to accept defeat…The rabid fans who rail against the losers on sports radio and threaten mayhem if the losing doesn't stop are the childish adults who never learned to distinguish between real life and a game.

As the victor of the 1982 War, 'Britain' was performed, at that juncture, through 'celebratory set pieces' in the tabloid press, replete with the usual invocations of 'patriotism' – such as in the *News of the World*'s 'Our boys caught Argies Napping' headline – and 'jokes' – such as in the *Sun*'s notorious 'Stick it up your Junta' headline (Latin America Bureau 1982, 119–20). Britain continues to be performed as the nation that accepted the reality of its role as victor and, as the nation still able to hold victory parades and still able to speak of the heroism of its soldiers, it has emerged from the War as the storyteller with the capacity to point out it won and to point out the loser, and a sore one at that. Argentina is easily portrayed as unable to grasp that the 'game' is up, that the reality of defeat must be accepted if it wants to be taken seriously on the world stage.

Standing up to the childish bully (of Buenos Aires)

For many British commentators, it is Argentina's aggressive 'bullying' stance that most characterizes recent tales of the Falklands-Malvinas. The idea of Argentina as a land of bullies frequently appears in online article reader comments and in the observations of political commentators. Falklands legislator Roger Edwards (in United Nations Department of Public Information 2012), who has accused Argentina of seeking to take away the rights of the Islanders, has asserted that, 'all that we ask for is the right to determine our own future without the bullying tactics of a neighbouring country'. British Foreign Secretary William Hague (in Wooding 2013) also recently stated that although there 'was a time in the 1990s when there was a dialogue…the current Government of Argentina has turned away from that dialogue into a pattern of bullying and intimidatory behaviour towards the Falkland Islands'; he also asserted that he wanted Argentina 'to know that this approach is completely counter-productive' (Hague in Wooding 2013).

Adults can be bullies, of course, and, in some settings, behavior that might constitute bullying is actually esteemed as a 'robust management style' and so forth. However, the bullying behavior of adults is often viewed as a power relation, as a way of gaining certain aims and objectives. In contrast to the agentic and proactive individual adult, however, the child bully, as a social being in the process of becoming and not yet an agentic social actor, is merely reacting to circumstances beyond its full comprehension. Thus, Hague's insistence that bullying is 'counter-productive' is more evocative of a teacher, or a parent, or any adult figure, telling a child that bullies never win, that one should not give in to intimidation rather than of a purposeful geopolitical strategy. The bully label thus casts Argentina as childish, as arrested in its development, and Britain as sensible and adult. In doing so, this supports the legitimacy of Britain's geopolitical claims about itself. To be rational is to be decisive, to be worthy of speaking and being listened to; to be a childish bully is quite the opposite.

Such discourses also work to conceal Britain's own bullying or rather to rehabilitate it as an adult practice; as the right to militarily defend itself from a more destructive and hostile party, much like the robust manager. The idea that Britain is a nation that bravely stands up to intimidation is symptomatic of a longstanding facet of British national identity that transcends the Falklands-Malvinas. Shortly after the 1982 War, Anthony Barnett (2012) argued that one of its most significant effects was to allow Thatcher and Thatcher's Britain to cling to 'Churchillism'; to simultaneously express 'ourselves' as the plucky underdog, a small island nation threatened once again by Nazism – this time in the form of Argentine fascism – while still being a significant world player that, given Britain's modesty (even in light of its military might), meant the world simply needed British leadership. In an updated edition, Barnett (2012) claims that this 'Falklands Syndrome', a development of Churchillism, has continued to foster a feeling of entitlement to demonstrate British military superiority whenever possible, and that any defeat or setback simply justifies this further. For Barnett, this political discourse of national identity facilitated recent ill-fated military 'adventures' in Iraq and Afghanistan, among others. Though the syndrome that Barnett identifies may have a longer heritage than the Falklands, 1982 and its anniversaries have represented particularly important opportunities for the re-articulation of Britain as 'Churchillian'. Contemporary British posturing over the Falklands-Malvinas may be in part about an Island in the South Atlantic and the people who live there, but it also facilitates the notion that Britain is a defiant, tolerant, and plucky nation that deserves to have a role of influence on the world (Barnett 2012). Argentina, in contrast, is a young, inexperienced nation that needs to 'grow up'. That Britain, an old power, continues to be discursively reproduced as a voice of reason in the face of the childish bullying of a fledgling former colony can only serve to reinforce this self-belief and projection.

Images of a bullying Argentina and a Britain respectful of the wishes of the Islanders were also prevalent following the outcome of a referendum in March 2013 in which just three Falkland Islanders voted against the Falkland Islands retaining their current political status as an Overseas Territory of the United Kingdom. The remaining 99.7% of voters voted in favor, and as there was a voter turnout of over 90% it was popularly concluded that the outcome was undeniably pro-British. British Prime Minister David Cameron (in *BBC News Online* 2013) responded in a speech to the press the next day that the 'Falkland Islands may be thousands of miles away but they are British through and through and that is how they want to stay…People should know we will always be there to defend them'.

President Cristina Fernández De Kirchner disagreed, though. Also invoking the idea of the 'childish', she questioned the very notion of an 'English territory more than 12,000 km away' and claimed that the question was 'not even worthy of a kindergarten of three year olds'[2] (Fernández De Kirchner in Alexander 2013). Here, the suggestion is that even children, beings of ongoing developmental cognition, would be able to comprehend the absurdity of Britain's claims to the Islands. The common response among British media sources, however, was to deride De Kirchner's statement as a 'Twitter rant'. Once again, her claims were marked out and denigrated as irrational, bullying, and childish.

It is not only Argentina but specifically Argentina's leader who is frequently accused of being a bully. Former aide to Margaret Thatcher, Nile Gardiner, has taken to calling Argentine President Cristina Fernández De Kirchner 'the bully of Buenos Aires' (Gardiner 2013) and the much-respected British Falklands War veteran, Simon Weston (in Beech 2013) has called her 'a sad lonely woman who's desperate to live out her dead husband's wishes'. As a 'bully' and a woman 'desperate' to fulfill her husband's legacy to regain Islas Las Malvinas for Argentina, Kirchner is at once gender nonconforming as a bully and gender conforming as the 'good wife'. In both cases, the representations of her, and of Argentina as an intimidating bully, are indicative of what Hutchings (2008, 33) calls a cognitive shortcut, something that resonates and resounds because it is part of the gendered and 'entrenched logic[s]' that pervade the wider political imaginary. The notion that Argentina and Kirchner are bullies is a cognitive shortcut to irrationality and child-ishness on their part. As well as working to undermine Argentina's claims, however 'legitimate' or 'illegitimate' they may be, and its right even to speak and be heard, Britain emerges as that which Argentina is not: the rational, adult speaker able to put forward claims built on reason. In standing up to the bully of Buenos Aires, Britain can only ever be the hero of this particular geopolitical tale.

This is also evident in other tales about the Islanders' right to self-determination, the right to remain 'British' should they chose to do so. Amid calls from the Argentine government in January 2012 for the United Kingdom to attend UN-led discussions over the future of the governing of the Islands, David Cameron (2012) told the British House of Commons that

> The absolutely vital point is that we are clear that the future of the Falkland Islands is a matter for the people themselves. As long as they want to remain part of the United Kingdom and be British, they should be able to do so. That is absolutely key. I am determined to make sure that our defences and everything else are in order, which is why the National Security Council discussed the issue yesterday…I would argue that what the Argentinians have said recently is far more like colonialism, as these people want to remain British and the Argentinians want them to do something else.

Though again asserting that military force is an option for the United Kingdom in supporting self-determination for the Islanders, Cameron's mention of Argentina's 'colonialism', and its assault on that self-determination, is suggestive of the very need to deal with a bullying Argentine aggressor, and militarily if necessary.[3] However, this discourse diverts attention from Britain's colonial past; away from how Britain's capacity to self-define as a plucky island nation, wishing to defend another of its own plucky islands, relies on the erasure of the violence of British Empire and its exploitation of the lands and bodies of others as an integral part of the nation, if not the national story. It also disguises the ways in which Britain's belief in self-determination has always been contingent. For example, between 1968 and 1973, the British government exiled all 1500–2000 inhabitants of Diego Garcia, a British overseas territory, to make way for a US military base (Vine 2009); and the 1982 war coincided with the ongoing deployment of British troops to Northern Ireland where self-determination was a right that was not extended to the people of that particular island when it was forcibly partitioned by Britain in the 1920s (Conroy 1987).

The notion of Argentine colonialism also obscures Britain's colonial practices in Latin America, including its initial desire to occupy, populate, and secure the Falklands-Malvinas to access Latin American markets and thwart a Spanish colonial monopoly. It overlooks its paternalistic economic relationship with Argentina in the period after its decolonization and well beyond (Latin America Bureau 1982) and how very little attention was paid by Britain, despite its self-identity as a key world player, to the inability of Argentines to determine their futures in 1982. Argentines were ineligible to vote and were governed by a military junta infamous for kidnapping, torturing, and murdering its own citizens. Moreover, although Britain was well aware of the human rights abuses in Argentina in the 1970s and the early 1980s, less than a year before Britain dispatched its troops to the Falklands-Malvinas, the then-Minister of Trade, Cecil Parkinson, led a trade delegation to Argentina. Prior to doing so, he insisted that 'trade with other countries should be determined by commercial considerations and not by the character of the governments concerned' (Parkinson in Latin America Bureau 1982, 84). Furthermore, British claims to respect the self-determination of the Islanders ought to invite critique. Though the military hostilities of 1982 were also characterized as a 'War of self-determination', where British troops fought for the rights of fellow British citizens to decide who would govern them, the Islands were governed at that time by a non-elected governor appointed by London (Latin America Bureau 1982). In the process of willfully forgetting its suppression or disregard for self-determination in some sites but not others, Britain has been able to contract and expand its borders at will; to re-assert its national identity, sovereign rights, and its right to secure both in particular ways.

Another tale that Britain tells about the 1982 Argentine invasion of the Islands and its subsequent decision to send troops to the South Atlantic is that the invasion was an act of aggression that had to be tackled so it did not set the troubling international precedent of a breach of sovereignty going unpunished. In a post-Afghanistan 2001 and Iraq 2003 world, the logics of this position are hardly difficult to critique, but neither was this a compelling yarn in 1982. From support for Chile's campaigns of violence within its borders and without in Central America, to its refusal to provide sanctuary to Latin American political refugees without the blessing of the CIA, 'Britain's less than illustrious record of standing up to international aggression…make its pretensions to an international policing role highly discreditable' (Latin America Bureau 1982, 104).

The notion that Britain 'stands up' to intimidation is, however, a productive one; it not only reinforces British claims about sovereignty but also about its right to militarily defend it and about its identity as a rational actor on the world stage. As a nation that can so readily demonstrate the rationality, resolve, and strength that have come to be widely associated with war and war preparedness, it is difficult to mark Britain as irrational and childish. Conversely, it is easy to characterize Argentina in this way in a geopolitical context where the idea that war is inevitable is considered common sense, despite being based on a notion of 'human' nature founded in the experiences of a small number of (white) men (*inter alia* Tickner 1992; Steans 1998).

War is not healthy for children and other living things[4]

[The] Tin-Pot Foreign General wanted to be important. He wanted to do something Historical so that his name would be printed in all the big History Books. So, one day, he got all his soldiers and all his guns and he put them into boats. Then he sailed them over the sea to the sad little island. There he stamped ashore and bagsied the sad little island for his own…Far away over the sea there lived an old woman with lots of money and guns…When this Old

Iron Woman heard that the Tin-Pot Foreign General had bagsied the sad little island, she flew into a rage. It's MINE! She screeched. "MINE! MINE! MINE! I bagsied it ages ago! I bagsied it FIRST! DID! DID! DID!" (Briggs 1984, 8–15)

As effective of social and political relations of power, discourses of the childish can also enable other tales, however. Renowned British children's author Raymond Briggs' particular tale of the 1982 Falklands-Malvinas War is of a childish squabble between the egotistical 'Tin-Pot' Argentine General Leopoldo Galtieri and Britain's richer but equally stubborn 'Old Iron Woman', the then-Prime Minister Margaret Thatcher. Though who 'bagsied' the Islands and when continues to ensure that tales of the past are dredged up to justify and articulate the present stand-off, and to envisage oppositional, divergent futures, Briggs' tale pokes fun at the futility of such squabbling by casting both Britain and Argentina as resembling the behavior of children. Though his depiction of Thatcher relies on sexualized caricature – for example, images of coins flowing out from Thatcher's iron breasts to pay for her war – and elides other ways to be a child, Briggs' tale could be regarded as what Agamben (2007; see also Basham and Vaughan-Williams 2013) calls a 'profanation'. In toying with the 'serious' activity of war and its associated claims about legality, territory, and political economy, by belittling it as a childish squabble, Briggs' story returns the war to the everyday; to performances and practices that take place in mundane spaces. While Briggs' book also highlights that the implications of such childish squabbles are far from innocent, comical, or silly – several pages of the book detail the deaths of the men shot, torn apart, and burned alive – it also unsettles more realist notions of war as an expression of rational, objective power, as self-evidently in the 'national interest', and as distinct from the social, the everyday (Tickner 1992).

Another way that 'childish' can come to unsettle more prominent – or more loudly shouted – geopolitical tales is by looking to actual lived experiences of childhood. The agency and everyday lives of children are frequently erased from geopolitical tales but also, as I have tried to show, in the very expression of what we come to recognize as childhood and the childish. Though the multiple ways in which Argentine, British, and Island children experienced the War, and how children continue to understand it, are beyond the scope of this particular article and warrant further research, there are still some stories that highlight the value of paying more attention to childhood and how it is militarized that can be considered here.

One such story is about some of the young men who fought. Despite the increased participation of women in the British armed forces, particularly over the past two decades or so, British service personnel have long been and are still frequently referred to as 'our boys' and the Falklands-Malvinas War was no exception. This collective moniker had and continues to have a number of political implications. As Helen Parr (2013) has argued, such mentions of 'our boys' during the Falklands-Malvinas War by politicians including the then-Prime Minister Margaret Thatcher, and by the British press, not only highlighted the fact that the Task Force was comprised exclusively of men – women were deployed but only in auxiliary roles, not combat – but also that these troops were not quite fully grown men. In being identified in this 'in-between' way but also as 'ours', British soldiers became sons of the nation. Their role as protectors of that nation may have motivated their deployment but, as always someone's 'boy', they were also in need of the protection provided by that nation. Indeed, after the British sank the *General Belgrano*, bringing about the deaths of 323 Argentine sailors, Thatcher told the House of Commons that, 'our first duty is to protect our boys' (cited in Parr 2013, 2). Violence, in the form of killing or being killed, perhaps becomes a little more palatable when the life of one's sons is at stake.

Another function of the invocation of 'our boys' to describe a body of men of very different ages is to conceal the fact that under-18s, boys in the literal sense of the word, were put in actual danger. Much has been made of the notion that the Argentine invading forces were comprised not only of ill-equipped and poorly trained conscripts but young ones at that (see Stewart 1991) and it is the case that many were 18, 19, and 20 year olds with limited training and combat experience. Though some stories tell of an Argentina united behind a popular invasion in 1982, one source of dissent came from members of the *Madres de Plaza de Mayo*, the group of mothers and other relatives who took to the streets to protest the 'disappearances' of children during the years of Argentina's military rule from 1976 to 1983. As one mother said:

> We were opposed to the Malvinas [War] because for us they were doing the same thing as they did to our children. They kidnapped those young soldiers as well, because they were sent there by force…We were against it because the military were using it to raise their prestige, to try to glorify themselves…They wanted to keep their hands soaked in the blood of our young people. (Carmen de Guede in Fisher 1989, 115)

Less has been made of the British deployment of 17 year olds into combat however, and that the youngest British soldier killed in Falklands-Malvinas War, Paratrooper Ian Scrivens, was just 17 when he died. He was killed in the same violent incident as fellow Paratroopers Jason Burt, who was also 17 years old, and Neil Grose, who turned 18 on the day that all three boys were killed. Britain remains the only state of the EU, Council of Europe, and United Nations Security Council Permanent Members that still recruits from age 16, and although under-18s in the British armed forces are prohibited from participation in armed conflict by official government policy, this policy can be overruled if 'military need' deems the deployment of minors necessary, or where it is considered impracticable to withdraw them before deployment (Child Soldiers International & ForcesWatch 2013).

Conclusion

Anniversaries marking 'events' associated with the 1982 Falklands-Malvinas War in social time have facilitated the telling of a variety of geopolitical tales about sovereignty, national identity, and security. Such stories have resurfaced 'periodically' with calendric markers and are likely to continue to resurface given that the war over the sovereignty of the Falkland Islands/Las Islas Malvinas, and its place in the national stories of Britain and Argentina, is far from settled. As I have attempted to demonstrate, one particularly salient story is of a sensible Britain standing up to an Argentine sore loser and bully; of an adult, rational, and ordered Britain that finds meaning in contradistinction to the muddled and frenzied activities of the childish Argentine other. Such metaphors and figures of speech invoking the 'childish' are, as Shapiro (1985, 195) argues, never 'mere adornments added to the cognitive meaning of expressions. They impose and order our reality insofar as they create meaning and value'.[5] Indeed, as I have tried to demonstrate, where childhood surfaces as metaphor in the ongoing war for the Falklands-Malvinas, it constitutes an attempt to determine the parameters for political action.

The functioning of a geopolitical order of rational actors also relies on routinized and assumed notions of Newtonian temporality. As a trauma, something that has the capacity to disrupt the continuity of everyday life, war has to be remade, retold as an integral, normal part of the national story. As Lundborg (2012) argues, to speak of war as an 'event' relies greatly on such suppositions that war has a clear before and after, a singularity, and coherence. These assumptions are not only reliant upon the materialization of a speaker who decides the boundaries of the 'event', however, but also on the erasure of multiple experiences of war as lived, ongoing, and resurgent, rather than contained. For the soldier with PTSD re-living each battle as a visceral experience for example, war is never a simple matter of before and after but is a constant, a continuum (Sylvester 2010).

When considered this way, the analysis of any 'war' necessarily entails paying greater attention to everyday social practices and processes that foster war preparedness and the prioritization of military force in societies as well as notions of 'war' itself (Cockburn 2012). Attempts to speak of the 74 days of military violence between Argentina and Britain in 1982 as an event can also be troubled by exploring traces of the geopolitical in the everyday. Even for Britain as the 'victor', something highly suggestive of a clear end-point to the war, the suicides and post-traumatic stress of veterans 'tell a different tale' (Edkins 2003, 1). Moreover, though maps, textbooks, memorials, and so on enable the reproduction of the Falkland Islands/Las Islas Malvinas in everyday settings in Argentina, Britain, and on the Islands themselves, the meaning and significance of these everyday artifacts cannot be assumed to be universally shared (Benwell and Dodds 2011). As others have also shown, expressions of 'everyday nationalism' suggestive of a degree of unity with national storytelling can also be temporally contingent (Benwell and Dodds 2011; see also Jones and Merriman 2009). They often rely on the 'heating up' of longstanding tensions to jog the memories of people consumed with more pressing daily matters (Benwell and Dodds 2011). Moreover, and importantly, though childhood and the childish as social discourses often elide the actual experiences of children and deny them a bona fide subjectivity, alternative tales depicting the childish behavior of supposed adults in facilitating childhoods marred by violence tell a different story.

War is not an inevitability therefore; neither is it a contained event. It is not in any way healthy for children and other living things. The reincorporation of war into a national story characterized by periods of war and peace conceals the role of that very state in the production of war and the ruptures it creates. However, by paying closer attention to the stories the state tells, and by looking to others, the state's reliance on a geopolitical story of distinct periods of war and peace for claiming authority via its capacity to provide continued security for its citizens becomes more visibly contingent (Edkins 2003). Claims about the 'childish' may have the potential to facilitate militarism; the telling of geopolitical tales of rational heroism in the face of sore losers and bullies may materialize war and its violence but, as geopolitical tales, other stories are always possible.

Acknowledgments

The author thanks two anonymous reviewers, the editors of the journal, and Alex Minton for their valuable comments on the article.

Notes

1. These three civilian women were mistakenly killed by British troops and weapons.
2. This is a rough translation. The original tweet reads: 'Territorio inglés a más de 12 mil kms de distancia? La pregunta no aguanta ni jardín de infantes de 3 años.'
3. In February 2012, the Royal Navy dispatched *HMS Dauntless*, a Type 45 destroyer and one of its most advanced warships, to the South Atlantic and the Royal Air Force deployed Prince William, heir to the British throne, to the Islands to carry out search and rescue duties. This was widely reported as having been interpreted by Kirchner's administration as an act of aggression. Cameron is also reportedly willing to send fast jets and troops to the Islands (Mason 2013).
4. This anti-war slogan was especially popularized by Lorraine Schneider's 1966 poster that displayed the slogan and a flower. It emerged in reaction to the Vietnam War.
5. See also Reeves (2013) on the political significance of metaphor.

References

Agamben, G. 2007. *Profanations*. Translated by J. Fort. New York, NY: Zone Books.

Alanen, L. 1988. "Rethinking Childhood." *Acta Sociologica* 31 (1): 53–67. doi:10.1177/000169938803100105.

Alexander, H. 2013. "Cristina Kirchner's Extraordinary Twitter Rant as She Lashes Out over Falklands." *Telegraph Online*, March 28. Accessed July 26. http://www.telegraph.co.uk/news/worldnews/southamerica/argentina/9959963/Cristina-Kirchners-extraordinary-Twitter-rant-as-she-lashes-out-over-Falklands.html

Ariès, P. 1962. *Centuries of Childhood*. Translated by R. Baldick. London: Cape.

Barnett, A. 2012. *Iron Britannia: Time to Take the Great out of Britain* e-ed. London: Faber and Faber.

Basham, V. M., and N. Vaughan-Williams. 2013. "Gender, Race and Border Security Practices: A Profane Reading of 'Muscular Liberalism'." *British Journal of Politics and International Relations* 15 (4): 509–527. doi:10.1111/j.1467-856X.2012.00517.x.

Bauman, Z. 1991. *Modernity and Ambivalence*. Cambridge: Polity.

BBC News Online. 2012. "Falklands War: UK and Argentina Mark Invasion 30 Years On." *BBC News Online*, April 2. Accessed July 26, 2013. http://www.bbc.co.uk/news/uk-17580449

BBC News Online. 2013. "Falklands: Cameron Says Argentina Should Respect Vote." *BBC News Online*, March 12. Accessed July 26. http://www.bbc.co.uk/news/uk-21752581

Beech, R. 2013. "Falklands War Veteran Simon Weston Slams Argentina President as 'Sad Lonely Woman'." *Wales Online*, January 4. Accessed July 26. http://www.walesonline.co.uk/news/wales-news/falklands-war-veteran-simon-weston-2496671

Benwell, M. C., and K. Dodds. 2011. "Argentine Territorial Nationalism Revisited: The Malvinas/Falklands Dispute and Geographies of Everyday Nationalism." *Political Geography* 30 (8): 441–449. doi:10.1016/j.polgeo.2011.09.006.

Briggs, R. 1984. *The Tin-Pot Foreign General and the Old Iron Woman*. London: Penguin.

Cameron, D. 2011. "'Engagements,' Oral Answers to Questions." *Parliamentary Debates House of Commons Hansard (session 2010–2012)* 529: 772–773.

Cameron, D. 2012. "'Engagements,' Oral Answers to Questions." *Parliamentary Debates House of Commons Hansard (session 2010–2012)* 538: 745–746.

Child Soldiers International & ForcesWatch. 2013. *One Step Forward: The Case for Ending Recruitment of Minors by the British Armed Forces*. Published by ForcesWatch (forceswatch.net) and Child Soldiers International (child-soldiers.org). Accessed July 26. http://www.child-soldiers.org/research_report_reader.php?id=650

Cockburn, C. 2012. "Gender Relations as Causal in Militarization and War: A Feminist Standpoint." In *Making Gender, Making War: Violence, Military and Peacekeeping Practices*, edited by A. Kronsell and E. Svedberg, 19–32. New York, NY: Routledge.

Conroy, J. 1987. *War as a Way of Life: A Belfast Diary*. London: Heinemann.

Dodds, K. 2012. "Stormy Waters: Britain, the Falkland Islands and UK–Argentine Relations." *International Affairs* 88 (4): 683–700. doi:10.1111/j.1468-2346.2012.01096.x.

Edkins, J. 2003. *Trauma and the Memory of Politics*. Cambridge: Cambridge University Press.

Femenia, N. 2000. "Emotional Actor: Foreign Policy Decision-Making in the 1982 Falklands/Malvinas War." In *Social Conflicts and Collective Identities*, edited by P. G. Coy and L. M. Woehrle, 41–66. Plymouth: Rowman and Littlefield.

Fisher, J. 1989. *Mothers of the Disappeared*. London: Zed.

Forrest, T. R. 1993. "Disaster Anniversary: A Social Reconstruction of Time." *Sociological Inquiry* 63 (4): 444–456. doi:10.1111/j.1475-682X.1993.tb00323.x.

Foucault, M. 2003. *Abnormal: Lectures at the College de France 1974–1975*. Translated by G. Burchell. London: Verso.

Gardiner, N. 2013. "Cristina Kirchner is the Bully of Buenos Aires. She is Dreaming if She Thinks the Falklands Will Ever Be Hers." *Telegraph Blogs*, February 5. Accessed July 26. http://blogs.

telegraph.co.uk/news/nilegardiner/100201379/cristina-kirchner-is-the-bully-of-buenos-aires-she-is-dreaming-if-she-thinks-the-falklands-will-ever-be-hers/

Goodheart, E. 2011. "Sports Allegory." *Society* 48 (6): 526–529. doi:10.1007/s12115-011-9476-x.

Holmer Nadesan, M. 2010. *Governing Childhood into the 21st Century Biopolitical Technologies of Childhood Management and Education.* New York, NY: Palgrave.

Hutchings, K. 2007. "Happy Anniversary! Time and Critique in International Relations Theory." *Review of International Studies* 33 (S1): 71–89. doi:10.1017/S0260210507007401.

Hutchings, K. 2008. "Cognitive Shortcuts." In *Re-Thinking the Man Question: Sex, Gender and Violence in International Relations*, edited by J. L. Parpart and M. Zalewski, 23–46. London: Zed.

Jenks, C. 2005. *Childhood.* 2nd ed. London: Routledge.

Jones, R., and P. Merriman. 2009. "Hot, Banal and Everyday Nationalism: Bilingual Road Signs in Wales." *Political Geography* 28 (3): 164–173. doi:10.1016/j.polgeo.2009.03.002.

Latin America Bureau. 1982. *Falklands/Malvinas: Whose Crisis?* London: Latin America Bureau.

Lundborg, T. 2012. *Politics of the Event: Time, Movement, Becoming.* Abingdon: Routledge.

Mason, R. 2013. "David Cameron: We Would Fight a Falklands Invasion." *The Telegraph Online*, January 6. Accessed July 17. http://www.telegraph.co.uk/news/politics/9783568/David-Cameron-we-would-fight-a-Falklands-invasion.html

Parr, H. 2013. "The Falklands War, Grief, Commemoration and Britishness." Paper presented at the BISA annual conference, Birmingham, June 20–21.

Peterson, V. S. 1998. "Feminisms and International Relations." *Gender & History* 10 (3): 581–589. doi:10.1111/1468-0424.00123.

Reeves, A. 2013. "State-Building and State Penetration: The Masculinised Metaphors of Post-Conflict Intervention." Paper presented at the 2013 South West international political theory workshop supported by the University of Exeter Great Western Four Social Science Regional Collaboration Fund (GW4), Bristol, June 7.

Shapiro, M. J. 1985. "Metaphor in the Philosophy of the Social Sciences." *Cultural Critique* 2: 191–214. doi:10.2307/1354206.

Simmel, G. 1971. *On Individuality and Social Forms.* Chicago, IL: University of Chicago Press.

Sorokin, P. A., and R. K. Merton. 1937. "Social Time: A Methodological and Functional Analysis." *American Journal of Sociology* 42 (5): 615–629. doi:10.1086/217540.

Steans, J. 1998. *Gender and International Relations.* Cambridge: Polity.

Stewart, N. K. 1991. *Mates and Muchachos: Unit Cohesion in the Falklands/Malvinas War.* Washington, DC: Brassey's.

Sylvester, C. 2010. "War, Sense and Security." In *Gender and International Security: Feminist Perspectives*, edited by L. Sjoberg, 22–37. London: Routledge.

Tickner, J. A. 1992. *Gender in International Relations.* New York: Columbia University Press.

Till, K. E. 2003. "Places of Memory." *A Companion to Political Geography*, edited by J. Agnew, K. Mitchell, and G. Toal, 289–301. Malden, MA: Blackwell.

Timerman, H. 2013. "Speech at the UN Special Decolonisation Committee, 20 June 2013." Accessed July 26. http://www.argentine-embassy-uk.org/PDFs/Argentina_Foreign_Minister_speech_at_the_Decolonisation_Committee_20_June_2013.pdf

United Nations, Department of Public Information. 2012. "Press Release: Special Committee on Decolonization Considers 'Question of the Falkland Islands (Malvinas),' Hears from Petitioners, Island Assemblymen, Argentina's President." Accessed July 26, 2013. http://www.un.org/News/Press/docs/2012/gacol3238.doc.htm

Vine, D. 2009. *Island of Shame: The Secret History of the US Military Base on Diego Garcia.* Princeton, NJ: Princeton University Press.

Wodak, R., R. De Cillia, M. Reisigl, and K. Liebhart. 2009. *The Discursive Construction of National Identity.* 2nd ed. Edinburgh: Edinburgh University Press.

Wooding, D. 2013. "Argies Will Never Bully Britain into Giving up Falklands Says William Hague." *The Sun Online*, February 10. Accessed July 17. http://www.thesun.co.uk/sol/homepage/news/politics/4787396/William-Hague-Argies-will-never-bully-Britain-into-giving-up-Falklands.html#ixzz2ZK3R80HP

Children, violence, and social exclusion: negotiation of everyday insecurity in a Colombian *barrio*

Helen Berents

School of Justice, Queensland University of Technology, Brisbane, Australia

Discourses on in/security are often concerned with structures and meta-narratives of the state and other institutions; however, such attention misses the complexities of the everyday consequences of insecurity. In Colombia's protracted conflict, children are disproportionately affected yet rarely consulted, rendering it difficult to account for their experiences in meaningful ways. This article draws on fieldwork conducted with conflict-affected children in an informal *barrio* community on the periphery of Colombia's capital, Bogotá, to explore how children articulate experiences of insecurity. It examines how stereotypes of violence and delinquency reinforce insecurity; how multiple violences impact young people's lives; and how children themselves conceive of responses to these negative experiences. These discussions are underpinned by a feminist commitment of attention to the margins and engage with those for whom insecurity is a daily phenomenon. The effects of deeply embedded insecurity, violence, and fear for young people in Colombia require a more nuanced theoretical engagement with notions of insecurity, as well as the complexities of connections and dissonances within everyday life.

Introduction

Colombia's current conflict has been ongoing for over half a century, fought between leftist guerrillas, right-wing paramilitary organizations, and the state. Between 3.9 and 5.2 million people have been internally displaced as a result of the long-running violence (UNHCR 2012; Watchlist on Children and Armed Conflict 2012). Children are particularly affected by the conflict, as approximately 30% of the general population is under 18. However, when considering those living below the poverty line (almost 40% of the population), this figure increases to more than half (CODHES 2010). The challenges of navigating the bureaucratic processes associated with being poor, marginal, and often displaced exacerbate these inequalities. Zea (2010, 11) notes that these people 'continue to live in social structures that reinforce discrimination and mask their past experiences and histories'. While some inequalities and security risks are present as a direct consequence of the conflict itself such as fighting, forced displacement, risk of recruitment, and death threats, others are more the result of underdevelopment perpetuated by the conflict, such as the absence of sufficient services, job opportunities, and education provision. These effects of protracted conflict are complex and interrelated. Frequently, however, they are seen as the by-products of conflict and not as conditions of ongoing insecurity that require negotiation by those forced to live with them. Insecurity becomes a condition of everyday life, reinforced by structural marginalization and experienced on and through the bodies of those who are socially excluded from protection and participation.

For children in these environments, the effects of insecurity can be acute. Poverty, lack of access to basic resources, and long-term dislocation from communities of origin disproportionately affect young people. For children living in situations of displacement and marginalization, there are also risks and insecurities including very high rates of physical violence and sexual assault, risk of recruitment to armed gangs, increased rates of teen pregnancy, limited space to attend school, and the pressures of contributing to household economies. Due to the multiple challenges of displaced communities, they are often seen as places of danger and the occupants are often stigmatized by the wider society as dangerous or the agents of broader social problems. Young people form the figurehead for much of these external understandings as these children are seen as a potential threat to the broader society. Such a construction is in contrast to the ideal concept of childhood that sees children as innocent and protected. In response to simple binaries and categorizations, this article takes a more complex view of young people. It argues that children competently negotiate and mediate the effects of insecurity and violence day-to-day as part of their everyday lives. Young people are both active and participatory, and are inherently worthy of attention in discussions of the violence and insecurity that characterizes their lived experiences on the margins of conflict and society in places like Colombia.

Concepts of security that focus on institutions cannot account for how people experience insecurity as a pervasive everyday phenomenon that contributes to their social exclusion. Luckham argues that discussions of security should be 'grounded more firmly in the lived experience of people who are insecure' (2009, 3). In response, this article seeks to locate discussions concerning conflict, violence, and insecurity within the Colombian conflict through the narratives and experiences of conflict-affected young people. Such recognition acknowledges the agency of those who experience insecurity and social exclusion and the ways they engage in and rely on everyday practices to respond to these challenges and contributes to a more thorough understanding of the everyday consequences of conflict.

The article is an attempt to center the margins and ground a discussion of the experience of insecurity within the everyday. I argue that a theorization of insecurity must move beyond privileged actors. Children – marginalized and affected by protracted conflict – not only face the challenges of being young, but the difficulties of negotiating violence and insecurity in their everyday lives. I first articulate an agential conception of childhood, locating it within the existing literature before exploring understandings of everyday insecurity and ways of conceptualizing children in these explorations. In doing this, I draw on arguments made by feminist security studies for attending to the margins and argue for the need for more grounded discussions of the causes and experiences of insecurity. Then I apply this theoretical discussion to fieldwork conducted with young people living in los Altos de Cazucá to ask how insecurity is understood by the children themselves who are often left out of discourses about security. The deeply embedded nature of insecurity, violence, and fear in many urban environments in Colombia has required residents to find new ways of coping with violence and insecurity in everyday life. Young people are aware of the complexities of such issues and articulate the connections and dissonances of an absent or harmful state, violence of local gangs, and ongoing consequences of stereotyping. These will be explored before finally looking at ways children seek security within their everyday life. In these situations, more complex notions of insecurity and *processes of securing* are rendered visible to inform explorations of insecurity and young people.

Theorizing everyday insecurity through children's lives

Koonings and Kruijt note that the 'syndrome of insecurity, violence and fear' has, within the urban Latin American context, caused 'a new brand of survival "know-how": coping with insecurity and violence in everyday life' (2007, 4). Globally, the population living in urban areas is increasing. In Colombia, the urban/rural ration is 70:30. For many of these people, experiences of urban life are experiences of poverty and exclusion, violence and insecurity. In 2012, UNICEF's annual report focused on 'Children in an Urban World'. It recognized the growing significance of negative indicators of rights including lack of secure tenure, lack of legal rights, lack of health provision, and inability to contribute to public debate as key challenges (UNICEF 2012, 3–6). The displaced and socially excluded communities on the edges of major cities in Colombia are exemplary of the myriad security challenges that children face in an increasingly urban world.

The focus of this article on the everyday insecurity of the lives of young people living in the urban periphery is underpinned by an understanding of children as competent actors in their own lives and is also informed by gendered critiques of security studies by feminist scholars, which highlight the absence of everyday concerns and individual experiences of insecurities in dominant discourses. These two foci are discussed and drawn together here.

What kind of childhood?

Skelton and Gough note that young people are 'part of the urban fabric' (2013, 463) yet they are discussed in ways that regularly reinscribe understandings of them as 'hood-lums and heroes, aggressors and achievers, wasters and workers' (2013, 459). In conflict-affected regions, similar dichotomies proliferate; McEvoy-Levy refers to this dominating view as reducing children to 'troublemakers or peacemakers' (2006), and Denov highlights the reliance on 'dangerous and disorderly' versus 'hapless victim' rhetoric when speaking about child soldiers specifically and conflict-affected children more broadly, also noting the propensity to render particular children 'heroes' (2010, 6–9). This dichotomization reflects the broader understanding of childhood across societies and situations, which sees children ideally as innocent and in need of protection. Children are universally conceived as incomplete, irrational, passive 'becomings' (Qvortrup 1994, 94) progressing toward a normative adulthood. If they fall outside this behavior, they can otherwise only be conceived of as transgressive and thus potentially dangerous and delinquent (see James and Prout 1990 for foundational discussion and critique of these ideas). In contrast to such reductive notions of childhood, academics within childhood studies and across disciplines have demonstrated that children are in fact competent actors and influencers of their everyday lives (see, among many others, Jenks 2005; Wyness 2006; Boyden 2004).

Dichotomies and stereotypes speak before young people themselves can offer alternatives. As a result, narratives of conflict and insecurity are largely articulated by adults and, consequentially, often perpetuate stereotypes about youth. Boyden notes this presupposes that children's insights 'have no relevance', are 'unreliable' testimony, and that they 'lack the maturity to hold and articulate valid views' (2004, 248). While work is increasingly been conducted within international relations (IR) broadly that takes a complex engagement with the notion of childhood seriously (Boyden 2004; McEvoy-Levy 2006; Denov 2010; Beier 2011; Watson 2006; Lee-Koo 2011; Pruitt 2013), children's participation and inclusion is not the norm. This article situates itself alongside these growing efforts to think about young people complexly as a way of accounting for and recognizing children's experiences of insecurity.

Insecurity in the everyday

Situating this exploration within the tensions caused by the 'syndrome of insecurity, violence and fear' described by Koonings and Kruijt in the Latin American context necessitates a questioning of how theoretical understandings of security and experiences of insecurity can locate and interrogate the lived experiences of children in these environments. A fruitful place to commence is within more critical engagements with the notion of security that move the focus away from states, weapons, and the macro-processes of conflict to the everyday lives of people themselves. In attending to the people usually rendered invisible in discussions of security, this article finds resonance with feminist explorations that take as their task a denaturalization of the inherent passivity and depoliticization of women and, by extension, children. Analyses and research by feminist IR scholars begin at the margins of political and social life but interrogate those who occupy the 'centers' and the exercise of power that perpetuates such inequalities and exclusions (Ackerly, Stern, and True 2006; see also Sylvester 1994). Feminist security studies draws attention to the bottom-up approaches that, as Tickner points out, are vital to understand issues of in/security and in helping 'emancipatory visions of security…[move] beyond statist frameworks' (2001, 48). In particular, D'Costa calls to attend to the insights of those marginalized in geopolitically marginal conflicts, and in spaces IR frequently tends to ignore (2006, 130–31). Tickner (2006, 29) argues that feminist scholarship, because of its situated awareness, necessarily focuses on the '"practical knowledge" from people's everyday lives'.

The spaces that children occupy are often similarly marginal to those occupied by women (although the oppression and frameworks of exclusion may operate in different registers); as a result, a framework that starts with feminist curiosity and attention can provide an important entry to considerations of security at an everyday level. There is an assumption made that those who occupy the margins are so far from the exercise of power that their opinions and voices could have little relevance (Enloe 1996, 186). Moreover, as Enloe notes, margins, silences, and bottom rungs cannot exist without someone occupying the center and these processes are not inherent but are the product of an exercise of power (1996, 186–89). Recognition that the margins are created and maintained through active processes of marginalization draws attention to the fact that the state is often complicit in perpetuating the exclusions and violences through systems of power and control that render the lives of individuals at the margins insecure in multiple, interconnected ways (see, among others, Shepherd 2008; Wibben 2010, 85). Marginalization is associated with 'economic and political weakness or powerlessness' and the resultant exclusion 'is the most dominant form of exclusionary practice by states or social groups over which marginalized groups have little or no control' (D'Costa 2006, 130). Considering young people who are marginalized, stigmatized, and excluded brings into sharp relief how insecurity functions as a collection of violences and exclusions.

Located within more critical engagements with notions of human security practices, Roberts posits a notion of the everyday in conflict-affected spaces as a 'reaction to chronic personal insecurity, as well as to a range of other contingencies' (2011, 412). He argues that this refocusing of the 'concept of security to concern people's everyday existences' may have profound implications for those most vulnerable people who live daily with significant insecurity (2008, 14). This requires a move away from a preoccupation with institutions and 'best-suited' actors, to focus on those actors who are marginalized. It also requires recognition that formal political processes and intimate, mundane everyday life are not distinct but inform each other. As De Certeau (1984, 14) argues, everyday life consists of repetitive and distinctive practices that push back against structural attempts at organizing life. People can, through everyday practices, take ownership over structures and use them to their advantage. Applying the idea of the everyday to security practice refocuses the way people use structures as well as relationships to recognize and respond to those things that make individuals feel insecure. The potential of considering these ideas on an everyday level is the ability to explore how individuals 'negotiate around violence, structural and overt, around material issues, or indeed deploys or co-opts these' (Richmond 2009, 331). Duffield (2007) recognizes that productive peacebuilding might stem from the idea of 'self-securing' that is contrasted against a notion of the state as the provider of security. While personal spaces might sometimes be 'partly secured' from violence by security sector reform, the most pervasive threats to everyday life are the effects of poverty; ill health; displacement from familiar surroundings; and lack of sufficient food, water, and sanitation. Such people, in attempting to secure their everyday lives, will prioritize solutions to these everyday threats, rather than be concerned about institutions of a distant, uncaring state.

In these contexts, which are *rendered insecure* by structural forces and the disregard of elites, it is the interrelationships between people that hold communities together. Accordingly, to speak of security – or insecurity – is to speak to structures of violence and of power, to discuss vulnerability, deliberate exclusion, and the interconnected nature of structural and direct violences. All these come together and are encountered within and on the bodies of those who are most affected, particularly children who are already structurally marginalized. While there is significant and important literature on repopulating the structures of violence and insecurity, there is a need to also (re)populate the discourse with an engagement with those for whom insecurity is a daily phenomenon.

Los Altos de Cazucá, Colombia

To explore these notions further, this article now turns to the fieldwork site of los Altos de Cazucá,[1] one of many informal communities that exist on the outskirts of Colombia's cities. Driven by high levels of displacement and overwhelmingly rural-to-urban migration patterns, since the 1970s communities of displaced and otherwise excluded people have been established around major cities in Colombia by those fleeing the conflict. These *barrio* communities occupy land illegally, constructing dwellings with whatever materials are available. The poverty and exclusion of such communities is immediately visible in the lack of paved roads, poorly constructed houses, presence of refuse, tangles of electricity lines, and general absence of curated public space. Cazucá in Comuna 4 of the city of Soacha is one such community and exists precariously on the steep hillside next to the highway south out of the capital Bogota. Comuna 4 is one of the highest recipient-communities in Colombia of internally displaced people (Medico Sin Fronteras 2005). The Municipality of Soacha recognizes that almost half the population of the city is classified as 'vulnerable' and in poverty conditions with the largest concentration of these people in Comuna 4. In these communities, there are high levels of poverty, low job opportunities, lack of access to services, and gangs associated with the broader armed conflict control much of the space. Families and individuals at times have to leave the community because their names are placed by the armed gangs on *listas negras* (black lists), which mark people for death. Employment is either in low-end service industries such as cleaning and laboring or on the informal market selling goods on the roadside. Many parents struggle to earn enough to provide for their families.

This article is informed by 4 months of fieldwork carried out from September to December 2010 with children from Cazucá. I gained access to the community through an organization that works with marginalized children around Colombia supporting education provision, nutrition programs, and community engagement. Working through a school supported by the organization, my fieldwork took the form of participant observation and semi-structured interviews with children aged between 10 and 17. Additional information was gained through interviews with adults from the community as well as with other organizations working on similar issues in other parts of the country. Names of all participants are pseudonyms to protect anonymity and safety. All interviews were conducted in Spanish by the author.

Ethical considerations of working with children who are often categorized as 'vulnerable' or 'marginal' were taken very seriously throughout the research. As discussed in detail above, this work is underpinned by a feminist ethic of attention to the margins and a commitment to validate and respect the experiences and voices of young people themselves. This meant that at times the process was fraught with both practical and ethical questions. Entering into this space in a position of privilege both as an adult and an outsider required ongoing reflexivity about my presence and also limited what I could claim as knowledge from the conversations with young people (for related discussion on reflexivity and power relationships, see Ackerly, Stern, and True 2006, 5; Punch 2002). Particularly in conducting research with conflict-affected children ethical questions of safety, participation, and power relations are particularly acute (Morrow and Richards 1996; Hart and Tyrer 2006; Freeman and Mathison 2009). Security concerns also meant I was unable to speak to children in the community who were not in school or were involved in the armed gangs; this necessarily limits the perspective that is engaged with here. However, any account is partial, and in recognizing the partiality this article respects the voices of those young people who did participate.

This article now turns to a consideration of young people's experiences and accounts of everyday insecurity to explore structural exclusion and violence before discussing young people's experiences of direct violence, fear, and insecurity. It then concludes with reflections by young people on ways of mitigating or responding to these structural and direct violences and insecurities.

Flattened narratives of childhood and structural violences

For the young people of Cazucá, overcoming the stigmatization of the community is an immense challenge. Of course, the young people of Cazucá are a distinctly heterogeneous collective of age, background, sexuality, employment situation, educational achievement, ethnicity, family position, personal desires, and aspirations. However, many authors note that adults generally tend to perceive these young people reductively as either 'transgressors' or as a 'problem' (Duque 2009; Villamizar Rojas and Zamora Vasquez 2005, 74; Pinzon Ochoa 2007, 288) and several teachers in the school in Cazucá echoed this sentiment, saying they felt that the challenges that exist for children generally are amplified in communities such as Cazucá because of the children's 'social status and geographic location' (teacher, in interview, November 2010). One teacher noted that while children's decision-making capacities are rarely recognized, in Cazucá 'they are often seen as delinquents and drug addicts' (in interview, November 2010) compounding opinions of children as incapable. Pinzon Ochoa (2007, 288) argues that the state is often criticized for 'interpreting the realities of young people as problems' particularly in sectors like Cazucá. More than this the government 'underline their [young people's] relationships with violence, insecurity and drug addiction, cataloguing the population as "high risk"' (Pinzon Ochoa 2007, 288). Hence, while the state has not been entirely absent in formulating responses and assistance, it has been carried out in the 'best interests' of an envisioned, imagined child. As a result, this idealized young person becomes 'representative, and thus [all] young people are represented' (Valderrama 2004, 166). Consequently, the actual realities and multiplicities of experience are erased. Not only this but in flattening experiences young people are both written out of the conversation and responses to the structures of violence that perpetuate insecurity for young people. For young people, faced with the consequences and experiences of both structural and direct violences and insecurities, it is the small practices within their everyday lives that are significant to them and that contribute to understanding local responses to insecurity. As Koonings and Kruijt note, coping with insecurity and violence in everyday life has prompted a new form of survival 'know-how', in which everyday threats are prioritized over the grand securitizing narratives of the state (2007, 4).

Multiple armed groups and criminal organizations characterize Colombia's conflict with presences in both rural and urban environments. The long-running conflict has been fueled by illegal trades such as drug and arms trafficking and complicated by the existence of multiple armed groups and the emergence of new urban criminal gangs, particularly in poor neighborhoods. The presence of such illegal armed groups in communities such as Cazucá is well known. Such communities provide pathways in and out of major cities for such groups to traffic drugs and arms to and from the wider conflict. Because of the utility of these spaces, they are fiercely held and contested by different groups. Often children are caught in the middle as they are particularly vulnerable to recruitment as well as exposed to surrounding violences. The presence of these illegal groups necessitates the involvement of the state, which occurs largely through the bodies of police and soldiers. Law enforcement often enters the community in highly securitized ways, conducting raids on suspected gang members, seeking drugs, and engaging in violent confrontations with illegal armed groups. This limited 'engagement' by the police or military reinforces external notions of inherent violence and perpetuates potentially violent interactions with the occupants. *All* members of the community become read as potentially violent, delinquent, and dangerous.

The consequences of such labeling are visible in accounts given by children themselves. For many Colombians beyond Cazucá, the images of raids and gang activity dominate their understanding of the community via television and newspapers. Andrea (age 11) explained how when her father went looking for work he was rejected when he told the potential employer where he was living (in interview, November 2010). Similarly, another student linked the difficulty of finding employment directly to the interventions of the government in the community and associated media coverage in a conversation during a lunch break at school with several students. One student told me of an incident a few weeks earlier where one of his older brothers was refused a job because he came from the neighborhood that had been on the news the previous day and thus was seen as potentially connected to the drug violence.

More than just stigmatization and its consequences, the security ostensibly provided by the state to its citizens is denied. Laura succinctly highlighted this in our conversation:

Laura (age 17):   the police are useless here on the hill (*la loma*). Their only use is as decoration. That's the truth.
    Researcher: *So the police are part of the problem?*
    Laura: Sometimes, yes.

The ongoing exposure to police, military, and gang violence renders people's lives fundamentally insecure. There is a profound structural violence at play also, visible in the disjuncture between the demands *on* the state by those living in marginalized and poverty-affected conditions, and the reluctance or inability *of* the state to provide adequate and necessary services.

While a majority of the occupants of the *barrio* are not involved in illegal activity and would prefer it not to occur, the violent interventions by the state security forces in which all occupants are seen as potentially violent and potentially involved only increased distrust of state forces. Such distrust increases the space in which the gangs can operate and decreases security for all members of the community. Violence and poverty become associated with particular neighborhoods or communities, marking them as *other*, and stigmatizing all those within them as violent or deviant. The effects of such configurations are processes of social exclusion that inscribe insecurity as a permanent fact of life. Pinzon Ochoa notes that in different *barrios* the threat varies – sometimes occupants are more affected by the local gangs, sometimes by targeted assassination and 'black listing', sometimes by paramilitary organizations or guerillas – however, the security of the population depends on their ability to exist in a state of 'generalized prevention' with people they do not know because they might be informants (2007, 284). In such an environment, contradictions, tensions, and insecurity contribute negatively to social cohesion and can result in increased levels of violence, both actualized and anticipated.

In Cazucá, paramilitaries associated with the broader conflict control the community through targeted threats and assassinations (Duque 2009; field notes, October 2010). Often this is done through the use of 'black lists' (*listas negras*), which serve as public notice of threat of death and generally result in the named party (and often their family) leaving the community. Several young women described this happening to a friend of theirs whose family was given 24 hours to leave:

Camila Andrea (age 14):   Yes, you have to go with your family, if you don't they kill them. This happened to one of our classmates.
    Laura (age 17):   Yes.
    Camila Andrea: It's that you have to go, you don't even know why. There is only one option: leave or get killed.

Rosa (age 15) also argued that this violence, which results in such precarious and insecure lived experience for many young people, is carried out without consideration of or care for the consequences:

Rosa (age 15):   There is a saying that they 'kill without knowing'. For example they kill someone and they don't know the pain that their mother feels, or they break windows in a poor family's house. It is all with impunity.

In children's lives, these acts manifest as profoundly destabilizing and insecure practices. Structures that should be secure, such as family and the home, are made into sites of potential danger. Evident in this situation is the precariousness and insecurity of life for young people, compounded by violence and death, which frustrates efforts to build more secure communities and lives (see also Riaño-Alcalá 2010 for detailed ethnographic work with young people in Medellin's *barrios*).

The presence of gangs and actors associated with the broader armed conflict in the community dramatically increases the sense of insecurity experienced by young people. The threat of violence is compounded by the stigma many children feel in response to narratives that characterize all young people as potentially involved in such groups. The public spaces of the community are circumscribed by both the threat and presence of armed actors (both illegal and state sanctioned). More than this, the domination of these actors occurs through acts of violence against the bodies of those who pass through these spaces; such acts include assassinations, robbery, sexual assault, extortion, and bribery. The consequences of these direct violences are discussed in the following section.

Fear, violences, and insecurity as a lived condition

As noted, exclusion and the specific forms of engagement by the state in the community permit the structures that impose multiple violences on the everyday lives of young people and render their daily existence insecure. Such experiences are not unique to Cazucá, but symptomatic of life in urban poor settlements across Latin America. McIlwaine and Moser (2007, 118–19), in conducting a large systematic survey of occupants of urban poor settlements in Colombia and Guatemala, found that violence of all types constituted between 40 and 50% of the concerns raised by respondents. These forms of violence and their associated fear and insecurity are articulated as relating to structural causes such as poverty and inequality; these people are also aware of how their marginalized position exacerbates violences (Moser and McIlwaine 2000). Arriagada and Godoy (2000) argue that within the context of Latin American cities widespread insecurity manifests as a result of the intersections of political violence with social and economic violence. In Moser and McIlwaine's (2000) study, young people were especially concerned with the drug problem in their communities, particularly the government's perceived lack of response, as well as generalized insecurity outside of the home. Young men mentioned gang violence while young women discussed these themes, as well as the risks of sexual assault on the street (2000, 25). Younger children identified violence outside the home, particularly men holding weapons, as a reoccurring theme in discussions (2000, 26). Such findings demonstrate the way in which specific instances of violence are embedded in a framework of insecurity that shapes everyday life and preoccupies the young occupants of these marginalized communities.

Fear of violence has 'gradually come to curtail, fragment and annul' (Restrepo 2004, 179) many of the crucial social spaces of the city, resulting in a weakening of social capital and the interactions between citizens that strengthen ties and sense of community. Daniela (age 16), when asked about the most difficult things about being young in Cazucá, replied without hesitation: 'insecurity … more than anything. Seriously. To be young'. In addition to this understanding of age as a risk factor, experiences of living in Cazucá are regularly described by the young people as specific experiences of insecurities. For example:

Yamila (age 11): Where I live, next to where I live there almost always are thieves.
Javier (age 11): Well, here it is bad because there are many robbers and there are many people who kill lots of people.

In response to being asked what they dislike about living in Cazucá, or what is difficult about living there, these three young people had immediate examples:

Paola (age 15): Well, what I don't like is the insecurity. You have to be very aware. Of everything and…
Alejandro (age 17): For me, well, no, it is that there are many thieves, and yes, the insecurity. That you can't even go to the corner sometimes.
Juliana (age 17): Yes, for me the insecurity also, more than anything; and the houses where no one lives.

A sense of insecurity, for these three, is not an abstract concept, but bound up in practices and places that they inhabit. Empty houses are seen by the community as potential sites of danger because they are not 'claimed' or sanctioned and so can be occupied by 'less friendly neighbors', as one teacher commented, referring to the criminal gangs, and the smaller scale drug vendors in the neighborhood. These varied violent actions circumscribe the space in which children can act, and cut threads of social cohesion and community. The consequence, beyond immediate risk of violence, is a precariousness and insecurity that becomes pervasive in young people's everyday lives.

Challenging flattened readings of insecure young people: responses to everyday insecurity

Amidst the insecure environments of their everyday lives, children find spaces and ways of being that actively resist the violence. These spaces include the school, spaces provided by NGOs, and at times collective community celebrations. Villamizar Rojas and Zamora Vasquez (2005, 70–71) point out that 'new forms of expression' arise in places of encounter that are often quite public. They point to the street or shops in which young people gather to claim particular ways of being and being recognized. These spaces, along with institutional spaces such as schools, also allow the establishment of normal routines. Collective engagements and routines form securing practices for children that are crucial in responding to persistent, daily insecurity. For children living among ongoing violence, maintaining routines increases a sense of autonomy and reinscribes the normalcy of everyday life and such practices are often linked to sites such as the home, the mall, or school and underscore coping mechanisms in young people (Pat-Horenczyk, Schiff, Doppelt 2006).

In responding to insecurity, many children recognized the school as a site that offers potential, a space where young people could pursue individual goals and also work collaboratively with others. Schools provide a sense of predictability and can foster 'enriched social networks' (Bentancourt and Khan 2008, 323). Such findings echo those of Villamizar Rojas and Zamora Vasquez (2005) as well as Burgess (2008, 273–84) to reinforce the ways in which sites such as the school can respond on a local, everyday level to ameliorate the sense of insecurity for young people. One of the teachers described the school as a space of 'refuge, where there is less violence' and argued this space allows children to form resilience and actively respond to difficult everyday environments. More than this, the actions of young people in this space are recognized and validated, and this creates a positive and collaborative environment:

> Researcher: *And why do you like school?*
> Susana (age 15): Because you are treated well. There are many good teachers, well not all, but most, and for example I have an attachment to almost all the teachers because they treat you well and are really lovely with us. They never raise their voice at me and treat you well and I understand the classes. And well, many places you don't have this. So that is why I like school.

> Researcher: *Do you like going to school?*
> Johan David (age 11): Yes! Because they teach well and all my friends are here and it is a good place to be for a child.

As well as teachers, strong friendship groups can be seen as a strength of the space of school. It is worth noting that in making use of the institution of the school young people are not simply perpetuating learned understandings of children as passive or innocent. Rather, these articulations demonstrate that many children are aware of the spaces available to them and make conscious choices to use them and access the support they offer. The space of the school can be conceptualized as a *site of opportunity* among everyday violence and insecurity (Berents 2014).[2]

Violence and insecurity limit young people's ability to move through the community and so young people modify their travels through the community to avoid these dangers, creating particular pathways in their everyday lives that are more secure. This involves walking to school past friends' houses and avoiding areas that are *caliente* ('hot', or dangerous) even if it means a longer walk. They speak with one another as well as adults to find the most recent information on potential insecurities in the community and will quickly act to respond either by stopping at a friend's house rather than continuing their walk home, altering their route, or passing on information to others who might be more affected. These practices are fundamentally everyday actions on a mundane level where young people actively respond to the insecurity that manifests in their lives.

Children in Cazucá both recognize the complexity of the issues facing their lives and argue for their inclusion in solutions. In these discussions, it was not local community but politicians or others in positions of power and privilege that were identified as having some culpability for the issues facing Cazucá, but also some ability to affect change.

> Researcher: *What do you have to contribute to these conversations [with adults, if they listened]?*
> Paola (age 15): Well, about the insecurity and everything, to try and fix this a little because this area [Cazucá] is often of very little concern to the politicians. It is like a tiny black dot on a sheet of paper… and so, to listen about how they can help the people who need it, because really now we see politicians that are worthless.
> Alejandro (age 15): Yes.
> Juliana (age 17): Yes, things are getting worse, well. [It would be better] that they pay attention to us, that older adults pay attention to the young people.

The challenges of the environment of Cazucá form the context in which both individual and collective efforts are located. Acute consciousness of the way Cazucá and the young people who occupy it are seen 'outside', coupled with the daily experiences of violence and conflict, make young people both highly motivated and defensive of their ability to achieve things in the future. This comment by Felipe (age 16) is indicative of these tensions and challenges:

Felipe: [after describing different forms of violence that 'never leave'] In part it is bad because it affects us and it does damage to us... but it is in part good, I guess, because it has taught us to support each other, to pull yourself forward and don't give up...

The efforts to affect change, located in everyday practices and supported through physical sites, such as educational institutions that assist in the amelioration of the insecurity of daily life, allow the potential for young people's daily routines to contribute to a sense of potential in the future. This is one compelling reading of Koonings and Kruijt's 'new brand of survival "know-how"' to negotiate violence in everyday life (2007, 4). It is the challenges of environments that are violent and insecure as well as attitudes that are dismissive of the capacity of young people that have the potential to annul these efforts.

Conclusion

This exploration of insecurity, through structural exclusion and stigmatization as well as direct violences, is not meant as a totalizing account of the lives of young people of the community. Rather, paying attention to how these encounters are experienced reframes how insecurity must be conceived through the lives and bodies of those living amidst conflict in their everyday lives. Responding to a feminist commitment to paying attention to the margins, this article has sought, through accounts of their own experiences, to contextualize discussions of the insecurity of Colombia's conflict-affected urban youth that tend to speak *for* young people. Emergent from these discussions of stigma, violence, and the resultant everyday fear and challenges is a more complex terrain of violence and insecurity. While children are not generally in a position to challenge the structures that actively marginalize them and their communities on a structural level, they constantly and actively seek ways of ameliorating the risks and violences to their lives. The act of belonging to the community is not straightforward; a sense of insecurity for many young people is not abstract but bound up in complex practices and places in young people's everyday lives – practices and places that are not accounted for by dominant security discourses.

Enloe notes that those who occupy the margins and 'bottom rungs' are assumed to have nothing relevant to contribute, an assumption that erases their agency and reinscribes presumed hierarchies of power. Understandings of security, or the insecurity of people's lives, that do not interrogate such assumptions are weakened. A critical feminist perspective that takes as central the importance and validity of the margins challenges narratives that disregard these sites as unimportant in theorizing security. Confronted with stigmatization and social exclusion as well as the direct and indirect violences of daily life, children negotiate their insecurity in multiple, active, and fluid ways. Riaño-Alcalá, in writing on children and youth in similar communities in Medellin, Colombia, makes explicit the 'shifting positions of youth', recognizing that they at different times, [serve] as sufferers of the loss of their loved ones or close friends, as perpetrators of violence, as carriers of hate and feelings of revenge, as active participants in democratic proposals, as witnesses to violence, or as participants in social movements and counter-cultural expressions. (2010, 13)

Paying attention to the lives of those who are insecure demonstrates that young people experience insecurity in specific ways. Because of their often-dichotomous characterization as innocent *or* delinquent, they are at the juncture of different securing practices, yet the lived complexity of their lives, not accounted for in simplistic formulations, renders them particularly exposed to pervasive insecurities.

This article does not attempt to imply that children's experiences and views provide a complete response to multiple understandings of insecurity. Rather, it argues that the ways in which insecurity pervades the daily lives of those who are made insecure are invisible in dominant discourses that attempt to diagnose these insecurities. Exploring how young people experience insecurities in their daily lives contributes to a fuller picture of what insecurity means in spaces made marginal and insecure by conflict. Understandings of insecurity cannot be flattened or read as straightforward but require – or even demand – closer engagement with the conditions and interrelations between processes and structures that render people insecure. Similarly, children's lives and engagements with their insecure lives must be read as complex, adaptive, and variable.

Notes

1. Inhabitants referred to the community simply as Cazucá, and this shortened form is used throughout this article.
2. As noted, this article focuses on those young people who are in school. It cannot speak for those who are unable or have opted out of education. It is important to note that other research highlights the self-securing role gangs can play in young people's lives, providing security, social cohesion and belonging (Duque 2009, 29–31; Pinzon Ochoa 2007, 283; Villamizar Rojas and Zamora Vasquez 2005, 70). This exploration is beyond the scope of this article, but draws attention to the fact that young people respond to everyday insecurity in a variety of ways and such activities merit further exploration.

References

Ackerly, B. A., M. Stern, and J. True, eds. 2006. *Feminist Methodologies for International Relations*. Cambridge: Cambridge University Press.

Arriagada, I., and L. Godoy. 2000. "Prevention or Repression? The False Dilemma of Citizen Security." *CEPAL Review* 70: 111–136.

Beier, J. M., ed. 2011. *The Militarization of Childhood: Thinking Beyond the Global South*. New York: Palgrave Macmillan.

Berents, H. 2014. "'Its About Finding a Way': Children, Sites of Opportunity, and Building Everyday Peace in Colombia." *The International Journal of Children's Rights* 22 (2): 361–384. doi:10.1163/15718182-02202006.

Betancourt, T. S., and K. T. Khan. 2008. "The Mental Health of Children Affected by Armed Conflict: Protective Processes and Pathways to Resilience." *International Review of Psychiatry* 20 (3): 317–328. doi:10.1080/09540260802090363.

Boyden, J. 2004. "Anthropology Under Fire: Ethics, Researchers and Children in War." In *Children and Youth on the Front Line: Ethnography, Armed Conflict and Displacement*, edited by J. Boyden and J. D. Berry, 237–261. New York: Berghahn Books.

Burgess, R. 2008. "Formal and Nonformal Education: Impacting the Psychosocial Well-being of Displaced, Violence-affected Children in Colombia." PhD diss., Teachers College, Columbia University.

CODHES (Consultoria para los Derechos Humanos y el Desplazamiento [Consultancy on Human Rights and Displacement]). 2010. *Número De Personas Desplazadas Por Departamento De Llegada* [Number of People Displaced by Department of Arrival]. Bogota: CODHES.

D'Costa, B. 2006. "Marginalized Identity: New Frontiers for Research in IR?" In *Feminist Methodologies for International Relations*, edited by B. Ackerly, M. Stern, and J. True, 129–152. Cambridge: Cambridge University Press.

De Certeau, M. 1984. *The Practice of Everyday Life*. Berkeley: University of California Press.

Denov, M. 2010. *Child Soldiers: Sierra Leone's Revolutionary United Front*. Cambridge: Cambridge University Press.

Duffield, M. 2007. *Development, Security and Unending War: Governing the World of Peoples*. Cambridge: Polity Press.

Duque, L. F. 2009. *Educacion Y Conflicto: Altos De Cazucá* [Education and Conflict: Altos De Cazucá]. Bogota: Fundacion para la Educacion y el Desarrollo (Fedes).

Enloe, C. 1996. "Margins, Silences and Bottom Rungs: How to Overcome the Underestimation of Power in the Study of International Relations." In *International Theory: Positivism and Beyond*, edited by S. Smith, K. Booth, and M. Zalewski, 186–202. Cambridge: Cambridge University Press.

Freeman, M., and S. Mathison. 2009. *Researching Children's Experiences*. New York: Guildford Press.

Hart, J., and B. Tyrer. 2006 "Research with Children Living in Situations of Armed Conflict: Concepts, Ethics & Methods." RSC Working Paper Series. Oxford: Refugee Studies Centre (RSC), University of Oxford.

James, A., and A. Prout, eds. 1990. *Constructing and Reconstructing Childhood*. Basingstoke: Falmer Press.

Jenks, C. 2005. *Childhood*. 2nd ed. London: Routledge.

Koonings, K., and D. Kruijt. 2007. "Introduction." In *Fractured Cities: Social Exclusion, Urban Violence and Contested Spaces in Latin America*, edited by K. Koonings and D. Kruijt, 1–5. London: Zed Books.

Lee-Koo, K. 2011. "Horror and Hope: (Re)presenting Militarised Children in Global North-South Relations." *Third World Quarterly* 32 (4): 725–742. doi:10.1080/01436597.2011.567005.

Luckham, R. 2009. "Introduction: Transforming Security and Development in an Unequal World." *IDS Bulletin* 40 (2): 1–10. doi:10.1111/j.1759-5436.2009.00016.x.

McEvoy-Levy, S., ed. 2006. *Troublemakers or Peacemakers? Youth and Post-Accord Peace Building*. Notre Dame, IN: University of Notre Dame Press.

McIlwaine, C., and C. O. N. Moser. 2007. "Living in Fear: How the Urban Poor Perceive Violence, Fear and Insecurity." In *Fractured Cities: Social Exclusion, Urban Violence and Contested Spaces in Latin America*, edited by K. Koonings and D. Kruijt, 117–136. London: Zed Books.

Medico Sin Fronteras. 2005. *Altos de Cazucá: Hasta cuando en el olvido*. Bogota: Medico Sin Fronteras.

Morrow, V., and M. Richards. 1996. "The Ethics of Social Research with Children: An Overview." *Children & Society* 10 (2): 90–105. doi:10.1111/j.1099-0860.1996.tb00461.x.

Moser, C. O. N., and C. McIlwaine. 2000. *Urban Poor Perceptions of Violence and Exclusion in Colombia, Conflict Prevention and Post-Conflict Reconstruction*. Washington, DC: The World Bank.

Pat-Horenczyk, R., M. Schiff, and O. Doppelt. 2006. "Maintaining Routine Despite Ongoing Exposure to Terrorism: A Healthy Strategy for Adolescents?" *Journal of Adolescent Health* 39 (2): 199–205. doi:10.1016/j.jadohealth.2005.11.021.

Pinzon Ochoa, N. M. 2007. "Los Jovenes De 'La Loma': Altos De Cazuca Y El Paramilitarismo En La Periferia De Bogota [Youth of 'The Hillside': Altos De Cazucá and Paramilitarism on the Periphery of Bogota]." *Maguare* 21: 271–295.

Pruitt, L. 2013. *Youth Peacebuilding: Music, Gender, Change*. New York: SUNY Press.

Punch, S. 2002. "Research with Children: The Same or Different from Research with Adults?" *Childhood* 9 (3): 321–341. doi:10.1177/0907568202009003005.

Qvortrup, J. 1994. "Childhood Matters: An Introduction." In *Childhood Matters: Social Theory, Practice and Politics*, edited by J. Qvortrup, M. Bardy, G. Sgritta, and H. Wintersberger, 1–24. Hants: Avebury.

Restrepo, L. A. 2004. "Violence and Fear in Colombia: Fragmentation of Space, Contraction of Time and Forms of Evasion." In *Armed Actors: Organised Violence and State Failure in Latin America*, edited by K. Koonings and D. Kruijt, 172–185. London: Zed Books.

Riaño-Alcalá, P. 2010. *Dwellers of Memory: Youth and Violence in Medellín, Colombia*. New Brunswick, NJ: Transaction Publishers.

Richmond, O. P. 2009. "Becoming Liberal, Unbecoming Liberalism. Liberal-Local Hybridity via the Everyday as a Response to the Paradoxes of Liberal Peacebuilding." *Journal of Intervention and Statebuilding* 3 (3): 324–344. doi:10.1080/17502970903086719.

Roberts, D. 2008. *Human Insecurity: Global Structures of Violence*. London: Zed Books.

Roberts, D. 2011. "Post-Conflict Peacebuilding, Liberal Irrelevance and the Locus of Legitimacy." *International Peacekeeping* 18 (4): 410–424. doi:10.1080/13533312.2011.588388.

Shepherd, L. 2008. *Gender, Violence and Security: Discourse as Practice*. London: Zed Books.

Skelton, T., and K. V. Gough. 2013. "Introduction: Young People's Im/Mobile Urban Geographies." *Urban Studies* 50 (3): 455–466. doi:10.1177/0042098012468900.

Sylvester, C.1994. "Empathetic Co-operation: A Feminist Method for IR." *Millennium - Journal of International Studies* 23 (2): 315–334. doi:10.1177/03058298940230021301.

Tickner, J. A.2001. *Gendering World Politics: Issues and Approaches in the Post-Cold War Era*. New York: Columbia University Press.

Tickner, J. A. 2006. "Feminism Meets International Relations: Some Methodological Issues." In *Feminist Methodologies for International Relations*, edited by B. Ackerly, M. Stern, and J. True, 19–41. Cambridge: Cambridge University Press.

UNHCR (United Nations High Commission for Refugees). 2012. *UNHCR Country Operations Profile – Colombia*. http://www.unhcr.org/pages/49e492ad6.html

UNICEF (United Nations Children's Fund). 2012. *The State of the World's Children: Children in an Urban World*. New York: United Nations.

Valderrama, A. 2004. "Una Mirada a Las Singularidades Juveniles [A Look at the Specificities of Youth]." *Maguare* 18: 161–195.

Villamizar Rojas, R., and S. Zamora Vasquez. 2005. "Vivir Juvenil En Medios De Conflictos Urbanos: Una Aproximacion En La Zona Colindante Entre Bogota Y Soacha [Living Young in the Middle of Urban Conflicts: An Approach in the Adjacent Zone between Bogota and Soacha]." In *Jovenes, Conflictos Urbanos Y Alternativas De Inclusion* [Youth, Urban Conflicts and Alternatives for Inclusion], edited by V. S. Ruiz. Bogota: Plataforma Conflicto Urbano y Jovenes, CIVIS Suecia & ASDI.

Watchlist on Children and Armed Conflict. 2012. *No One to Trust: Children and Armed Conflict in Colombia*. New York: Watchlist on Children and Armed Conflict.

Watson, A. M. S. 2006. "Children and International Relations: A New Site of Knowledge?" *Review of International Studies* 32 (2): 237–250. doi:10.1017/S0260210506007005.

Wibben, A. T. R. 2010. "Feminist Security Studies." In *The Routledge Handbook of Security Studies*, edited by M. Dunn Cavelty and V. Mauer, 84–94. London: Routledge.

Wyness, M. 2006. *Children and Society: An Introduction to the Sociology of Childhood*. Houndsmills: Palgrave Macmillan.

Zea, J. E. 2010. "Internal Displacement in Colombia: Violence, Resettlement, and Resistance." PhD diss., Portland State University.

Shifting the burden: childhoods, resilience, subjecthood

J. Marshall Beier

Department of Political Science, McMaster University, Hamilton, ON, Canada

Despite broadening of its boundaries over the past two decades, Security Studies has so far paid very little attention to childhood and its relationship to status quo circulations of power, to children as possessed of bona fide political subjecthood, and to the under-interrogated ideational commitments that have made these exclusions appear relatively unproblematic. In contrast, the rise of resilience thinking across a range of disciplines in recent years has attracted considerable attention from security scholars and practitioners alike. This article takes a critical perspective on the idea of resilience in connection with children's (in)security, arguing that the failure to take seriously children's political subjecthood has dire implications for the figuring and assignment of responsibility for traumas visited upon young people in a range of contexts. Moving beyond zones of conflict to consider also the everyday of (post)industrial societies of the Global North, it finds that resilience thinking together with an impoverished conception of childhood agency may move even the most benignly conceived interventions in cases of real or presumed childhood trauma to place responsibility for the work of forbearance on children themselves.

Introduction

This article brings into articulation two important new literatures recently emergent in Critical Security Studies, both of which draw on longer lineages and intersections in other disciplines and fields of study. The first, inquiring into issues of children and childhood, has thus far seen some significant contributions by an as yet small community of scholars and from a variety of points of intervention. The second new and growing body of literature also engages an idea (or, more accurately, a field of ideas) already very well established in, among others, various scholarly, professional, vocational, and clinical settings: resilience (see, for example, Folke 2006; Windle 2011; Zolkoski and Bullock 2012; Panter-Brick and Leckman 2013). Though, like children and childhood, it too came late to Security Studies, resilience got almost immediate traction and, in fact, has become something of a buzzword in recent years. The value in reflecting on children/childhood and resilience together, as I set out to do herein, is that each is productive of important insights regarding the other and apropos to thinking about how both might fit into critical currents of thought about security. It is the aim of this article to highlight something of this and, in particular, to raise some important and troubling implications of an insufficiently critical embrace of resilience thinking. In this sense, I will sketch something of a cautionary tale about a darker side of resilience thinking and how it may become bound up with childhood insecurity in highly problematic ways.

But, before proceeding, a caveat is in order regarding the approach to be taken here. Even within the relatively narrow delineations marked by their emergence in Security Studies, it is beyond the scope of this article to attempt a comprehensive survey of the literatures dealing with either children/childhood or resilience, let alone both. Accordingly, in what follows, I address a common theme identifiable across several seemingly disparate contexts of childhood insecurity wherein resilience thinking functions to confer an ersatz subjecthood on young people in ways that risk downloading responsibility to them for their own (in)security whilst withholding their empowerment as bona fide political subjects. The point of this is not to issue a broad indictment of the work being undertaken in the name of resilience and, indeed, I will highlight some of its promising expressions and directions. Rather, by reflecting on the (in)security subject/ object positions occupied by children as child soldiers in zones of conflict, as victims of natural disasters and in abject material circumstances, and as clients of social services in the midst of family strife, we catch some glimpses of how resilience thinking can help to expose important circuits of power that sustain and reproduce children's disempowerment and subjugation – and how, if we are insufficiently sensitive to this, it may work to deepen these processes and exacerbate their consequences. To this end, I will draw from the relevant newly emergent literatures in Critical Security Studies to make particular points, but make no pretence to an exhaustive treatment of either of these bodies of new scholarship, both of which are also due our careful attention on their own terms for all they have to tell us that is beyond the particular issues of concern in this article.

Beings/becomings, subjects/objects

Thinking about children and youth in relation to (in)security immediately poses problems where it is overcome by hegemonic and 'common sense' understandings of childhood, which, despite their historical specificity, can be remarkably resistant to the need to 'unlearn' them. Among the issues raised in recent contributions on children and childhood in Security Studies, questions of agency and subjecthood loom large (see, for example, Beier 2015; Jacob 2015; Macmillan 2015). These are inseparable from dominant ideas about the very 'nature' of childhood itself, which, in turn, bear directly on children's (in) security in myriad ways and contexts. Constructed in a paradoxical space between 'human being' and 'human becoming,' the universal child of hegemonic imagining poses a problem for dominant and emancipatory discourses alike where actual lived childhoods exceed or otherwise defy its very limited and profoundly limiting vision of young people as pre-political beings whose entry into social life must await passage through prefatory developmental stages. Fraught with indeterminacies and close ties to a particular late-modern (post)industrial historical context, the idea of innocent childhood and of children as 'human becomings' encodes, among other things, deeply entrenched assumptions about the limits of and need to regulate young people's agency. This follows from an underlying view of children as lacking the capacity for moderation and full faculties of reason, expressed most famously by Rousseau ([1979] 1762) and enduring still in his formidable and lasting imprint on liberal pedagogies and beyond – an outlook which militates strongly against recognition of children as bona fide political subjects.

For Rousseau, canonical instruction was not to be productively undertaken until early adulthood, following prior stages of education wherein learning takes place through a young person's accumulation of first-hand heuristic experience guided – but not directed –

by adults (Rousseau [1979] 1762, 168). On first gloss, this seems to centre the child as thinking and acting subject inasmuch as it is evocative of what we would today call 'student-centered learning': an approach that rejects what Paulo Freire (1970) famously denounced as the 'banking' method of conceiving students as empty vessels awaiting 'deposits' of knowledge imparted by the teacher, treating them instead as active co-participants in discovery. Read in its fuller context, however, Rousseau's is an impoverished conception of the young pupil's subjecthood in light of how staunchly he defended his assumption of an as yet unrealized capacity for rationality (Rousseau [1979] 1762, 60). More recent insights and advices of critical pedagogues notwithstanding, the logics and exigencies of systems of linear-progressive tutelage in our own time are such that scholarship and higher education more broadly belong almost entirely to the adult world. It is important to make explicit note of this, even if it might at first seem a rather prosaic statement, and to recognize that Security Studies is, perforce, in and of the adult world. Its core commitments and narratives count no children's voices among their authors, and the same may be said of other fields and disciplines. This might seem uniquely problematic in the case of Childhood Studies, since it is conspicuously 'about' children, but the fact is that all academic fields are about children and childhood in important ways, even if this is seldom acknowledged and notwithstanding the absence of children's voices.

For its part, the most straightforward sense in which Security Studies is 'about' children inheres, perhaps self-evidently, in the fact that children are part of the social worlds through and upon which visions and practices of security are predicated. Traditional formulations that make the state the referent object of security, for example, encode implicit claims about what is therefore in the security interests of the people, including children, who reside within. A breach of the physical security of the state, it is assumed, imperils fulfilment of its role as guarantor of security, and children and adults alike are among those taken to be reliant upon the provision of this critical social good. Similarly, human security approaches encompass children as irrevocably part of the aggregate referent in whose name security is variously defined and pursued. Somewhat more visibly, children populate key empirical subject matters and issue areas of interest to Security Studies as well. They appear, for instance, as simultaneously dangerous and endangered child soldiers. Children are counted among and frequently highlighted emblematically as the hapless 'collateral damage' of drone strikes in conflict zones and, just as readily, rendered ominously in worries about potentially destabilizing demographic 'youth bulges.' In short, Security Studies' near-complete neglect of children finds no vindication in any even minimally persuasive claim that the field is not at all 'about' them. In virtually every rendition, it very much is in some fashion or another.

More abstractly, *childhood* may be even more congenitally bound up in core commitments and ideas of Security Studies. Though much more broadly sited, hegemonic ideas about childhood are constitutive of operant ontological terrains upon which myriad projects both within and without the field depend for their intelligibility. To the extent that Security Studies unproblematically operates on this ontological terrain it also reproduces it and, with it, a particular understanding of childhood that, like Rousseau's, does not admit of engaging children as political subjects. Nowhere is this more profoundly the case than where the trope of innocent childhood is concerned. Both mainstream and critical discourses in Security Studies draw on and reproduce this trope in various ways, as do the politics, practices, and projects – from emancipatory or resistance struggles in everyday life to the prosecution of interstate wars – that security scholars study. Drawing on deeply held common senses and assumptions, the idea of childhood as a time of innocence and children as, therefore, bereft of responsibility and deserving of protection, manifests instrumentally as a potent political resource when purposefully deployed (see, for example, Moeller 2002; Watson 2011) and, more generally, fixes limits on imaginings of political life and its beings – in itself an (in)security practice, not unlike those that have rightly been challenged in recent decades for operating along exclusionary lines of gender, race, or class.

Whether in the campaign literature and deployed semiotics of the movement to ban landmines, vulgar war propaganda posters, or hackneyed appeals to 'our children's future' made by candidates for public office, children appear almost irresistible as devices to motivate political action. That they may be productively invoked in a full spectrum of political purposes speaks to their metonymic utility as unambiguous markers of embodied innocence and virtue. Importantly, the connection does not require elaboration – audiences can be counted on to decode childhood in this way, and this is revealing of just how deep-rooted its hegemonic renderings are. Together with the concomitant understanding of children as vulnerable and in need of protection, the idea of innocent childhood sketches political worlds wherein adults occupy subject positions and the subjecthood of children, as human becomings, is held in deferment. Essentialized as the protected objects of adult protectors, children constituted on the basis of hegemonic understandings of childhood thus become an enabling condition of adult political subjecthood. It is important, in light of this, to recognize that allusions to childhood allude also to adult–child relationships (Johansson 2011, 102) and, besides underwriting particular political projects, encode power relations that constitute adults as socio-political actors.

None of this is to say that children's agency is not frequently (made) visible in discourses and enactments of everyday political life as well as in the more rarefied colloquy of academe, including Security Studies. The agency of child soldiers, for example, on whose behalf much ink has been spilt over that past two decades and whose plight has been taken up in a proliferation of increasingly high-profile civil society campaigns, is very explicitly foregrounded in most iterations of their lot. It arguably is also the most pervasive phantasm of child/youth global political actors – more broadly, an area of acute myopia for security scholars who see few other child agents of potential global political import. Indeed, the lone, gun-toting, prepubescent and, typically, African, male child soldier is now rightly counted among the iconic images of contemporary global politics, especially in connection with the much discussed 'new wars' (Kaldor 1999) of the post–Cold War era. It is, of course, this quintessential child soldier's capacity to act as an agent of political violence that imbues the image, and the panoply of child/youth experiences for which it purportedly stands,[1] with substantive content. Elsewhere, much excited talk of 'youth bulges' (see, for example, Urdal 2012) is animated by anxieties about what young people – and, in particular, a critical mass of young people – might 'do.' Similarly, moral panics about (presumed) dangerous children and youth in various contexts (see, for example, Basham 2011) turn vitally on fears of their agency and how it might be brought to bear. A litany of other such examples could readily be cited here also, but the point is that children's agency is nowhere seriously in question – even if security scholars have made little note of it – and expressions of it abound.

The ubiquity of child/youth agency exemplars does not mean, however, that children are understood as political subjects in their own right. If 'agency' refers to the capacity to act, 'subjecthood' bespeaks mastery of one's own agency or the idea that actions are products of one's (at least relatively) autonomous choices. It is here we may trace the lapse that is diminutive of children as political beings in prevailing social imaginaries, for they tend not to be understood as legitimately the authors of their actions. Once again, the construction of child soldiers is instructive. Their manifest agency notwithstanding, it is not normally imagined that child soldiers act of their own volition. Rather, as famously and dramatically demonstrated in the abortive 'Kony 2012' social media campaign mounted by the San Diego-based group, Invisible Children, the dominant narrative is one in which some nefarious figure or figures of the adult world have compelled or confounded children whom they have purposefully put under arms, inducing them to fight and die for projects that are not their own. As young perpetrators of unspeakable violence, child soldiers are conspicuous agents of bloodshed in some of the world's most troubled places. At the same time, however, as abductees and victims of horrific abuse, they appear more as powerless instruments of the brutality of their adult captors.

To be sure, it is difficult to dispute the ineluctable dimension of child soldiers' various lived experiences that is their victimization. But to reduce them to victimhood alone is to affect erasure of other aspects that constitute them as subjects and not merely objects of the depredations of adult others. Even in extreme cases, human subjects are always more complex than the ascriptions of victimhood allow. To lose sight of this is to foreclose possibilities of and spaces for autonomous resistance, thereby defining those upon whom violence is visited as little more than bodies in need of protection. Mystified in all of this are the unequal power relationships by dint of which victim/object and victimizer/subject are mutually and co-constituted and which those relative positions function to sustain. And effacement of subjecthood may be affected anew in even the most benignly conceived remedial responses where protection reinscribes victim/object as protected/object.

Interrogating the politics of protection with an interest in attendant circulations of power has much to tell us about subject formation and about what is at stake in the struggles that take place around it (Jacob 2015, 15). Something of the interpellation of subject and object positions by way of protection is evident in, for example, well-intentioned advocacy on behalf of adult inmates at the Guantanamo Bay detention camps, which, in centering their vulnerability, obviates any possibility of their autonomous resistance, divesting them of political subjecthood in the process (see Beier and Mutimer 2014). This is not in any way to suggest that the inmates are not vulnerable, but is, rather, to highlight the fact that all persons, child or adult, are potentially vulnerable and that it is unequal power relationships that make this essential characteristic of human experience politically meaningful. It is important to recognize as well that the act of defining other bodies on the basis of vulnerability and the urge to protect those thus marked also encode relations of power and instantiate subject/object correlations.

Guantanamo is revealing too as regards the discursive pull of childhood inasmuch as we can see how the protective inclination may be muted in the case of adult vulnerability to the extent that containment of a subjecthood *a priori* deemed illegitimate (in the present example, that marked by the ascription 'unlawful combatant') is taken by many to justify what might otherwise seem unjust treatment without due process. The logics at work here insist upon the clear subjecthood of the detainees since it is that very delegitimized subjecthood which detention is intended to regulate and restrain. It is significant in this regard that the case of Canadian detainee, Omar Khadr, just 16 years of age when he arrived at Guantanamo,[2] has occasioned so much political struggle around efforts to define him as either a child or adult (see Foran 2011) or, put another way, as, respectively, a vulnerable object of politics in need of protection or a dangerous political subject in need of confinement – in the former construction, the object of (in)security and, in the latter, the subject of (in)security.

Where those unambiguously defined as children are concerned, protection is apt to operate even more potently, driven simultaneously by the condition of vulnerability which rationalizes protection and the trope of innocent childhood which demands it, activating responsibility on the part of adult protectors. The view of children as vulnerable and in need of protection has deep cultural purchase, especially in advanced (post)industrial societies of the Global North. We can see this expressed in, among other places, myriad cultural artefacts. The recurrent theme of orphanhood and abandonment, prevalent in children's literature from the Brothers Grimm to J.K. Rowling's *Harry Potter*, for example, turns on and reproduces anxieties about children's insecurity in the absence of benevolent adult protectors. The idea of the child alone in the world – or in the forest – functions as a device by which to build tension, explore issues of responsibility, and assign various subject and object positions to characters. But to achieve any of this, it relies first on audiences' shared understanding of childhood as a period of vulnerability as well as on a concomitant disdain of adults who abrogate the socially assigned responsibility to provide protection.

Similarly revealing in the wake of the devastating April 2015 Nepal earthquake is a photo widely circulated on social media showing what was purported to be a four-year-old boy comforting his palpably frightened two-year-old sister in the quake's aftermath. But the image, powerfully evocative of overwhelming vulnerability and of the tragic circumstance of a preschool age boy thrust unnaturally into the role of protector of his even younger sister, turned out not to have been from Nepal at all. In fact, it was taken years earlier in northern Vietnam and, according to the photographer, the little girl's fear was of him: an unfamiliar man who had appeared suddenly with a camera. Elsewhere and at other times, the same photo had been circulated and the children pictured in it described as Burmese orphans and as young civilians caught in the Syrian civil war (Pham 2015). The apparent ease with which these two very young children have been presented and accepted as metonymic expressions of various situations of acute vulnerability and insecurity is telling of prevailing assumptions about childhood which allow children's transmogrification into semiotic markers easily deployed in the service of the security rationalities encoded in the political projects of others, whether in calls for humanitarian aid or to vilify one side or the other in a war zone. Importantly, the photo was read as vulnerability and victimization in every context contrived for it and, indeed, its semiotic functioning relied on a widespread predisposition to read it in precisely that way.

Resilience/responsibility

Victimhood foregrounds the subjecthood of victimizers on the one hand and summons the subjecthood of protectors on the other. But whether beset by vulnerability or enclosed by protection, children's subjecthood is lost. Also lost is a fuller understanding of the political and of much of what we might expect security scholars, and critical scholars in particular, would seek to apprehend. Returning to the example of child soldiers, the denial of subjecthood leaves little room for serious engagement with the possibility that some young people might choose participation in armed conflict as an autonomously reasoned survival strategy. Moreover, directing our gaze instead toward the presumed 'real' subjects – those adults in the name of whose projects child soldiers fight – also leaves us potentially inattentive to the material conditions that could motivate a young person to see such a choice as an opportunity for improved circumstances. In any event, where some measure of voluntary participation appears to be the case, the echoes of Rousseau linger in the inclination to question the young person's competence to legitimately choose in the first place – and, once again, attention is directed away from the material determinants of the choice.

It is here that the rise of resilience thinking holds out some promise of a salutary corrective and an opportunity to recover children's subjecthood from overly simplistic and reductive ascriptions of victimhood (see Gilligan 2009). The idea of children as resilient has made a major imprint and has had vast influence in both scholarly and clinical fields dealing with issues of child trauma, mental health, and well-being. Challenging the idea of irreducible vulnerability, resilience thinking has the potential to imbue children with positive substantive attributes upon which greater appreciation of their subjecthood could be founded. Of course, children's resiliency might seem paradoxical in light of the deeply entrenched idea of childhood as a time of acute vulnerability. But children are, in fact, increasingly coming to be understood as exemplary resilient subjects. This draws on discourses and ideational commitments about children as human becomings: presumed still to be subjects in the making, the idea of adaptive life paths is more readily at ease with social imaginaries which have long held that it is the 'old dogs' who do not so easily assimilate 'new tricks.' As will become clear, however, the idea of resilience does not raise as much of a challenge to hegemonic constructions of childhood as it might at first appear.

Still, the importance of approaching child subjects with a view to positive substantive content, as resilience thinking seems to better position us to do, can scarcely be gainsaid. It is an effective counter to the developmental model of childhood that followed in the Rousseauean tradition, essentially equating age with graduated levels of presumed capacities and competencies, and which has largely given way to a strengths-based approach in Childhood Studies (see McNamee and Seymour 2013). As Birnbaum and Saini (2013, 279) argue, placing the accent on children's deficits, in effect defining them according to presumed absences of the attributes normally ascribed to adults, excludes them from participation in aspects of social life directly affecting them, while focusing on strengths has the potential to promote such participation. Resilience is discursively appealing for the inherent foregrounding of strengths in the orientation it has toward uncovering factors that might account for outcomes which are better than might otherwise be expected in the face of excessively challenging or even dire circumstances. It thus seems to hold significant promise by virtue of the centering of subjectivity that is at least implicit in the emphasis it places on an agent's own capacities to adapt and overcome adversity, even to the extent that we might begin to identify the emergence of a security paradigm transcending victimhood (Chandler 2012).

But, as suggested earlier, resilience thinking is neither without serious drawbacks nor, consequently, detractors. Mark Neocleous (2013), for example, calls for outright resistance to resilience thinking, which, he argues, is 'subsuming and surpassing the logic of security.' Across a wide range of contexts, resilience has emerged as the organizing principle for political (in)action in ways that may be disenabling of just as wide a range of resistance strategies. Neocleous (2013) notes, for instance, how austerity measures that disproportionately impact the poor are recast as vital to building their resilience: 'The beauty of the idea that resilience is what the world's poor need is that it turns out to be something the world's poor already possess; all they require is a little training in how to realize it.' There is much at work here as regards the assignment (and the confinement) of subjecthood. Note that responsibility to build resilience is sited with the poor themselves, whilst the requisite competencies to do so are proffered from on high in a double move that assigns responsibility to the poor without conferring full political subjecthood on them. It is a political manoeuvre reminiscent of the White Man's Burden and shot through with the core logics of patriarchy. And it underscores the importance of bringing into relief the unequal power relations that enable and sustain it.

More fundamentally, what seems foreclosed here is the very possibility of resistance inasmuch as the thrust is to abide material circumstances, not to remake them. Proceeding from the normalization of disaster, deprivation, or pathology, then, resilience thinking manifests as a rationalization for the acceptance of abject circumstances. Indeed, it may readily cast abjection as inescapable. Pathology is ontologically given such that its (eventual) realization is taken for granted and the full range of agential possibility is thus confined and defined by the imperative of survival and recovery. Avoidance or mitigation of harm thereby fades from view as the naturalized harm itself becomes determinate of the given framework for action and reaction. The resultant sketch of subjecthood is one whose measure conforms in direct proportion to the relative distribution of power resources. Despite the emphasis on strengths, their application is limited to the imperative of adjusting to circumstances made or unmade by other, more empowered political subjects. The framing is such that a resistance politics may actually be delegitimized as an errant or intransigent refusal to be resilient.[3]

Needless to say, all of this has weighty implications for possibilities of raising and sustaining (or resisting and overcoming) concrete political projects. In a striking example, Alison Howell (2015) reveals how resilience training for soldiers and their families (see, for example, Chapin 2011; Saltzman et al. 2011; Easterbrooks, Ginsburg, and Lerner 2013; Simmons and Yoder 2013) is explicitly tied to the aim of reducing the healthcare costs of war – an objective which, to the extent that it can be realized, has the potential to affect the calculus regarding the viability of recourse to war. Resilience in this context becomes identifiable as an enabling condition of the mobilization of organized political violence by the state. And it falls to soldiers and their families, the 'wetware' of advanced militarized power, to do the work of building resilience in order to facilitate this. For Neocleous (2013), resilience thinking can be understood as 'a new technology of the self' and, importantly, is about surviving not just the initial harm, but 'whatever political measures the state carries out' in response. We might think here of the 'primary' harm of terrorist attacks (in respect of which, we are told, we must be resilient) and the resultant 'secondary' harm of the surveillance state and the loss of our civil liberties (in respect of which we must also then be resilient). Crucially, there is no room in any of this to imagine either alternative futures or a capacity to resist those that are called into being and naturalized by others and we therefore want for a subject position in respect of both harms, save for the impoverished one that issues from our individualized responsibility to be resilient in the face of them both.

Prior and Hagmann (2014, 296) urge us to consider that, 'the resilience agenda effectively. . .refers to a larger political process, namely societal decisions about whose and what kind of resilience is addressed, and political conclusions about who assumes what task and what responsibility in the production of a secure and resilient society.' It is therefore of critical importance that we pay close attention to whom, in various contexts, is being asked and relied upon to do resilience work. Returning to issues of childhood and security, it turns out to be children to whom the real work of resilience building in the face of insecurity very often falls, though they remain disadvantaged by unequal power relationships at the same time. The situation is complicated by the to and fro of subject formation and ascription in resilience work, which, as discussed earlier, may give the appearance of bona fide subjecthood but within such rigid confines as to make it politically inconsequential.

A further problem is that resilience is coded in contradistinction to what we might identify as pathology, but pathology is too often coded in terms of symptoms exhibited by the individual rather than the material and social determinants (that is, the condition of insecurity) of those symptoms. Again, resilience thinking hardens harms into ontology and looks to individualized strengths that enable survival and promote adaptation to harm, not transcendence of it. Resilience, from this perspective, is itself an abjection. Despite the promise it seems to hold for recovery of a more fulsome kind of political subjecthood, this may turn out to be remarkably circumscribed, amounting to little more than the capacity to forbear conditions which are themselves placed beyond the reach of any kind of remedial action. Moreover, it involves an individualization of responsibility for forbearance of harm, which is anathema to an ethos of support and of community. Instead, external supports aim at promoting the resilience work undertaken by individuals on their own behalf. The real work of resilience is in *being* or *becoming* resilient.

Resilient child/responsible child

All of these strands can be drawn together in connection with everyday ways in which children confront and are confronted with (in)security. In doing so, it is useful to move from highly conspicuous experiences of insecurity, like those navigated daily by child soldiers and others in zones of conflict, and to turn our focus to some comparatively mundane ways in which insecurity is faced by children living even in the most privileged areas of the (post)industrial Global North. Doing so helps to expose the circuits along which inequalities between the child and adult worlds, particularly as regards subjecthood, are sustained and reproduced. This is revealing of how deeply held many of our ideas and commitments about childhood are and how they inhere even in the most benevolently conceived practices and interventions. If they are to be confronted, it is vitally important that they be confronted here too, lest we repeat the mistake of proceeding as though children's insecurity is a problem that belongs only to the fraught places of the Global South and without any meaningful connection to ideas and practices performed into being elsewhere.

It is important to bear in mind, however, that the traditional preoccupations of Security Studies do not easily accommodate the full range of connections that can be drawn here. In part, this owes to the persistence of hegemonic ideas about childhood, but it is equally for reason of dominant understandings of both the objects and substantive content of 'security' itself. Howell (2014) challenges the arbitrary distinction between social security and international security, revealing how processes in these allegedly discrete spheres are co-constitutive and operate in ways that are not just complementary but mutually sustaining, and according to shared logics as strategies for the defence of populations. Parceling off 'social security' as a discrete realm unto itself thus removes from the agenda great swathes of social life wherein (in)security processes, projects, and practices operate inseparably from those gathered under the rubric of 'international security.' Like dominant views concerning childhood, this separation operates at the level of ontology, giving rise to a strong cognitive predisposition, arguably expressed in such things as the apparently easy collapse of a more nuanced human security agenda back into a preoccupation with somatic violences.

Similarly, Security Studies' inattention to childhood as an idea intimately and inextricably bound up in both the production of security discourses and the framing of (in)security issues, projects, and practices urges reflection on how resilience thinking has been taken up in the field. That resilience has come much more readily into currency with security scholars than childhood is curious for many reasons, including those sketched earlier, but all the more so in light of the genealogy of resilience as a concept. As noted at the outset of this article, the rise of resilience thinking is traceable through a range of disciplinary contexts, many of them thoroughly engaged with the idea long before Security Studies came to it. Particularly noteworthy, however, is the tremendous debt owed by contemporary discourses of resilience to mid-twentieth-century research into child and youth psychosocial well-being, which marked a shift from the centering of risk to an emphasis on resilience (see, for example, Werner, Bierman, and French 1971; Werner and Smith 1982, 1992). Taking these origins seriously promises not only a richer and more nuanced understanding of resilience but also a corrective to the privileging of international security over social security and their arbitrary separation.

Thus, a perhaps unlikely point of inquiry – for Security Studies, if not for literatures and clinical practices concerned with resilience – is friction and family reorganization associated with parental separation and, in particular, therapeutic interventions made with the intention of promoting children's resilience through what most would assume is a very trying experience. Admittedly, the same logics to be highlighted here can be found at work also in other, perhaps more arresting, situations of children's insecurity – schoolyard bullying or domestic violence, for example – but it is precisely for its ability to speak to a more mundane, less overtly somatic conception of (in)security that family reorganization is particularly instructive. In this sense, it helps us to avoid repeating something akin to the mistake of allowing the physical violence associated with child soldiers to occlude the acute insecurity of their broader material circumstances. Just as important, moving into the everyday challenges the association of (in)security with exceptional circumstances, which, in turn, exposes the equally quotidian power circulations sustaining and sustained by children's resilience work across a wide range of settings.

Parental separation can be a profound insecurity event in a young person's life and undoubtedly most children experience it with at least some measure of this sense. At the same time, for the majority of cases, children exhibit a high degree of innate resilience. Reflecting this, since the 1970s, scholarly and therapeutic approaches have moved from the centering of risk to the embrace of a resilience paradigm (see Kelly and Emery 2003) – a move that bears striking parallels with and which presaged much in the way of the more recent turn to resilience in security discourse. Longitudinal studies of children's adjustment to family reorganization show that, while there is a spectrum of short-term adverse reactions that children may exhibit to greater or lesser extents as they adjust to their new circumstances, 'the vast majority are resilient and able to cope with, or even benefit from their new life situation,' and the most effective supports during the period of adjustment are non-interventionist: positive social environments at school, amongst peers, and so forth (Hetherington 2003, 234).

However, well-intentioned interventionist strategies abound and may frequently have the effect of pathologizing children's quite normal and expected reactions, raising the specter of inadvertently communicating to the child that the problems in need of redress reside with them. Besides reinforcing the individualization of responsibility for resilience work, there is the further danger that internalized feelings of responsibility for conflict between the parents may likewise be reinforced – the intervention is, after all, in the life of the child, not the adults. Significantly, a recent review of published studies of the effectiveness of school-based interventions for 'children of divorce' raises methodological concerns over, among other things, an emphasis on psychopathology and insufficient attention to the presence of coping mechanisms (Rose 2009). The centering of measures that focus on psychopathology is particularly noteworthy in the sense that it is consistent with the 'common sense' that children undergoing family reorganization are unusually at risk, something which flows together with and impels the therapeutic impulse whilst elevating the risk associated with the intervention itself.

Parental separation is often regarded as a social 'problem' – particularly in connection with conservative discourses lamenting greater diversity in forms of family structure – wherein children are constructed as 'victims' (Coltrane and Adams 2003). Even where there is less enduring attachment to the traditional ideal of the 'nuclear' family, hegemonic notions of childhood innocence and vulnerability may still exert an impetus for separating parents to seek therapeutic intervention for their children. Notwithstanding that most parents might undertake this course with the best of intentions, perhaps guided by a culturally informed intuitive sense that children are vulnerable and require support, it is once again revealing of where the operant subjecthood is located – here too, with adults who decide on the course and undertake to place children in therapy. It is important to recognize also that not all therapeutic interventions are benign, the upshot of which is that children may be subjected to unnecessary risk for exhibiting symptoms that, although worrying for parents, are wholly normal and expected responses by any child to a situation not of their making and not within their control. In light of this, a more appropriate course might be to place the emphasis instead on the adults' need to do their own resilience work under the stress of separation, counselling parents who exacerbate their children's stress (Jamison et al. 2014) because they cannot or will not moderate conflict, co-parent cooperatively, or cultivate appropriate parent–child relationships.

Once more, it is attention to the play of power and subjecthood that brings problems into relief. For example, while much attention has been devoted in recent years to research participants' full and informed consent and right to withdraw at any time, precious little thought has been devoted to appropriate handling of a child's dissent from participation in counselling processes (Ulvik 2015, 196), which are wont to be far more personally intrusive. This becomes a matter for concern when considered alongside the fundamentally unequal power dynamic that can manifest even between a therapist and an adult client and which is greatly exacerbated in the absence of free and sustained consent (see Szasz 1998). More than two decades ago already, the therapy setting was described as a 'mirrored room' in which liberal ideologies obfuscate power circulations and material inequalities whilst gendered, raced, and classed discourses still circulate in 'common senses' and assumptions that condition the relations within the room (Hare-Mustin 1993). In the same way, hegemonic ideas about childhood set up the power dynamic between child and therapist. The move away from developmentalism in Childhood Studies has yet to be matched by a commensurate change in some therapists' attitudes towards children's competencies and capacity for consent (McNamee and Seymour 2013, 158). This is most problematic where therapists might not give due weight to risks of iatrogenesis (negative side effects the child might experience as a consequence of participation in therapy) or self-labelling and social stigma risks (see Jensen, Regis McNamara, and Gustafson 1991) and there is an identified need for more intensive research designed to engage rather than gloss over instances of negative effects or a lack of identifiable benefit from therapeutic interventions (Barlow 2010). Though perhaps less conspicuous to disciplinary sensibilities than more overtly somatic violences, (in)security is nevertheless fundamentally at issue in all of these relationships and effects.

We can draw a clear parallel here with the sorts of 'secondary' harms identified by Neocleous (2013). Also revealed are the complex processes of subject construction and maintenance at work, all of which belie the presumed or implied stability of operant ontological categories and commitments and which are simultaneously revealing of important circuits of power, domination, and control. The urge to therapy performatively (Butler 1990) objectifies the child as victim (or perhaps 'collateral damage'). And it also performatively constructs the conscientious, caring parent(s). Victimhood and vulnerability activate protector responsibility, but efface the subjecthood of those constructed as victims. The focus on an individually expressed symptomatology draws the identification of what is pathological away from the social circumstances and locates it with reactions to those circumstances – reactions that may be wholly appropriate to circumstances that are pathological. In effect, the symptom of pathology is rendered *as* the pathology. If the child appears not to be abiding the circumstances well enough, or even if she is but hegemonic ideas about childhood nevertheless insist upon her inherent vulnerability, the logic of the intervention is that it be with the child. The implication once again is that there is some failing of the 'wetware' that does not abide the social pathology as well as some others (appear) to do. The therapeutic impulse downloads onto the child responsibility to better abide the real pathology (see O'Reilly 2015), whilst the whole exercise continues to withhold recognition of her robust subjecthood, which, if exercised in the manner of resistance to circumstances foisted upon her by others, might itself come to be pathologized as intransigence.

When brought together with resilience thinking, the very logics of the therapeutic intervention are such that the child bears practical responsibility for the resilience work that must be done. And while this might appear to entail a *de facto* instantiation of subjecthood, it is sharply circumscribed and highly contingent. On the strength of enduring Rousseauean/developmentalist ideas about childhood, resilience is divested of its potential for recovery of child/youth political subjecthood. This enjoins us to theorize children and adults alike as simultaneously beings *and* becomings (Uprichard 2008) and thereby to unsettle the exclusive location of political subjecthood in the adult world.

Conclusion

The United Nations Convention on the Rights of the Child explicitly upholds children's right to security and invests both parents and the state with responsibility in this regard. As we have seen, however, resilience thinking in combination with dominant ideas about childhood as a time of innocence, vulnerability, and becoming can give rise to subtle processes of responsibility delegation without commensurate empowerment or a fuller recognition of children as autonomous political subjects in their own right. From zones of conflict to the comparatively privileged everyday of life in the (post)industrial Global North, the same knowledge commitments and practices operate largely unseen (though very much in plain view) to constitute children/youth outside of political life. That the rise of resilience thinking bears important similarities in its implications for children thus constructed despite their being separated by geography, material circumstances, and lifeways recommends inquiring beyond our accustomed ways of thinking about the production of (in)security, its subjects, and its referent objects.

Equipped with this insight, we quite readily find that plying areas largely unfamiliar to Security Studies is indeed a productive approach by which to reveal something of the pervasiveness of ideas and practices inseparable from lived experiences of insecurity, domination, and resistance across a vast array of diverse sociopolitical settings. Therapeutic intervention in cases of family reorganization and/or parental conflict, for example, may ultimately end up shifting a significant burden of resilience work to children without providing them any means to exert meaningful control over the circumstances in which they find themselves – a move not so very different from promoting resilient forbearance of austerity by the poor. Though therapy might be imagined to be empowering of children in the sense that their voices are heard (and it undoubtedly achieves that very thing in many cases, especially in the absence of other supports), it has the potential to manifest a downloading of responsibility. It also ignores other contexts in which the young person might be raising her voice already, simultaneously effacing both the subjecthood and responsibility of those in whom she has confided in deference to the centering of the therapist as the intervenor of import: in some cases, other professionals might activate this deference themselves in the hope or even genuine belief that it is the therapist's exclusive role to address the oft times difficult issues at hand. The effect, in such cases, is to narrow the sort of non-interventionist social supports that have been shown to have the most positive effects in sustaining innate resilience, as opposed to delegating resilience work.

Resilience thinking *appears* to offer a promising avenue towards the recovery of subjecthood, but, in many cases, and particularly in the case of children/youth, this appearance may be akin to a parlour trick. The subjecthood seemingly recovered in the move to resilience is an impoverished one to the extent that the 'subject' position is confined mostly or entirely to forbearance: abiding social pathology while the social pathology is naturalized and placed beyond the subject's ability to affect change. Resilience thinking thus runs the considerable risk – indeed, may be predisposed toward – downloading responsibility to be resilient in the very abject sense of abiding the naturalized social pathology. In the same instant, those subjects possessed of actual power are absolved of responsibility to address, remediate, and resolve the social pathology, while the impoverished should-be-resilient 'subject' is denied the possibility of doing so herself – again, hers is to forbear. Far from being transcended, situations of acute insecurity might thus be entrenched.

Clearly, there is good reason for healthy scepticism about the rise of resilience. As I indicated at the outset, however, my aim is not to issue an absolute indictment of resilience thinking but, rather, to caution against its adoption without sustained critical refection on the political possibilities it enables or disenables, and for whom. How, then, might we reimagine the terrain of engagement with and through this increasingly ubiquitous discourse such that it might be recaptured as a counterhegemonic political resource? It would seem that an essential first step lies in highlighting innate resilience as a characteristic common to all human subjects while taking care always to critically scrutinize resilience-*building* projects and the subject/ersatz subject relationships they activate and sustain. Alison M.S. Watson (2015) finds children's bona fide political subjecthood in innate resilience, which she understands as being resistance in its own right. This is a qualitatively different subjecthood than the ersatz form conferred from sites of power and delimited by projects issuing therefrom. The call for resilience *work*, in contrast, runs the risk of being a demand for others to accommodate themselves to the political projects of the comparatively powerful.

Perhaps it is the case that thinking about resilience without simultaneously thinking about victimhood, and vice versa, is inherently problematic. It may well be that this is one of those situations in which we should not be thinking in terms of some definitional/conceptual resolution or endpoint at which we can hope to arrive, finding one or the other of vulnerability and resilience somehow more critical than the other. Rather, reflection on underinterrogated issues of child/youth (in)security suggests that we need to sustain affirmation of both, holding them visibly in tension. For reasons of victimhood's diminution of subjecthood, we should not want to be implicated in reducing children confronting insecurity to mere victims, but neither should we endorse the wholesale denial of victimization since, as we have seen, to do so has weighty implications for the naturalization of harm and the (re)assignment of responsibility. And this becomes especially problematic where a shifting of the burden of responsibility comes to absolve sites of power and thus to mystify structures and practices of domination and control together with the violences, both spectacular and mundane, that they necessarily entail. Recalling the ways in which Security Studies, like other fields and disciplines, is about children, the manner of our theorizations and invocations of resilience is itself rightly counted among the constitutive practices both of (in)security as children's lived experience and of childhood itself.

Acknowledgements

Research for this article was supported by an Insight Grant from the Social Sciences and Humanities Research Council of Canada.

Notes

1. Much is occluded by standard imagery of child soldiers, not least the involvement of girls (see Mazurana and McKay 2001; Fox 2004). From a postcolonial perspective, Lorraine Macmillan (2009) and Catarina Martins (2011) problematize the dominant, Northern image of the child soldier and its implication in the reproduction of both a particular privileged understanding of innocent childhood and colonial discourses about the Global South.
2. Omar Khadr was fifteen years of age when he was captured by US forces in the aftermath of a firefight in Afghanistan, in which he was severely wounded. He was held briefly at Bagram Airfield in Afghanistan before being transferred to Guantanamo Bay where he remained until his repatriation to Canada in 2012.
3. I am indebted to Marc Doucet for drawing this insight to my attention.

References

Barlow, D. H. 2010. "Negative Effects from Psychological Treatments: A Perspective." *American Psychologist* 65 (1): 13–20. doi:10.1037/a0015643.

Basham, V. 2011. "Kids with Guns: Militarization, Masculinities, Moral Panic, and (Dis)Organized Violence." In *The Militarization of Childhood: Thinking Beyond the Global South*, edited by J. M. Beier, 175–193. New York, NY: Palgrave Macmillan.

Beier, J. M. 2015. "Children, Childhoods, and Security Studies: An Introduction." *Critical Studies on Security* 3 (1): 1–13. doi:10.1080/21624887.2015.1019715.

Beier, J. M., and D. Mutimer. 2014. "Pathologizing Subjecthoods: Pop Culture, Habits of Thought, and the Unmaking of Resistance Politics at Guantanamo Bay." *International Political Sociology* 8 (3): 311–323. doi:10.1111/ips.12059.

Birnbaum, R., and M. Saini. 2013. "A Scoping Review of Qualitative Studies About Children Experiencing Parental Separation." *Childhood* 20 (2): 260–282. doi:10.1177/0907568212454148.

Butler, J. 1990. *Gender Trouble: Feminism and the Subversion of Identity*. New York, NY: Routledge.

Chandler, D. 2012. "Resilience and Human Security: The Post-Interventionist Paradigm." *Security Dialogue* 43 (3): 213–229. doi:10.1177/0967010612444151.

Chapin, M. 2011. "Family Resilience and the Fortunes of War." *Social Work in Health Care* 50 (7): 527–542. doi:10.1080/00981389.2011.588130.

Coltrane, S., and M. Adams. 2003. "The Social Construction of the Divorce 'Problem': Morality, Child Victims, and the Politics of Gender." *Family Relations* 52 (4): 363–372. doi:10.1111/j.1741-3729.2003.00363.x.

Easterbrooks, M.A., K. Ginsburg, and R. M. Lerner. 2013. "Resilience Among Military Youth." *The Future of Children* 23 (2): 99–120. doi:10.1353/foc.2013.0014.

Folke, C. 2006. "Resilience: The Emergence of a Perspective for Social-Ecological Systems Analyses." *Global Environmental Change* 16 (3): 253–267. doi:10.1016/j.gloenvcha.2006.04.002.

Foran, J. E. 2011. "Interrogating 'Militarized' Images and Disrupting Sovereign Narratives in the Case of Omar Khadr." In *The Militarization of Childhood: Thinking Beyond the Global South*, edited by J. M. Beier, 195–216. New York, NY: Palgrave Macmillan.

Fox, M.-J. 2004. "Girl Soldiers: Human Security and Gendered Insecurity." *Security Dialogue* 35 (4): 465–479. doi:10.1177/0967010604049523.

Freire, P. 1970. *Pedagogy of the Oppressed*. New York, NY: Herder and Herder.

Gilligan, C. 2009. "'Highly Vulnerable'? Political Violence and the Social Construction of Traumatized Children." *Journal of Peace Research* 46 (1): 119–134. doi:10.1177/0022343308098407.

Hare-Mustin, R. T. 1993. "Changing Women, Changing Therapy: Clinical Implications of the Changing Role of Women." *Journal of Feminist Family Therapy* 4 (3–4): 7–18. doi:10.1300/J086v04n03_03.

Hetherington, E. M. 2003. "Social Support and the Adjustment of Children in Divorced and Remarried Families." *Childhood* 10 (2): 217–236. doi:10.1177/0907568203010002007.

Howell, A. 2014. "The Global Politics of Medicine: Beyond Global Health, Against Securitisation Theory." *Review of International Studies* 40 (5): 961–987. doi:10.1017/S0260210514000369.

Howell, A. 2015. "Resilience, War, and Austerity: The Ethics of Military Human Enhancement and the Politics of Data." *Security Dialogue* 46 (1): 15–31. doi:10.1177/0967010614551040.

Jacob, C. 2015. "'Children and Armed Conflict' and the Field of Security Studies." *Critical Studies on Security* 3 (1): 14–28. doi:10.1080/21624887.2015.1014675.

Jamison, T. B., M. Coleman, L. H. Ganong, and R. E. Feistman. 2014. "Transitioning to Postdivorce Family Life: A Grounded Theory Investigation of Resilience in Coparenting." *Family Relations* 63 (3): 411–423. doi:10.1111/fare.12074.

Jensen, J. A., J. Regis McNamara, and K. E. Gustafson. 1991. "Parents' and Clinicians' Attitudes Toward the Risks and Benefits of Child Psychotherapy: A Study of Informed-Consent Content." *Professional Psychology: Research and Practice* 22 (2): 161–170. doi:10.1037/0735-7028.22.2.161.

Johansson, B. 2011. "Doing Adulthood in Childhood Research." *Childhood* 19 (1): 101–114. doi:10.1177/0907568211408362.

Kaldor, M. 1999. *New and Old Wars: Organized Violence in a Global Era*. Stanford: Stanford University Press.

Kelly, J. B., and R. E. Emery. 2003. "Children's Adjustment Following Divorce: Risk and Resilience Perspectives." *Family Relations* 52 (4): 352–362. doi:10.1111/j.1741-3729.2003.00352.x.

Macmillan, L. 2009. "The Child Soldier in North-South Relations." *International Political Sociology* 3 (1): 36–52. doi:10.1111/j.1749-5687.2008.00062.x.

Macmillan, L. 2015. "Children, Civilianhood, and Humanitarian Securitization." *Critical Studies on Security* 3 (1): 62–76. doi:10.1080/21624887.2015.1014696.

Martins, C. 2011. "The Dangers of the Single Story: Child-Soldiers in Literary Fiction and Film." *Childhood* 18 (4): 434–446. doi:10.1177/0907568211400102.

Mazurana, D. and S. McKay. 2001. "Child Soldiers; What about the Girls?" *Bulletin of the Atomic Scientists* 57 (5): 30–35. doi:10.2968/057005010.

McNamee, S., and J. Seymour. 2013. "Towards a Sociology of 10-12 Year Olds? Emerging Methodological Issues in the 'New' Social Studies of Childhood." *Childhood* 20 (2): 156–168. doi:10.1177/0907568212461037.

Moeller, S. D. 2002. "A Hierarchy of Innocence: The Media's Use of Children in the Telling of International News." *The Harvard International Journal of Press/Politics* 7 (1): 36–56. doi:10.1177/1081180X0200700104.

Neocleous, M. 2013. "Resisting Resilience." *Radical Philosophy* 178. http://www.radicalphilosophy.com/commentary/resisting-resilience

O'Reilly, M. 2015. "'We're Here to Get You Sorted': Parental Perceptions of the Purpose, Progression and Outcomes of Family Therapy." *Journal of Family Therapy* 37 (3): 322–342. doi:10.1111/1467-6427.12004.

Panter-Brick, C., and J. F. Leckman. 2013. "Editorial Commentary: Resilience in Child Development – Interconnected Pathways to Wellbeing." *Journal of Child Psychology and Psychiatry* 54 (4): 333–336. doi:10.1111/jcpp.12057.

Pham, N. 2015. "Haunting 'Nepal Quake Victims' Photo from Vietnam." *BBC News*, May 4. Accessed 5 May. http://www.bbc.com/news/world-asia-32579598

Prior, T., and J. Hagmann. 2014. "Measuring Resilience: Methodological and Political Challenges of a Trend Security Concept." *Journal of Risk Research* 17 (3): 281–298. doi:10.1080/13669877.2013.808686.

Rose, S. R. 2009. "A Review of Effectiveness of Group Work With Children of Divorce." *Social Work With Groups* 32 (3): 222–229. doi:10.1080/01609510902774315.

Rousseau, J. J. [1979] 1762. *Emile; Or, on Education.* Translated by Allan Bloom. New York, NY: Basic Books.

Saltzman, W. R., P. Lester, W. R. Beardslee, C. M. Layne, K. Woodward, and W. P. Nash. 2011. "Mechanisms of Risk and Resilience in Military Families: Theoretical and Empirical Basis of a Family-Focused Resilience Enhancement Program." *Clinical Child and Family Psychology Review* 14 (3): 213–230. doi:10.1007/s10567-011-0096-1.

Simmons, A., and L. Yoder. 2013. "Military Resilience: A Concept Analysis." *Nursing Forum* 48 (1): 17–25. doi:10.1111/nuf.12007.

Szasz, T. 1998. "Discretion as Power: In the Situation Called 'Psychotherapy.'" *British Journal of Psychotherapy* 15 (2): 216–228. doi:10.1111/j.1752-0118.1998.tb00444.x.

Ulvik, O. S. 2015. "Talking with Children: Professional Conversations in a Participation Perspective." *Qualitative Social Work* 14 (2): 193–208. doi:10.1177/1473325014526923.

Uprichard, E. 2008. "Children as 'Being and Becomings': Children, Childhood and Temporality." *Children & Society* 22 (4): 303–313. doi:10.1111/j.1099-0860.2007.00110.x.

Urdal, H. 2012. "A Clash of Generations? Youth Bulges and Political Violence." *Department of Economic and Social Affairs, Population Division, Expert Paper No. 2012/1.* New York, NY: United Nations.

Watson, A. M. S. 2011. "Guardians of the Peace? The Significance of Children to Continued Militarism." In *The Militarization of Childhood: Thinking Beyond the Global South,* edited by J. M. Beier, 43–60. New York, NY: Palgrave Macmillan.

Watson, A. M. S. 2015. "Resilience is its Own Resistance: The Place of Children in Post-Conflict Settlement." *Critical Studies on Security* 3 (1): 47–61. doi:10.1080/21624887.2015.1014687.

Werner, E. E., J. M. Bierman, and F. E. French. 1971. *The Children of Kauai: A Longitudinal Study from the Prenatal Period to Age Ten.* Honolulu: University of Hawaii Press.

Werner, E. E., and R. S. Smith. 1982. *Vulnerable, But Invincible: A Longitudinal Study of Resilient Children and Youth.* New York, NY: McGraw-Hill.

Werner, E. E., and R. S. Smith. 1992. *Overcoming the Odds: High Risk Children from Birth to Adulthood.* Ithaca: Cornell University Press.

Windle, G. 2011. "What is Resilience? A Review and Concept Analysis." *Reviews in Clinical Gerontology* 21 (2): 152–169. doi:10.1017/S0959259810000420.

Zolkoski, S. M., and L. M. Bullock. 2012. "Resilience in Children and Youth: A Review." *Children and Youth Services Review* 34 (12): 2295–2303. doi:10.1016/j.childyouth.2012.08.009.

Index

For Product Safety Concerns and Information please contact our EU representative GPSR@taylorandfrancis.com Taylor & Francis Verlag GmbH, Kaufingerstraße 24, 80331 München, Germany

T - #0187 - 270225 - C0 - 246/174/8 - PB - 9780367026264 - Gloss Lamination